W9-CFV-329

# Islamic Terror and the Balkans

# Islamic Terror and the Balkans

Shaul Shay

The Interdisciplinary Center, Herzliya

The International Policy Institute for Counter-Terrorism

Transaction Publishers
New Brunswick (U.S.A.) and London (U.K.)

This book is printed on acid-free paper that meets the American National Standard for Permanence of Paper for Printed Library Materials.

Library of Congress Catalog Number: 2006040467
ISBN: 0-7658-0347-X (alk. paper)
978-0-7658-0347-4
Printed in the United States of America

Library of Congress Cataloging-in-Publication Data

Shay, Shaul.
Islamic terror and the Balkans / Shaul Shay.
p. cm.
Includes bibliographical references.
ISBN 0-7658-0347-X (alk. paper)
1. Terrorism—Balkan Peninsula. 2. Terrorism—Balkan Peninsula—History. 3. Terrorism—Religious aspects—Islam. 4. Islam—Balkan Peninsula—History. 5. Balkan Peninsula—Ethnic relations. 6. War on Terrorism 2001- I. Title.

HV6433.B35S43 2006

My thanks to Professor Gideon Biger, Dr. Michael Roman, and Ms. Jennie Lebel for their illuminations and comments which greatly contributed to the writing of this book.

# Contents

# Introduction

Since the dissolution of Yugoslavia and the outbreak of ethnic conflicts, the area of the Balkans became a focal point of attraction to Islamic terror entities, particularly for some of the Afghan "alumni." In the course of the civil war in Bosnia, the Muslim world rose to the aid of the Muslim minority, and countries like Iran, Libya, and Saudi Arabia sent money, humanitarian aid, and weaponry to the Muslim side, thus circumventing the UN embargo on arms shipments to the fighting parties. In the framework of the mobilization of the Muslim world on behalf of the struggle of the Muslim minority in Bosnia, volunteers arrived in the country, mainly Afghan "alumni," and their numbers were estimated at several thousand fighters.[1]

Initially, the volunteers joined the various Bosnian militias that fought the Serbs, but they were quickly incorporated into special units that were established for them (the Mujahidin brigades), with the blessing of Ilia Izetbegovic, leader of the Muslims in Bosnia, who appointed himself their honorary commander.

The Islamic volunteers' contribution to the success of the Muslim Bosnians was significant. They helped to boost the morale of the Bosnian fighters, infused them with enthusiasm and a fighting spirit, and deepened their consciousness and Islamic knowledge. The volunteers fought on the various fronts, but also dealt in the training of the Muslim Bosnian fighters. The Mujahidin brigades were active throughout the country and carried out many military campaigns in which their daring and considerable operational skills were demonstrated.

The Islamic volunteers were also involved in many atrocities and cruel acts against the Serb forces and the Serb civilian population, for which three of the Mujahidin brigade commanders are currently being tried in The Hague for crimes against humanity.

In the framework of the mobilization of the Arab world in favor of the Muslims in Bosnia, Bin Laden's men also arrived in Bosnia and established infrastructures for the Al Qaida organization in the Balkans.

In 1994, Bin Laden published an article in response to the "ethnic cleansing" carried out by the Serbs among the Bosnian Muslims. His article stated the following: [2]

> … The world has witnessed all this, and not only does it not react to these evil incidents, but it also prevents these helpless people from purchasing the firearms required for their self-protection. All of this is a conspiracy between the United States and its allies, sponsored by the infidel UN.

Bin Laden's claims raise many questions regarding the complex conflict raging in the Balkans, as the United States and the European community both directly and indirectly supported the Muslim side in the confrontation, and they enabled the Muslim side to receive military aid in the form of firearms and fighters by turning a blind eye.

In November 1995, the war in Bosnia ended in the Dayton Agreements and Bosnia-Herzegovina was divided into two political identities, a Croatian Muslim federation with a Muslim majority and a Croatian minority, and the Serb Republic (SRPSKA) with a Serb majority.

At the end of the war, the Bosnian government was required to disarm the Mujahidin brigades and expel them from the country, but the Bosnian government ignored this demand, claiming that Bosnian law makes anyone who fought for the independence of Muslim Bosnia eligible for Bosnian citizenship, and also these fighters are eligible for citizenship due to the moral debt that the Muslim society in Bosnia owed those who came to its aid during wartime.

Thus, Bosnia dismantled the Mujahidin brigades but most of the volunteers remained in Bosnia, established families, and became part of the Muslim Bosnian society. According to estimates, some 1,000 Mujahidin remained in Bosnia and settled in the cities and villages. They also built their own villages, incorporated local supporters, and established autonomous societies governed by the Sharia and strict Islamic lifestyles. Today, Bosnia serves as a focus for the activities of Musim extremists due to the government's weakness, the lack of public security, unenforced law and order, economic backwardness, corrupt public institutions, and extensive infrastructure of organized crime.

These reasons, alongside the existence of border crossing points, most of which are not under any effective government control, turn Bosnia into a convenient focal point for criminal and terrorist activity. For the moment there is no indication of significant terror activity on Bosnian soil, mainly due to the aspiration of extremist Islamic entities to use Bosnia as a haven and safe passage for terror activists.

Following the September 11, 2001 attacks and the U.S. declaration regarding the war on terror, increased pressure was placed on the Bosnian authorities to take action against Islamic terror entities that had found a haven in their country. The United States and Britain have been acting independently (although with the authorities' knowledge) to arrest suspected terrorists in the framework of the international peace force stationed in Bosnia. As noted, the involvement of the Islamic terrorist entities in the Balkans has continued after the end of the war in Bosnia, and these entities took an active part in the war in Kosovo in 1999 and, subsequently, in Macedonia as well in 2001.

It would appear that in the course of the last decade, which was characterized by conflict between the Muslims and the Serbs in the Balkan, terror entities succeeded in establishing a firm organizational infrastructure which currently serves these organizations for the purpose of their terror activity in Europe and in other world focal centers, with the Western countries headed by the U.S. experiencing difficulty coping with them.

Aside from Islamic terror organizations like Al Qaida, Iran has also played a central role in supporting Muslims in the Balkans and has established a widespread infrastructure of terror and intelligence entities which stand at its disposal to promote its goals in the European continent.

It is evident that not only Bosnia, but also additional Muslim focal points in the Balkans such as Albania, Kosovo, and Macedonia (FYROM), have become havens and hothouses for radical Islamic terror entities and will continue to serve as a focus for the threat of Islamic terror against the West.

Thus, this study attempts to illuminate the processes that caused the Balkans to become a focal point of Islamic terror in Europe and the threats that are posed due to this phenomenon.

This study analyzes the roots of radical Islamic terror in the Balkans as well as the processes that led to the strengthening of Islamic terror infrastructures in this region.

The book does not discuss history or provide an analysis of the wars in the Balkans (in Bosnia, Kosovo, and Macedonia), but chooses to focus on the contribution and impact of Islamic terror organizations in the Balkan arena upon the course of the wars and their consequences, and to discuss how Iran and these organizations took advantage of the wars in the Balkans to reinforce infrastructures that serve them today in their activities in Europe and worldwide.

## Notes

1. Yosef Bodansky, Bin Laden , the Man Who Declared War on America, Forum Roseville, California 1999, p. 100.
2. Ibid.

# Section One

## Background—The Development of the Global Jihad Phenomenon

# The Development of Radical Islam—From Local Jihad to Global Jihad

The September 11 attacks were the fruition of meticulous and ongoing planning based on the infrastructure of the global Jihad that developed in the final decade of the twentieth century on the basis of the global Islamic Dawa infrastructure.

It would be impossible to understand the September 11 attacks, the background leading to the attacks, the motivation that inspired the attackers, and the repercussions felt throughout the world in general, and particularly in the Muslim world, without understanding the development processes of the Jihad from local Jihad movements with goals defined on the national, state, and regional level, to the global Jihad movement with its globally defined goals.

Only by comprehending the roots of the global Jihad phenomenon, its formation and Islamic religious foundation, as well as the popular and logistic support received from the Islamic community, is it possible to grasp the dimensions of the worldwide terror conspiracy that horrifically culminated in the September 11 attacks.

The joint vision shared by all of the Jihad organizations is based on the concept of the "Umma" (the establishment of the Islamic community of believers that will unite all Muslims worldwide). The instruments for realizing this vision are the Jihad (Holy War) and the Dawa; both terms being taken from the world of classic Islamic concepts and reflecting a yearning for the glorious days of Islam. From the Islamic point of view, the world is divided into two parts: The first part—Dar al Islam, which includes territories controlled by Islam, and the second—Dar al Harb, which is controlled by the infidels. These two means—the Dawa and the Jihad—are mutually supportive and complementive of each other. But while the Dawa is based on non-violent means aimed at rectifying Islamic society through the education systems, preaching, and social aid, the Jihad aspires to achieve its aims through extreme violence.

These two means developed at different paces during the twentieth century. Due to the fact that the Dawa is moderate, tolerant, and less threatening, it spread worldwide. Any place where there are Muslim communities in which Islamic institutions/mosques and centers existed, the Dawa activity, aimed at expanding the influence of Islam way beyond its territorial boundaries, thrived. This is true to such an extent that it is noteworthy that on the eve of the Islamic revolution in Iran in 1979, the Dawa infrastructure had already spread to many countries worldwide. In contrast, during the twentieth century, the Jihad movement was active mainly on the local or regional levels with the aim of exiling a foreign power from their land or, in order to remove what they deemed as infidel governments, and replace them with Islamic regimes.

The following review will endeavor to clarify how a local, radical religious struggle was transformed into a "Holy War" machine, the global Jihad that currently poses the greatest threat against the Free World.

## The Local Jihad—Initial Stages

A central cornerstone of the development of radical Islam in the modern era was laid with the foundation of the "Muslim Brotherhood" movement in 1929 by Hassan Albana in Egypt. The movement's goals were to expel the British from Egypt, amend the secular constitution introduced under the British influence, and establish an Islamic state to be run according to the Sharia. The means to achieve these goals was the use of the Jihad. The latter constituted one of the three central foundations of the Muslim Brotherhood's concepts: Knowledge, Education, and Jihad. Albana succeeded in convincing his followers that death in Allah's name is desirable, and he who sacrifices his life in the name of Islam will enjoy eternal life in Paradise. During the thirties and forties the Muslim Brotherhood launched subversive and terrorist activity against the Egyptian regime, the British presence in Egypt, as well as cultural and entertainment sites identified with Western culture.

From the thirties onwards, Albana's teachings began to take root in the Muslim world and offshoots of the Muslim Brotherhood (or parallel organizations) began to crop up throughout the Muslim world and among Muslim communities all over the world. The organizations quickly established Dawa infrastructures, which met the communities' needs in the areas of education, welfare, relief, and, mainly, in the areas of faith and spirituality. Due to the fact that the nature of these movements' activities was essentially religious and social, most of the countries did not stop them as long as they did not veer to political issues or violence.

Following Hassan Albana's death in 1949, the movement's leadership split up. His disciples were of one mind regarding the goals and vision related to the establishment of a religious Islamic state, but could not agree about how to bring it about:

1. **The "moderate" faction which believed in the Dawa approach** – Hassan al Hadibi, who headed this faction, chose to compromise with political reality, be it democratic or tyrannical, and advocated that the Jihad should be adopted according to the spiritual and non-violent meaning of the word. He believed that the population should be won over in amiable ways rather than by unleashing violent force. Therefore, this faction believed that information and education (the Dawa) are the main tools to be applied in the transformation of society.
2. **The extremist faction that believed in the Jihad –** based itself on the radical philosophy of Sayyid Qutb that called for an uncompromising struggle against the corrupt and ignorant government (Jahilli) through the Jihad. Qutb characterized the maladies of Muslim society, analyzed its components, and came to the conclusion that only activism, Jihad and revolution, whose message is carried by "true believers," have the ability to being about the establishment of a religious Islamic state. He emphasized that there is a sharp contrast between two images, two ideologies, two societies, two forms of government, and a conflicting truth. Islam and ignorance (Jahilliya), faith and heresy, truth and lies, good and evil, God's government or that of man, God and Satan, etc. One side cannot exist if it does not eradicate the other, and there is no room for compromise or mediation between the two. The change, according to Qutb, can only be achieved through revolution, terminating the leaders of the infidels and placing faithful leaders in their stead.

The followers of Qutb's aggressive, Jihad oriented theories—Shukri Ahmad Mustafa, founder of Jamaat Al-Hijra and Al-Takfir, and Abd Salaam Faraj, one of the founders of the Jihad movement in Egypt, developed Qutb's radical line and adopted the Jihad as a means to topple "the corrupt governments" and establish religious Islamic states.

These people believed that it was their duty to build an alternative society upon the rubble of the Jahilli society, by educating and informing the masses on the one hand, while waging a violent and unbending battle against whoever stood in their path on the other.

In 1979, Abd Salam Faraj established the al-Jihad Organization in Egypt. His organization was responsible for the assassination of President Sadat on October 6, 1981. Faraj hoped that chaos would prevail in Egypt in the aftermath of the assassination, thus enabling his organization to seize the reins. One of Faraj's disciples is Ayman al Zawaheiri, Osama

Bin Laden's deputy and cohort. To summarize, the local approach characterized the Jihad Movement until the end of the 1970s. Although the characteristics of the Jihad and its goals had become more radical, they still operated in internal state and regional arenas. The Jihad movements maintained collaborative ties to a certain extent. In contrast, the Dawa spread out a network of means and agents throughout the world. One of the prominent philosophers who advocated the Jihad was Abdullah Azzam.

Azzam conducted fundraising campaigns in the Western world in order to raise money in support of the Jihad in Afghanistan, including in Muslim communities in the United States.

Azzam regarded the Jihad as the main tool to achieve Islamic victory and the establishment of Islamic rule on earth. For a period of time he even joined the Mujahidin that fought in Afghanistan. He became the symbol and leader of the Jihad movements and of the radical Islamic circles worldwide, and his impact on the world Jihad movement transcended the time and place of his lifetime. Azzam's concept of Jihad constitutes the theoretical basis for the modern Jihad movements. It affected the development of several phenomena and processes in radical Islam as follows:

1. The establishment of an Islamic "Internacionale" on the basis of recruitment of volunteers from all over the Muslim world on behalf of the Jihad in Afghanistan.
2. The creation of an international network of Islamic terror cells supported by radical Islamic organizations worldwide.
3. The victory of the Mujahidin in Afghanistan created an aura and ethos of bravery around the Muslim fighters and serves as an inspiration for Muslims all over the world.
4. A broad cadre of Islamic fighters motivated by a sense of mission and combat experience came into existence and turned into the spearhead in struggles between radical Islam and its foes, conspiring to continue the Jihad in various global arenas mainly connected to the West.

## Bin Laden and the Implementation of the Global Jihad Concept

Osama Bin Laden's radical worldview was influenced by the writings of the radical Egyptian Islamists and by Wahhabi Islamic concepts from his land of birth, Saudi Arabia, taking form during his years in Afghanistan. Bin Laden was particularly influenced by the doctrine of the Palestinian Abdullah Azzam, champion and mentor of the global Jihad concept, with whom he cooperated in the running of an organization in Peshawar that dealt in the recruitment of Islamic volunteers for the

Jihad in Afghanistan as well as their training and the provision of arms, ultimately followed by their relocation to fight in Afghanistan. However, conflict subsequently arose between the two. Bin Laden parted ways with Azzam and began to recruit, train, finance, and operate volunteers independently in the Jihad frameworks.[3]

The Islamic organizations that dealt in the "Dawa" dedicated resources to humanitarian relief but at the same time they also dealt in Islamic indoctrination in the communities in which they were active. In contrast, the Jihad movement, whose activities had become increasingly radical, continued to act locally or regionally in Muslim countries against Muslim rulers or foreign occupiers.

The situation changed in the aftermath of the Islamic revolution and the war in Afghanistan in 1979. From that point onward the concept of a global Jihad began to crystallize. It was developed by Abdullah Azzam, who, at the time, was active in Afghanistan, but more importantly, it was implemented by Bin Laden and the Afghan "alumni," who founded the global Jihad in 1998 and declared the U.S., Christianity, and Judaism as main targets of the global Jihad.

The rapid development and expansion of the Jihad movement was based on the infrastructure of the Dawa networks that had been spread out all over the world since the 1930s.

## The Dawa and its Role in Promoting the Global Jihad[4]

The global Jihad, including its lethal branches, would not have succeeded in reaching its current dimensions, expanding its bases, recruiting supporters and terror activists, and conducting terror activity worldwide (particularly the September 11 attacks) if not for the prior global network of the Dawa system which included logistics, financial channels, and its community of benevolence. The infrastructure of charities, as well as the system of religious and communal services that they had established over several decades, served as an anchor and foundation for the activity of the global Jihad's cells and branches.

Members of Islamic terror organizations in general, and Al Qaida in particular, mainly originate from populations characterized by radical Islamic consciousness. This Islamic consciousness is not the fruit of a momentary epiphany but rather the result of ongoing indoctrination carried out by the organizations and their messengers, whether through Muslim states which believe in disseminating the Islamic message worldwide, or through official and semi-official religious establishments in Muslim countries. Communities, groups, or individuals in Muslim countries or

Muslim communities worldwide (where the Dawa infrastructure was established during the twentieth century), were exposed to the Dawa activity for years. These entities constitute the main human resource that feeds the Islamic terror organizations.

These audiences are more attentive to the calls to volunteer for Jihad in order to save the Islamic nation, even if the war is being waged far away from their countries of origin. The Mujahidins' success in Afghanistan, and the incorporation of the Afghan "alumni" in world Islamic terror organizations, encouraged the continuation of activity along the same course. It is important to perceive that the Afghan "alumni" are actually an "Internacionale" of Islamic extremists from all over the world who went through the radical Islamic melting pot in Afghanistan.

Many of the Afghan "alumni" found their way back to local terror organizations and to other Islamic areas of conflict, and some of them joined the ranks of the global Jihad. It is noteworthy that the activity of the Dawa, at many focal points in the Muslim world, was extremist by nature. Alongside the social and humanitarian activity of the Dawa organizations, the Muslim believers were expected not to be content with merely strengthening their faith but also to take action in the defense of Islam and, from there, making the leap to adopting Jihad concepts was not great. The mobilization for Islamic terror organizations and the global Jihad among these audiences bears a procedural similarity to the model of the Afghan "alumni."

1. **Stage 1:** Dawa activity, education and welfare that brings the people closer to Islam.
2. **Stage 2:** Responding to the call for Jihad to save Islam in areas of conflict addressed to both members of the Jihad movements and audiences that have been exposed to Dawa activity. Supportive Islamic countries and charities along with Islamic institutions dispatched the latter to combat areas and training camps. These entities financed their travels, provided the necessary fake papers and referred the recruits to training camps.
3. **Stage 3:** Increased exposure and a closer link between the recruits at the Mujahidin training camps and Jihad radical indoctrination.
4. **Stage 4:** Strengthening the link between the recruited fighters and terror organizations at various conflict areas in the world, both due to joint formative experiences alongside veteran terrorist activists during combat and also as a result of the creation of interpersonal relationships.
5. **Stage 5:** Recruitment to terror organizations under the umbrella of global Jihad and the perpetration of terror attacks in that framework.

## The Link between Global Dawa and Global Jihad[5]

The Dawa infrastructure all over the world was constructed by three central entities:

1. Muslim states that directly built and nurtured the Dawa.
2. Semi-official Islamic institutions and charities established and operated Dawa infrastructures in their countries of origin and worldwide.
3. The Jihad organizations and movements that also developed Dawa infrastructures as a support foundation for their activities.

The Soviet invasion of Afghanistan generated mobilization of the Muslim and Western world on behalf of the Afghan Mujahidin. This mobilization on behalf of the Jihad in Afghanistan forged the link (which was granted widespread legitimacy) between the Dawa mechanisms that originally offered humanitarian aid to the Afghans and the Jihad entities that recruited fighters for the campaign. This integration that actively worked, and led to the trouncing of the Soviets in the Afghan arena, contributed to the crystallization of the global Jihad concept in the hands of Abdullah Azzam and Osama Bin Laden.

In the aftermath of the war in Afghanistan, and following the formulation of the concept of continued Jihad in other arenas worldwide, Bin Laden and his associates had at their disposal tested and effective infrastructures which had earlier served the war in Afghanistan and, upon its completion, were free to support new Jihad arenas such as the Balkans, Chechnya, Kashmir, and more. The cooperation, the joint work at the Dawa centers, the direct contact between the charities and the Mujahidin fighters, and the interpersonal relationships that had been forged as the result of their joint activities, all constituted the basis for the continuation of this pattern of activity when the terror organizations began to act against Western targets and others, particularly against the United States.

This worldwide system enables optimal flexibility for diverting funds, combat means, and fighters from one arena of activity to the next all over the world while maintaining operational discipline and high levels of secrecy, without any need for reorganization.

### An Analysis of the Reciprocal Relationship and Cooperation between the Dawa Factors and the Jihad on the Local Level

When placing the emphasis on the state entity, the Dawa factors mentioned earlier in this chapter developed the Dawa infrastructures both inside the state and in Muslim communities abroad which served

Dawa activities abroad. An examination of the reciprocal relationship between the three factors on the level of the individual Islamic center abroad plainly clarifies the role played by the Dawa centers and infrastructures in the rapid dispersion of the global Jihad. The following is a characteristic example that illustrates the relationship model between global Dawa and global Jihad.

1. **Stage A –** An Islamic state takes a decision to build an Islamic center abroad, and allocates funds for this purpose.
2. **Stage B –** The center is built and dedicated by government representatives.
3. **Stage C –** Responsibility for running the center is transferred to Islamic charities and institutions.
4. **Stage D –** The state continues to support the center's activities and maintains control through representatives at embassies abroad. At this stage the institutions/charities begin to recruit personnel (teachers, preachers and lecturers) to run the center.
5. **Stage E –** The center attracts Islamic audiences and conducts Islamic indoctrination activities based on the permanent staff; it occasionally summons special staff to teach seminars and organize Islamic conferences at the center. In cases such as these, the presence/arrival of a charismatic radical Imam at an Islamic center turns him into a magnet for extremist Islamic target audiences.
6. **Stage F –** The global Jihad identifies the potential that lies in the center and acts to recruit into its ranks activists from among the center's visitors.
7. **Stage G –** As time passes, the center turns into a gathering place for global Jihad and a base for recruitment and logistics. Around and inside it, members of the global Jihad are actively dealing in identification, mobilization, and the training of new recruits. They depart for terror attacks from this location, where they conduct Jihad indoctrination. From this point onwards, the Dawa center becomes a focal point for global Jihad activity alongside the state and semi-official Dawa entities and means involved in the center's activities.

## The Dawa, the Jihad, and Global Islamic Terror

The radical Islamic organizations view terror as the most effective tool to achieve their goals in the modern era. Thus, it is no coincidence that since the 1980s, following the Islamic revolution in Iran, and even more markedly during the 1990s (following the Mujahidins' triumph in Afghanistan), Islamic terror has become a leading factor and a source of emulation for terror organizations worldwide.

International terror organizations in general, and Islamic terror organizations in particular, must develop worldwide infrastructures and secret action patterns in order to ensure their survival and low-key activity. An international terror organization like Al Qaida acts on the basis of four basic principles:

1. Secrecy and compartmentalization
2. Decentralization
3. Logistic and financial infrastructure
4. Collaboration with local terror organizations.

The terror organization has a secret command center within the organization's logistical, financial, and operative setups. The logistical and operational infrastructures are spread out all over the world in autonomous, regional, and local terror networks that are linked to the organization's command through regional "operators."

The organization has recruitment points based on agents who are planted in mosques and Islamic cultural centers as well as in Muslim communities worldwide.

The recruitment process of a volunteer is accompanied by in-depth investigations regarding the recruit, as well as training and indoctrination, culminating in the demand for the recruit's oath of allegiance.

The terrorists' training is conducted at the organization's training facilities. The volunteers come to the facility, undergo training connected to their missions, and are sent back to their lands of origin or to the destination countries.

The financial and logistic system is required to provide financial resources and means, and to send them to the terror networks in order to sustain their activities.

Mega terror attacks like those perpetrated on September 11 are the result of the existence of a worldwide terror infrastructure based on a logistic and financial system backed by abundant resources as well as planning and implementation capabilities.

These are the product of the accumulation of capabilities and many years of experience. To summarize, an international Islamic terror organization like Al Qaida can obtain results like those achieved on September 11 on the basis of extensive infrastructures which can only be provided directly or indirectly by a state entity.

## The Advantages of a Global Terror Organization

The implementation of the global Jihad concept necessitates worldwide infrastructure and alignment. The following advantages can be attributed to the international terror organization:

1. The spreading of the infrastructures generates survivability and superiority. The distance and deployment of the organization create a situation whereby the headquarters and sub-headquarters are spread out in safe places (Bin Laden and his headquarters continue to be active to this very day). The training areas are situated in other places and the logistic infrastructures are also decentralized. As a result, the organization has maximum survivability even if the infrastructure is damaged at one location.
2. A global terror organization can prevent effective surveillance by a single country. This would necessitate international cooperation, something that is almost impossible to implement on a global scope. The global terror organization has the ability to recruit and/or move terror activists all over the world so that surveillance activities related to their movements and activities would necessitate global control and supervision that simply do not exist. For example, it is possible to restrict the entry of citizens of certain countries to the United States, but the terrorists can always enter by using documentation of countries whose citizens are allowed entry.
3. The global terror organization has maximum flexibility when choosing targets. The organization can act against targets of a certain country on its soil or all over the world (embassies, corporations, etc.). The organization has the ability to attack by recruiting terrorists in the target countries or by collaborating with local terror organizations.
4. Due to the fact that the international terror organization can choose any place it desires as an attack arena, this prevents the possibility of effective defense because it is impossible to provide a global response to this type of challenge.
5. The international terror organization has the ability to raise financial resources and to transfer them all over the world by using the world finance system to feed and operate terror infrastructures.
6. The global terror organization also operates by building sleeping infrastructures that are incorporated within the population of the target country and are activated when needed. The chance of discovery is non-existent prior to the stage when they begin acting in subversive patterns.
7. Modern media empower the advantages of the global terror organization and enable it to operate according to a global action plan including gathering intelligence regarding targets in the country of destination, transferring information to headquarters for planning purposes, transferring terror campaigns to the destination within a short amount of time, and managing decentralized headquarter work, which makes it harder to thwart.
8. The global terror organization has the ability to investigate, learn, draw and implement lessons from one terror attack to the next on the other side of the globe. There is no doubt that the September 11 attacks were based on lessons drawn from other attacks perpetrated by Al Qaida all over the world.

Only by understanding the advantages at the disposal of a global terror organization is it possible to comprehend and explain how Bin Laden planned and executed the September 11 attacks through Al Qaida from his hiding place in the wilds of Afghanistan by activating a worldwide system of activities that brought the American superpower to its knees.

## The Dawa and the Global Economic Jihad

The violent (terrorist) Jihad is accompanied and backed by the Economic Jihad, which on the one hand serves to finance and aid the infrastructures and the terror perpetrators, and on the other hand constitutes a parallel arena of contention against the enemies of Islam with the focus on the West.

Over the years, Al Qaida has built an extensive economic infrastructure that serves as a sort of "shadow economy" which acts alongside and within the free economic system that is characteristic of the twentieth and the twenty-first centuries. Most of the organization's budget is designated for the funding of local terror organizations in order to expand the alignment of the global Jihad; part of it is used as payment for host countries such as Sudan and Afghanistan, and the rest is spent on the terror attacks.

The economic infrastructure that serves as Al Qaida's foundation includes a complex and extensive network of entities, the majority of which are "legitimate" such as economic corporations, charities, Islamic banks, religious and educational institutions, and private organizations that contribute to the organization and its activities. Thus, part of the organization's revenue comes from sources and means connected to the Dawa, both from sources controlled by the Islamic state and via those controlled by Islamic associations and institutions. The transfer of funds to the organization is achieved through sophisticated camouflage, cover up and laundering, as well as through legitimate businesses. This method of using businesses as a cover for transferring funding to the movement was made possible by the basic capital infrastructure that Bin Laden possessed as well as his access to business. Over the years he weaved and established a global network of commercial companies through which he succeeded in laundering funds, creating revenue and capital profit, providing work to the organization's members and supporters, and funding its activities. The cornerstones of free society, including freedom of speech and religion, freedom of occupation, freedom of movement, and the principle of a free economy make it easy for the terror organizations to act within this system, exploit it for their own purposes, and ultimately act against it in order to undermine the state-oriented system upon which it rests. The desire to preserve the free and democratic character of the West's economic and political system places many restrictions on the security and law enforcement agencies when contending with terror which aims to undermine the foundations of democracy.

The economic Jihad claims a high toll from the Western world and poses a grave challenge to its continued freedom-based existence:

- Immediate damage stemming from attacks (the direct damage of the September 11 attacks)
- Indirect damage inflicted by attacks (damage to aviation, tourism, insurance, etc.)
- The threat of terror necessitates the investment of huge sums of money for protection against it (changing security procedures in aviation, establishing the DHS, etc.)

Another heavy blow inflicted by the global Jihad in the West stems from the need to carry out steps to thwart this activity. These steps affect the economic system and endanger the foundations of the democratic system.

## Summary

The Jihad waged in Afghanistan against the Soviets generated processes of historical importance that altered the appearance of modern radical Islam:

1. The Dawa and Islamic organizations rushed to help the Islamic movements in Afghanistan, and with the aid and support of the Muslim (and Western) world established systems that provided humanitarian aid to the Afghan population.
2. Islamic fighters from all over the Muslim world arrived in Afghanistan in order to participate in the Jihad against the Soviet Union.
3. The provision and training of fighters, supplying them with weapons and sending them to the battlefield with the help of the infrastructures of Islamic organizations that were active in the arena.
4. The combination of the Dawa centers and infrastructures upon which the Jihad infrastructures were constructed created a highly efficient system that proved to be successful in the Afghan arena and has served as a model in other arenas worldwide.
5. The Jihad in Afghanistan created three central phenomena:

**First phenomenon** – Globalization of the Jihad and Jihad movements, while prior to the Jihad in Afghanistan these entities generally acted locally in Jihad movements (sometimes on the basis of local or regional mutual aid) in order to topple the regime in their country. The Afghan Jihad brought about a direct encounter between the members of the Jihad movements from all over the world and generated "a brotherhood of comrades-in-arms," and joint formative experiences which at the end of the Jihad in Afghanistan created a sort of worldwide "Jihad Internacionale."

**Second phenomenon –** A systematic model incorporating the Dawa and Jihad infrastructures on a global scope and their activation as a coordinated and integrated system to promote the Jihad's goals. Abdullah Azzam (Bin Laden's spiritual mentor) and Bin Laden himself both played key roles in molding the concepts and systems of the global Jihad whose basic components are described above.

**Third phenomenon –** The construction of a "learning system" that accumulates experience, learns lessons and incorporates them within the planning processes of the attacks and realizes them in the implementation.

The contribution of the Islamic institutions and the charities to the development of Al Qaida as a global terror organization was essential and stemmed from the fact that the Dawa infrastructure had been spread all over the globe prior to the concept of global Jihad. When this idea came to full maturity and implementation by Bin Laden, it grew on the foundation and infrastructure of the global Dawa system that was anchored in a worldwide alignment of Islamic centers, mosques, preachers, funding and logistic sources. On the eve of September 11, the global Islamic Dawa infrastructure included thousands of Islamic institutions and sites spread out among Islamic communities all over the world, and even if only a handful of them dealt in radical Islamic indoctrination this would suffice to enable the rapid expansion of the global Jihad.

The Dawa activity provided the platform which the global Jihad, founded by Bin Laden, needed, and, among other things, it provided the following:

1. **Fundamentalist indoctrination –** A central theme in the activity of the Islamic institutions and the state institutions. Through institutional and advanced dissemination means the latter enhanced Islamic consciousness among Islamic communities as well as the motivation of these populations to take part in a war defending Islam. These entities also molded public opinion in favor of the terror activity against the West in general and the United States in particular.
2. **The logistic infrastructure –** The Dawa entities, including the Islamic institutions and the charities, built and operated a logistic infrastructure

that provided shelter, a refuge and an address vis-à-vis spiritual and material help for the Jihad activists. At the same time, this infrastructure recruited young Islamic men and dispatched them to various combat zones. It purchased combat means and equipment for the forces (uniforms, medical equipment, vehicles, etc.) The Dawa entities also helped with the maintenance of the training camps in various combat areas, with emphasis on Afghanistan.

3. **Financing –** Islamic institutions and charities provided direct and indirect funding for the terror organizations through deception, concealment and money laundering while carefully covering up any link between the financer and the terror organization.

It is noteworthy that the Muslim states that are acquainted with the reciprocal ties between the Dawa and the Jihad apply tight supervision over the Dawa means and entities due to the fact that it will provide the infrastructure which the Jihad needs for its development. The West, which only saw the humanistic side of the Dawa and was unaware of the powerful ties between global Dawa and global Jihad, did not restrict the Dawa activity, thereby enabling the consolidation of global Jihad upon the infrastructure of global Dawa.

Al Qaida succeeded in tapping the potential inherent to the Dawa infrastructures worldwide, became integrated within them and harnessed them to promote the terror campaign it was planning, based on its familiarity with and exploitation of vulnerabilities inherent to the democratic American society, with the aim of causing grave damage to the most sensitive and painful sites in the United States and the Free World as a whole.

## Notes

1. Yoram Schweitzer and Shaul Shay, The Globalization of Terror, Transaction Publishers, New Brunswick, U.S.A., 2003, p 13.
2. Ibid, pp 14-16.
3. Rohan Gunaratna, Inside Al Qaida, Global Network of Terror, Columbia Unioversity Press, New York, 2002, pp 3-4.
4. This part was developed with Dr. Eitan Azani from the ICT.
5. Ibid
6. Ibid

# Section Two

## The Balkans and Islam—<br>An Historical Background

# The Balkans—Historical Milestones

Yugoslavia is a mountainous country in the northern Balkans. The state till 2006 has been composed of two republics: Serbia and Montenegro.

The geographical region situated in the central and western Balkans, which became the Yugoslavian entity, is the most complex from the aspects of its ethnic composition and territorial affinity, and is the most representative of the "Balkan situation." It is where two fault lines cross, the one drawn between Orthodox Christianity (for example, the Serbs and the Macedonians) and Catholicism (Slovenians and Croatians), and the other drawn between the Christians and the Muslims (Bosnians and Albanians). The variety of population groups is much larger because the link between religious affiliation and ethnic or language-related identity is not always unequivocal. Thus, for example, the Muslims, defined as Bosnians, are mostly of Slavic descent and they speak Serbo-Croatian. The fact that there are many other ethnic groups also contributes to the wide diversity—particularly those at the margins of this area (Hungarians, Bulgarians, etc.).[1]

The picture is no less complex from the aspect of spatial alignment, as the ethnic cocktail is not only found in the distant periphery or at urban junctions, but also in many of the rural areas which are situated within the nuclear regions of the main population groups.

There are two diametrically opposed schools of thought regarding the Balkans' historical role. The first outlook, which is advocated by Samuel Huntington, [2] regards the Balkans as a typical focus of the competition between civilizations (see elaboration in Section Seven), while the other outlook views the Balkans as a transit area and as a bridge between different cultural worlds, a range through which people, ideas, and merchandise passed, thus stimulating the cultures located on the various sides of the peninsula. The "city-polis" Dubrovnik, which existed under the Venetian and Ottoman regimes as an autonomous Christian-Catholic city, is presented as a place which more than any other symbolizes the "positive" role of the Balkans as an area of passage and a meeting place for Catholics, Orthodoxy, Muslims, and Jews.

The Serb bombardment of Dubrovnik during the Serb-Croatian War (1991-1992) is presented as a deliberate attempt to destroy the delicate fabric that had been woven there for years as well as the pluralistic character of all of the Balkans. [3]

Those who choose to regard the Balkans as a meeting place view the bridge, as the structure that symbolizes this role. Indeed, the Ottoman bridge built in the form of a semi-circular arc which stands on a base of several arcs over the foaming river, often serves as a symbol signifying the Balkans as a meeting place and passageway between cultures where people of different faiths coexist peacefully and speak different languages. [4]

The first independent Serb kingdom, which was established in 1169 under the leadership of Stefan Dushan, developed and controlled the majority of the Balkan Peninsula.

This kingdom ceased to exist after the Ottomans defeated the Serb army in the Kosovo Campaign of 1389. From that time until the end of the ninteenth century, the entire region became part of the Ottoman Empire. The Ottoman Empire, which at its peak reached the gates of Vienna, was the homeland of many peoples and religions in which Christians, Jews, and others coexisted for hundreds of years under the control of the Muslim majority. However, this coexistence did not prevail due to a modern concept of tolerance, nor was it based on the acceptance of differences and the offer of equality to all, but rather it stemmed from a feeling of superiority that regards others as entities worthy of tolerance, despite their inferiority. Thus, although the Turks, or the Muslims, were a minority in certain parts of the empire, they maintained control due to their status as the Muslim master, while the various Christian groups (and Jews) were all demoted to the status of "protected residents" ("Demis").

The Christians and others who preferred to become assimilated in the Ottoman system by converting to Islam, using the Turkish language, and serving in the state army, soon became an integral part of the Ottoman culture, even when they preserved their ethnic affinity and their mother tongue. [5] During their years of power, the Ottomans were faced with a dilemma: On the one hand, it was in their economic interest to squeeze the "Demi" taxpayers, and in order to do so they had to leave the invaded population where it was and refrain from evicting it or forcing it to convert to Islam. But on the other hand, military and security needs dictated that measures be taken to make certain that the Muslim population was large enough to ensure loyalty to the empire. In the Balkans, the Ottomans were inclined to follow the second path. They decided to deport the local population and settle their own people, or other occupied peoples, in their place. Thus they ascertained that it would not occur to any local minority to rebel when surrounded by a Muslim population. The "Islamization" process was particularly apparent in Bosnia due to mass conversion of the local population. The new Muslims quickly became the worst oppressors of their former fellow believers, to the extent that the Bosnians earned a bad reputation due to the positions they filled in the Ottoman government and in the military, particularly in the Yanichari brigades. [6]

At the Berlin Congress in 1878, it was decided to establish Serbia and Montenegro as two independent monarchies and a border was drawn between them and the other areas of the Empire, however this line changed over the years.[7]

In 1912 Serbia, Montenegro, Greece, and Bulgaria joined forces against the Ottoman Empire in the "First Balkans War," defeated it, and banished it from most of its strongholds in Europe. That same year a first attempt was made to bring to fruition the concept of "a greater Albania," when Albania declared its independence and won the support of the Western European powers. These entities aspired to clip Serbia's wings due to its ties with the Czarist Russian Empire.

Albania's independence was granted recognition at the London Conference in 1913, and an international committee was set up to demarcate its borders. However, before the committee began its deliberations, the "Second Balkans War" broke out and Bulgaria attacked its former allies and was defeated.

To a significant degree, the results of this war formed the Balkans boundaries as we know them today. [8]

The international conference that determined Albania's borders finally completed its task, and due to pressure exerted by Serbia, the Kosovo Region, whose population was made up mainly of Muslim Albanians, was left inside Serbia's borders. The Serbian claim was that it had strong historical links with Kosovo due to the battle in which they were defeated in 1389. In this resolution, which was made in consideration of the European power balance at the time and under pressure exerted by the Austro-Hungarian Empire, the boundary was delineated between Serbia and Albania, and the seeds were sown for the war in 1999.

After World War I (1918) the state incorporating Serbia, Croatia, and Slovenia (the kingdom of the Serbs, the Croatians, and the Slovenians) was founded. The international conference continued its work in defining the boundaries and only completed its work in 1925, but Yugoslavia's boundary with Albania was never changed. Thus a multinational country was created in the Balkan Peninsula in which Serbs, Orthodox Christians, Catholic Croatians, Macedonians, Muslims, Slovenians, Bulgarians, Hungarians, Montenegrins, and Albanians coexisted.[9]

The guideline for the definition of the unifying and inclusive identity for each of the groups was focused on identity and linguistic similarity. The name of the "Serb, Croatian and Slovenian Kingdom" was changed in 1929 to "Yugoslavia" (the State of the Southern Slovenians), although the latter included a significant number of additional groups in light of the concept that necessitated the creation of a large enough territory to possess economic and geopolitical resources. The Serbs were the demographic and territorial nucleus of the new entity because they had enjoyed independence even prior to the war and they were the dominant group.

However, it was this aspiration to base the extensive entity on Serbian centrality that generated growing opposition on the part of the Croatians and other nations and, consequentially, the centrifugal forces that aspired to undermine the joint framework intensified. Thus, during the Nazi invasion Croatia was separated from Yugoslavia and turned into a German protectorate country (a state of affairs which was terminated after the war). [10]

Between the two world wars and also in their aftermath, with the establishment of the Yugoslavian Republic under Tito's leadership, the external boundaries of Yugoslavia were not altered and it succeeded in maintaining a balance between the various components of the population for several decades.

Immediately following World War II, as a lesson learned from the experiment of the first "Yugoslavian" model that had failed, an additional attempt was made by Tito which constituted a sort of compromise between the traditional multiethnic reality and the aspiration to establish a centralized nationalist country. Tito united all of the ethnic groups under the slogan of "affinity and unity" within one governmental entity.

The Communist ideology, which stood at the basis of the new entity, approached the question of nationality with a mixture of censure and recognition of the cultural and ethnic differences. The version adopted by the new Yugoslavia was, therefore, the recognition of pluralism and self-definition for the main groups—a recognition reflected in the federative structure of the state from the aspect of community and territory. The six republics that made up the federation were Serbia, Croatia, Slovenia, Bosnia, Montenegro, and Macedonia. Within the framework of the Serbian Republic, two entities were granted the status of autonomy, that of

Wivodena (which has a significant Hungarian minority) and Kosovo (whose main representation was Albanian). Thanks to delicate balancing, the controlling ideology, and the prestige of leadership at the federal center, Yugoslavia enjoyed years of stability. The religious and ethnic foundation in this atheist country was considerably weakened. Even in Sarajevo, which was at the meeting place of the community "fault lines," Christians separated themselves from Muslims as follows: "While we don't go to church, the Muslims don't go to mosques." In contrast to the Middle East, mixed marriages between Muslim Bosnians and Serbs or Croatians became frequent, and there were many who defined themselves as "Yugoslavians." [11]

The deterioration of the "Yugoslavian system" began in 1980 with Tito's demise and the collapse of the Communist order—two processes that intensified the centrifugal forces and reignited the traditional community foundations at the basis of the Balkanization. The first to break away from the Federation was the Northern Slovenian Republic. As the most homogeneous and developed entity, which regarded itself as part of central Europe, it preferred its own interests over the federative structure, which included areas that necessitated the allocation of significant federal resources, such as the distant south which was poor and torn by conflict or nearby Bosnia. It is to be noted that in order to balance Serbia's weight in comparison to the other republics, some of the mixed areas that contained Serb population were included in nearby Croatia and Bosnia. Thus, in the name of this demand for segregation and self-definition, the Serbs in Bosnia and Croatia aspired to be annexed to Serbia and realize the concept of a homogenous state for "a larger Serbia." The main means to achieve this goal was through ethnical cleansing.

The reignition of the pure national concept as the main political theme and guideline from the aspect of the territorial breakup brought to a head not only the question of the periphery and the boundaries of the Serbian space but primarily the attitude toward the historical and symbolic nucleus of the Serb entity. This nucleus is situated in the Kosovo region where, as stated earlier, the Muslim Ottomans defeated the Serbs in 1389. This event became a formative experience from both national and territorial points of view. But at this location the Serb population constitutes a minority in retreat in the face of the demographic growth and population expansion of the Muslim Albanians. [12]

At the end of the 1980s the nationalist Serbian leader Slobodan Miloshevich rose to power in Yugoslavia. He made frequent use of nationalist and religious motifs to promote his political agenda. His policy incited considerable tension between the Serbs and the Albanians in Kosovo.

The spark that ignited Serbian nationalism was kindled in 1989, on the occasion of the 600th anniversary of the Serbs' defeat. To mark the event, the Serbs in the region were granted preference and powerful positions while at the same time the autonomy given to the Albanian majority in the framework of the federative arrangement was abolished.

In 1991, after Croatia declared its independence, fighting broke out between the Serbs and the Croatians. After a bitter battle between the Serb and Croatian forces in the area of Vukovar in Croatia, the two countries signed a ceasefire agreement through U.S. mediation. In 1991, Bosnia-Herzegovina (which has a Muslim majority and a Serb minority) declared independence and in April 1992 it was granted UN and U.S. recognition. Serbia refused to recognize the Bosnian independence and rushed to the aid of the Serbian minority in this republic that opposed the establishment of an independent state in the form of Bosnia-Herzegovina. The Serbs invaded Bosnia and surrounded Sarajevo, the Bosnian capital. They continued the invasion and the "ethnic cleansing." Some of the incidents of mass murder perpetrated among the Muslims were carried out in concentration camps built by Miloshevich's army in Bosnia. Nevertheless, it is important to note that in the course of the war the Muslims also carried out massacres among the Serbian population.

Thus, the "Balkanization" [13] process swept on. It began in the northern part of the former Yugoslavian Federation—in Slovenia and Croatia—which were the most developed countries that were the first (as stated earlier) to break away from the Yugoslavian Federation. The process subsequently spread to the Bosnian region in the center—where the population is the most diverse—and from there moved southwards to Kosovo, "the focal point of the historical memory spaces."

Further south, in the region of the new Macedonian Republic (FYROM), [14] the competitive and identical territorial demands were no less problematic and even more deviated from Yugoslavian soil: In addition to the new Macedonian identity, the battle over the Macedonian entity also involved the Serbs, the Albanians, the Bulgarians, as well as the Greeks, who claim the heritage of Alexander the Great as their own.

From the start, Yugoslavia suffered from a lack of international interest, which allowed the level of violence to rise and acts to be perpetrated that can be defined as crimes against humanity, without the intervention of the international community. Despite the increasing reports in world media regarding massacres, rapes, and looting, as well as the establishment of concentration camps, the international community chose to remain silent.

Only when the dimensions of the tragedy became catastrophic did entities in the international system wake up and begin to actively intervene in the conflict. In the course of the war in Bosnia-Herzegovina 200,000 Muslim Bosnians were killed and another two million became refugees. Only in 1995, after the Serbs were accused of massacring 7,000 Muslims in the city of Serbernica in Eastern Bosnia, did significant Western military intervention begin (including NATO attacks against the Serbs from the air). Through U.S. mediation, the Dayton Accords was signed at the end of 1995. According to the agreement, Bosnia was divided into two political entities—the Serbian Republic and the Bosnian-Croatian Federation, with a multinational force enforcing the agreement on the two parties to the conflict.

The war in Bosnia did not signal the end of the ethnic confrontations in the Balkan, but only their beginning. The struggle of the Muslims in Bosnia, and their support on the part of the West and the Muslim world, served as a source of encouragement and inspiration for the Muslims in Kosovo.

For about a decade, the tension between the Muslim-Albanian majority and the Serb minority rose. At the heart of the controversy was the demand of the Muslim population in Kosovo to restore the autonomous status that the area had enjoyed before it was revoked during Miloshevich's regime.

In the framework of the Muslim struggle against the authorities in Belgrade, a Muslim terror group called the KLA (Kosovo Liberation Army) was established. The KLA perpetrated terror attacks against the authorities and the Serb population in Kosovo. The ruthless Serb response caused considerable suffering to the civilian Muslim population in Kosovo. In the beginning of 1999, an attempt was made to resolve the conflict under the patronage of the European Union in talks that were conducted between the parties in Rambuie, France (February 1999).

Following Miloshevich's rejection of the compromise that Kosovo would remain under Yugoslavian sovereignty but be granted extensive autonomy, he initiated military steps to enforce Serb control of the region and conducted "ethnical cleansing" within the Muslim population.

Under U.S. leadership, NATO responded sharply to the Serb actions and after its ultimatum to Miloshevich was rejected, launched a bombardment from the air against Serbia that ultimately forced Miloshevich to give in to NATO's demands.

The Serb/Muslim confrontation in Kosovo, which at the present time has been suspended due to NATO's intervention and the dispatch of a multinational force to maintain order, has yet to be resolved. Moreover, a short time after the end of the confrontation in Kosovo, tension and violence bubbled in Macedonia between the Macedonian majority and the Muslim minority that is supported by the KLA in Kosovo.

In summary, it would appear that the Balkans will continue to constitute an ethnic and cultural confrontation point between the Muslims and their opponents in the foreseeable future. According to Samuel Huntington, this process is part of the cultural war that characterizes the end of the twentieth century and the beginning of the twenty-first century.

## Islam in the Balkans during World War II [15]

World War II constitutes both a traumatic and formative period in the history of the Balkan peoples and serves as a source for "historical reckoning" between the adversaries today.

Modern Yugoslavia, which was founded after World War II under the leadership of Marshal Tito who had led the struggle against the Germans and their allies in Yugoslavia during the war, strived to repress the issues of the past and forge a united federation in the Balkans. This attempt was successful during Tito's lifetime but the Yugoslavian Federation collapsed after his demise.

The collapse of the Yugoslavian Federation reignited the ethnic, national, and cultural conflict among the Balkan peoples. Historical issues in general, and the traumas of World War II in particular, play a central role in the present confrontations.

Among other aspects, World War II honed the confrontation between the Muslims in the Balkans and their adversaries, and provided an opportunity for the infiltration of radical Islamic influences from the "breeding house" of the Mufti Hajj Amin al Husseini. [16]

This chapter will address the sensitive issue of the Balkan Muslim support of Nazi Germany during World War II.

Following the German invasion of Yugoslavia in 1941, parts of its territory were distributed among neighboring countries that had collaborated with Germany during the invasion. Among the recipients of these territories were Hungary (large areas of the Bechka region), Bulgaria (Macedonia), Italy (part of Slovenia and the Dalmatian coast on the Adriatic Sea), and Albania, which was under the patronage-conquest of Italy until September1943. The Germans directly controlled large sections of Slovenia and Serbia, and under the German patronage, a puppet government led by Milan Nedic was established.

On April 10, 1941, four days after the outbreak of the war and prior to the Yugoslavian surrender, the Germans handed over the reins of government in Croatia to their recent collaborators, the Fascist "Ustase"

Organization headed by Dr. Ante Pavelić. On the same day the establishment of the "Independent Croatian State" (ICS). which also included Bosnia-Herzegovina, was declared.

A short time after the Ustases ascended to power they initiated the physical extermination of "government opposition," including the murder of Serb Jews in cruel death camps, the most infamous of which was Jasenovac. The Ustases' cruelty shocked their Italian allies who initiated activities to save the Jews by smuggling them out of ICS territory to Italy or to the Yugoslavian territory that was under their control.

Due to the Ustases' terror regime, there was a popular uprising which the Croatian government had trouble subjugating. The latter was forced to request German aid. In exchange for their assistance, the Germans demanded the recruitment of Croatian manpower on behalf of the German war efforts at the various fronts where its forces were fighting. As a result of the Croatian government's acquiescence to the German demand, Croatian divisions were established and sent mainly to the eastern front in the Soviet Union.

Croatian President Pavelic, who was interested in preserving his regime's stability, understood that he must try to gain the trust and "conquer the hearts" of the Muslims whose numbers approached one million in the Balkans. Thus, on the first anniversary of Croatian independence (on April 10, 1942), he appeared in public wearing a fez, which was characteristic of the Muslim population. Many Muslims were recruited into the Ustases' ranks, whether willingly or under duress. In August 1942, the weekly Osvit, which appeared in Sarajevo, published an interview of its correspondent in Rome with Hajj Amin al Husseini, and it was widely quoted in all of the ICS newspapers.

The weekly described the Mufti as the standard-bearer and protector of millions of Muslims worldwide, and placed special emphasis on his links with the Fuehrer. In a cable sent by the German Ambassador in Zagreb to his superiors in Berlin, the Mufti's words in the interview were highlighted:

> The Muslims' position is clear. In their struggle for freedom they stand alongside Germany, Japan and their allies. Their struggle against Great Britain will continue until the final collapse of the British Empire, as well as against the Soviet Union, Islam's foe for hundreds of years ... the triumph of the Axis powers will also be that of the Islamic people.

On October 15, 1942, a four-member delegation of the Muslim action committee on behalf of an autonomy in Bosnia-Herzegovina set out from Mostar, the capital of Bosnia-Herzegovina, to Rome in order to meet with

Hajj Amin who was Mussolini's guest of honor at the time. Thus, the Bosnian links with the Mufti were renewed. These ties had already been forged in December 1931 at a pan-Islamic conference in Jerusalem.

The talks in Jerusalem focused on the question of autonomy for the Muslims in the framework of the ICS and the handling of their adversaries, mainly the Partisans or the Serb Chetniks.

Although not all the Muslims necessarily opposed Tito or the nationalist Serb Colonel Draža Mihailović's forces, Hajj Amin succeeded in persuading the members of the Muslim delegation that the goals of the Muslims would be attained only by joining forces with the Axis.

Two weeks later, on November 1, 1942, the popular committee of the Muslim isolationist circle in Bosnia-Herzegovina sent a memorandum to Adolph Hitler asking him to sponsor and protect them. The memorandum was written in German and was addressed to "his Highness Adolph Hitler, Leader of the German people" and it begins with the words:

> Our Leader:
>
> In Berlin, capital of the great German Reich, there are many of the leaders of the Islamic peoples from the east. They came to you in the name of their peoples to seek protection and succor from you, to help them in their war against the despised British and English yoke, under which they live.
>
> The situation of these emissaries and refugees and their efforts are simple and clear: They seek freedom, their liberty- which is among the spoils of the British Imperialism, against whom the German people also fights under your leadership. It is logical that your aid to the oppressed Islamic people will not be denied: However, this memorandum-request that we are dispatching to you is a sensitive matter and at first glance may seem complicated too because it comes from us, the "Boshniaks," meaning the Muslims from Bosnia and Herzegovina, whose homeland is within the framework of the state that was established based on your desire and consent; But when we clarify the matter with proof, it will be impossible to refute the facts. Then our issue-request will be clear and logical, mutual and beneficial, similar to the other emissaries of the Muslim east who have come to you requesting assistance.

The memorandum's authors pointed out that the Muslims in Bosnia-Herzegovina are an inseparable part of the Islamic peoples whose numbers come to some 300 million, and that their liberation can only be obtained with the aid of the Germans and their great Fuehrer in the joint battle against British Imperialism, Judaism, the Free Masons, and Bolshevism.

It is worthy of notice that the memorandum's authors wrote that the Muslim hopes in the ICS had been betrayed at great personal risk. They clearly stated that instead of feeling liberated, ICS had brought a terrible disaster upon them—some 150,000 Muslims had been murdered to date. Their statement clearly raised an accusatory finger at Pavelić, who had forcefully annexed Bosnia-Herzegovina to his own country.

The memorandum also dealt with the issue of "the purity of race" and the Bosnians stated their version regarding their origins and historical development, while offering Hitler concrete proposals regarding the realization of their national goals, which they maintained matched those of the Third Reich.

> We, the Muslims in Bosnia, are not devoted to the German people because of our momentary distress and interests. Although we live in this land, whose majority is composed of Slavic peoples, and despite the fact that we speak Bosnian, which is similar to Serbian-Croatian, we are not Slavs. Our origins are Gothic. We, the Bosniaks, came to the Balkans from the north during the Iliric Province in Rome in the third century, in the form of a German tribe, the "Bosnis." In the sixth century, the Roman name of our country was changed to the popular name "Bosna."
>
> In our ancient language the word "Bosn" means a good man, while "Beisen" means a bad man. We called our new homeland only "Bosna," similar to the name that we gave the main river in our land.
>
> In the sixth century the Slavs—the Serbs and the Croatians—came to our country, and our forefathers employed them as serfs on our estates. To this very day, the differences between us, the Bosniaks, and the Slavic, Serb, and Croatian nations, have been preserved in spiritual and anthropological characteristics. Ninety percent of the Bosniaks have thin blond hair, blue eyes and light skin, while 80 percent of the Serbs and Croatians have thick black hair, black eyes and dark skin …
>
> After their arrival in the Balkans, the Serbs accepted the Eastern Christian religion, the Croatians, Roman Catholic Christianity, while we, the Bosniaks, preserved our ancient Gothic Aryan religion. We preserved this religion, which calls us "Bogomils" (beloved of God), until the arrival of the Turks in 1463 …
>
> The Bosniaks adamantly held on to their swastikas, which they had brought as Goths to Iliriya (i.e. Bosnia), and we decorated our graves with this sign. Although Islam forbids the placing of non-Islamic signs on tombs, we preserved the swastika and some of our graves bore that sign even after the conversion to Islam …
>
> World War I linked us in blood ties with Germany and with Turkey- the Islamic religion and history. We had thought that we were facing a brilliant future: As Muslims, we would serve as the bridge between our blood brothers from the west—and the Islamic east, where 300 million Muslims live … "

## The Incorporation of Muslims in SS Divisions

Up until 1940 Hitler did not trust Himler and decided that the number of SS units would not exceed 10 percent of all German military forces. In August 1940, Hitler changed his attitude and approved the establishment of the SS elite units—the Waffen SS, which were made up solely of volunteers. In this framework it was decided to establish the Waffen SS 13th Division (in a directive issued on February 10, 1943). The formation directive did not mention that the Division would be based on Muslim recruits or that it was planned as a Croatian Division. Three days later, on February 13, 1943, Himler informed General Arthur Phleps, Commander of the Waffen SS 7th Division (Prinz Eugen), of this decision. The latter division had previously accepted ethnic German volunteers (Folkdeutsche) from the Banat region in the former Yugoslavia who spoke the country's language fluently. (During the monarchy, many of these volunteers had served as a fifth column for the Germans.) The rumor regarding the arrival of the Prinz Eugen soldiers in Bosnia-Herzegovina aroused great fears among the Muslims because the Folkdeutsche were known for their hatred of Muslims because of the fact that they are Semites.

The German Ambassador in Croatia, Ziegfried Kasche, was informed of this by the German Foreign Minister von Ribbentrop who demanded that he notify the ICS government of Hitler's decision to set up a new Waffen SS Division by recruiting volunteers, primarily those who had served as volunteers in the Royal Emperor's Austro-Hungarian Army (KUK) during World War I.

On February 18, 1943, the German Ambassador Siegfried Kasche reported to his superiors in Berlin that General Phleps had already visited him and that the ICS Foreign Minister, Dr. Meaden Lorkovi , also attended the meeting. He informed them that the Croatians had welcomed the idea and recommended that the Division's name be the "SS Croatian Ustasen Division." He added that they had raised no objection to the fact that Muslim recruits would serve as the Division's nucleus, but they could not agree to German handling of the mobilization.

Following Kasche's letter, a consultation was held on March 5, 1943 in Zagreb regarding mobilization for the soon to be established Waffen SS unit. It was decided that both Croatian Catholics and Muslims would serve in the Division, mainly from the area of Bosnia-Herzegovina, because that was where "the best Croatian military human material existed." At this opportunity various issues were raised such as the language of the commands and the details regarding uniforms and symbols. The ICS government ultimately granted its permission to establish the "Kroatische Waffen-SS Freiwilligen Division." It was decided to designate no less than 46,000 individuals for this purpose, starting with those born in 1908.

Subsequently, the ICS Secretary of State, Dr. Vjekoslav Vrancic, held work meetings with Dengek, Letsch, Ulrich, and Von Krempler, all leaders of the SS, in order to facilitate the matter.

The Germans estimated that the majority of the Division would be made up of Muslims and, therefore, understood that they would need to find a charismatic leader who would encourage Muslim recruitment. Thus, the Germans welcomed Hajj Amin al Husseini's offer to come to ICS prior to the establishment of the Waffen-SS 13th Division. (The German Ambassador to Croatia, Siegfried Kasche, only learned about the matter in a conversation with Foreign Minister Lorkovi . He was informed that the Mufti wished to pay "a short private visit" to ICS quite soon. Kasche emphasized that the Mufti had not been invited, but rather had requested that an invitation be extended to him).

## The Involvement of the Mufti Hajj Amin al Husseini in Recruiting Muslims for the German SS Divisions in the Balkans[18]

On March 30, 1943, Hajj Amin al Husseini arrived in Zagreb on a German aircraft accompanied by Dr. Mile Budak, the ICS Ambassador to Berlin, five SS officers and two family members: Dr. Mussa Abdullah al Husseini and Zafout Yunes al Husseini. He was received in Zagreb by Dr.Ante Paveli . He was escorted by Akif Handzić, the Zapwat Ustasen "mufti," and Professor Ibrahim Ruzdić on his visit to Bosnia-Herzegovina, Sarajevo, and Banja-Luka.

During his stay in Sarajevo, Hajj Amin al Husseini met with representatives of Muslim and Catholic organizations, religious clerics, and social figures, in the presence of the Germans and the Ustases. Hajj Amin delivered a sermon at the city's main mosque and called upon the Muslims to demonstrate their unity at every opportunity and to respond to the call to volunteer for the SS-Waffen Divisions. Hajj Amin returned to Berlin on April 15, 1943 and immediately sent a detailed report about his visit in the Balkans to the German Foreign Ministry. Hajj Amin wrote that in light of his discussions with the Muslim representatives in Bosnia-Herzegovina, it became clear that the Muslims had welcomed the entry of German forces into Bosnia-Herzegovina in April 1941, and for that reason the Serbs called them "a fifth column." He claimed that, immediately following the outbreak of the war in the east (meaning the Soviet Union), Serb gangs had initiated mass murders of Muslims and the torching of their homes.

The Muslims' disappointment grew when they learned that "certain elements" among the Axis powers were aiding Draźe Micailović's Chetnik Serbs (a heavy allusion to Italy). The Muslim anger against their adversaries increased over time due to the lies that they spread, according to which the Muslims maintained ties with the Partisans, while in truth they fought them in Yugoslavia as well as on the eastern front as volunteers against Bolshevism, and many of them worked in factories throughout Germany, supporting the German "war machine."

Hajj Amin noted that thanks to his considerable efforts, he had succeeded in convincing the Muslims of the importance of active cooperation with Germany, and they understood that it was worth their while to volunteer and be incorporated in the establishment of the SS-Waffen Divisions.

Therefore, the Mufti asked the Germans to recognize and support his position regarding the Division's role, as he stated in several points. He also demanded that collaboration with the Chetniks cease and that they be disarmed. Another request was to curb the Catholic Church's influence. The Mufti reported that up to the time that the report was written, over 12,000 volunteers had registered and stated that the ICS government was incapable of putting an end to the uprising sweeping over Croatia.

The Mufti believed that a statement made by Anthony Eden in the British House of Parliament on January 27, 1943, according to which the British and the Soviet governments were helping the revolutionary forces in Serbia and Croatia, alluded to a possible invasion of the Balkans by the Allied Forces. In addition, he claimed that the uprising in Croatia might serve as an example for other countries under the control of the Axis powers.

At the end of the report, the Mufti wrote that the Axis powers and their allies, including some 4.5 million Muslims in the Balkans, must cooperate closely in order to suppress the uprising as quickly as possible and avert complications that could affect the results of the war. Many parts of Mufti's report to the German Foreign Ministry are almost identical to the content of the memorandum written by the Bosnian isolationist Muslims whom, as stated earlier, was sent to Hitler on January 1, 1942. The only topic that Hajj Amin refrained from mentioning was the conflict between the Muslims and Pavelić, and he had to be satisfied with stating that action should be taken to improve the Muslims' conditions in the ICS in keeping with the Reich's strategic interests.

The Foreign Ministry forwarded the report to the SS main headquarters. With Hajj Amin's assistance, Hitler and Himler killed two birds with one stone: On the one hand, they almost completely curbed Muslim recruitment to Tito's Partisan units, while on the other hand they achieved extensive mobilization of Muslims to active service on behalf of the Germans. This enabled them to send significant parts of their forces to other fighting arenas in the occupied areas of Yugoslavia or at other European fronts. The Germans also believed that the recruitment of Muslims in the Balkans would contribute to improved ties with Turkey.

The first Muslim division to be established in the ICS was called "Handzar," meaning a spear or a dagger. The division was also known as SS Division No. 13.

There are testimonies about the dissatisfaction expressed by some of the fighters in the units that were sent to Germany for training and subsequently to France as well. The soldiers claimed that their families in Bosnia-Herzegovina suffered not only at the hands of their main enemy—the Partisans, but also at the hands of the Serb population and even Croatians, and therefore asked to be posted in their own country. According to reports, an uprising took place in several of the units that was ruthlessly oppressed. In order to improve morale Hajj Amin visited these units several times in Croatia, France, and in Neuhammer, Shlezia.

Upon their return to the territory of former Yugoslavia, the Handzar soldiers rained terror upon the civilian population everywhere that they were posted and perpetrated many war crimes, mass killings, rapes, the burning of complete towns with their inhabitants, robbery, and looting.

The Handzar soldiers were presented with a pamphlet called "Islam and Judaism" (Islam und Judentum) written by Hajj Amin al Husseini. The pamphlet served as a "Holy Scripture" for the soldiers who regarded Hajj Amin as a "saint" and did not doubt the purity of his motives. As they were not fluent in German and could not understand its content, the pamphlet was translated into Croatian for the Handzar Division and called "Islam I Zidovstvo." This edition was published in 1943. The pamphlet featured two pictures of the Mufti speaking at the opening of the Islamic Institute in Berlin on December 18, 1942, with Dr. Josef Goebbels, the German Propaganda Minister, at his side. The pamphlet started with the following words:

> For us, the Muslims, it is below our dignity to mention the word Islam in one breath with Judaism, because Islam is so much loftier than its corrupt foe.

The pamphlet closes with a quotation from Bukhari-Muslim by Abu-Khureira:

> The Day of Judgment will come, when the Muslims will crush the Jews completely: And when every tree behind which a Jew hides will say: "There is a Jew behind me, Kill him!"

The Waffen-SS 13th (Handzar) Division was not the only one to be established on Yugoslavian territory on the basis of Muslim recruits and the Mufti's intervention.

In telegram no. 234 dispatched on February 12, 1944, General Gottlieb Berger stated that the Albanians ("Volks-Abaner") must be "plucked out" of the Waffen-SS 13th Bosnian (Handzar) Division so that they could serve as the nucleus of a new Waffen-SS Division in the Kosovo region. The "Muslim Albanian nucleus" did, indeed, arrive and in March 1944 mobilization began in Kosovo. The Waffen-SS 21st Division, which was established quickly, was named after the Albanian national hero from the fifteenth century—Skander-beg. The Division was founded on the basis of Albanians from Kosovo and Sanjak who had been assigned to the 13th Division until then.

The first operational activity of the 21st Division was on May 21, 1944; the "Skander-beg" soldiers raided Jewish homes in Pristina, the capital of Kosovo, arrested them, and handed them over to the Germans who sent them to Bergen-Belzen where many of them perished.

At the initiative, and with the active assistance of, Hajj Amin, an attempt was made to establish another Waffen-SS division in ICS territory, the third in number.

At that time, Hajj Amin's friend, Professor Nesad Topcic, was active in the area. Topcic served as the commander of the "Green" Fascist Militias and conspired to establish Bosnia-Herzegovina autonomy under the patronage of the Third Reich. General Gottlieb Berger regarded Professor Topcic as someone who could be useful to the Germans.

In the beginning of May 1944, Germany invited him to attend talks. In June 1944 Topcic flew to Berlin where he was hosted by Hajj Amin for three days. Talks held in Himler's headquarters were also attended by his friend, Hajj Amin.

At the command issued by Himler's headquarters on June 10, 1944, it was decided to establish a new Muslim division in ICS territory. In order to coordinate policy, Topcic flew to Germany again and met with General Berger in June 1944.

Topcic met with Berger and other generals several more times in Budapest (July 3, 1944) and Zagreb (August 1944) and subsequently visited Berlin again as Hajj Amin's guest in order to finalize the details regarding the establishment of the division.

Despite the prolonged labor pains, the Waffen-SS 23rd Division named "Kama" was finally founded.

Due to the approach of the Partisans and the Red Army, the preparations for the establishment of the Division were not completed in Yugoslavia. On June 24, 1944, it was transferred to Hungarian territory where it was supposed to stay until the end of December 1944. For reasons that are unclear, the members of the Skander-beg and Kama Divisions were dispersed among other Waffen-SS divisions in Hungary due to a directive issued on September 24, 1944, and for all intents and purposes the Muslim Divisions ceased to exist.

About one million Serbs, 80,000 Jews, and some 25,000 gypsies, were killed in Yugoslavia during World War II. The Muslim Divisions played a central role in eradicating the Jewish communities. They were renowned for great cruelty towards the Jews, gypsies, and Serbs. [19]

Fifty years later, in the framework of the war between the Muslims and the Serbs in Bosnia, the Muslims established a division based mainly on foreign Muslim volunteers. This division was called "Handzar," like the Waffen-SS Division No. 13 (Handzar), which, as stated above, was established during the years 1943-1944. Despite the differences in time and context, it is impossible to ignore the implications and the horrendous memories connected to the choice of the name of the Muslim division in the current conflict.

## Notes

1. Biger, Gideon The Historical Geography of Kosovo, Ma'archot Issue 371, July 2000, p. 2.
2. Samuel Huntington, the author of the "Clash of Civilizations and the Remaking of World Order," Simon and Schuster, New York, 1996.
3. Gineo Eyal, Islam and the Muslims in the Balkans: Orientalist Concepts, Myths and Memory, the Hebrew University, Jerusalem, 2000.
4. Ibid.
5. Rafi Yisraeli, From Bosnia to Kosovo: The re-Islamization of the Balkans, Nativ, Issue 6-77, June 2000, p. 41.
6. The Yanichari Brigades were Ottoman cavalry units.
7. Biger, Gideon, The Historical Geography of Kosovo, Ma'archot , Issue 371, July 2000, p. 2.
8. Ibid.
9. Ibid.
10. Michael Roman, Ethnicity and Territorialism in the Balkans, Ma'archot, Issue 371, July 2000, p. 8.
11. Ibid
12. Michael Roman, Ethnicity and Territorialism in the Balkans, Ma'archot, Issue 371, July 2000, p. 8.
13. "Balkanization" as an expression of conflict and separatism on an ethnic, religious and nationalist basis.
14. Former Yugoslav Republic of Macedonia (FYROM).
15. This chapter is based on the following sources: Jennie Lebel's book, Hajj Amin and Berlin, published by Technosdar Ltd., Tel Aviv, 1996. See also an article by Carl Savich, The Holocaust in Bosnia-Herzegovina 1941-1945, www.srbianna.com.
16. Hajj Amin al Husseini was the Mufti of Jerusalem who collaborated with the Nazis in World War II.
17. The Independent Croatian State—ICS
18. This chapter is based on Jennie Lebel's book, Hajj Amin and Berlin, Technosdar Publishers Ltd., Tel Aviv, 1996.
19. John Rams, "Serbs, Jews and Bosnia—A Holocaust Survivor Speaks," *Jewish Week*, New York, July 28, 1995.

# Section Three

## The War in Bosnia-Herzegovina

# The Background

Bosnia-Herzegovina is a mountainous country in the Balkan that is divided into two historical geographic regions—the Bosnia region in the north and the Herzegovina region in the south.

Slavic tribes settled in the area in the seventhy and established several principalities, the most prominent of which were the Hom principality (later to become Herzegovina) and the Bosnian principality.

Greek Orthodox Christian influences penetrated the principalities from the Byzantine (and subsequently from Croatia), while the Ottoman invasion at the end of the fifteenth century brought about a huge wave of conversion to Islam on the part of the Serbs and Croatians in the principalities, thus creating the Bosnian nationality.

In 1878, the Berlin Congress placed the Bosnia-Herzegovina region under the control of Austro-Hungary. Following World War I, Serbia annexed the region into its territory, and at the end of World War II Bosnia-Herzegovina became one of the six republics of Yugoslavia. Three conflicting religious-ethnic groups coexisted in the Republic of Bosnia-Herzegovina: the Muslim Bosnians (Bosniaks), the Greek Orthodox Christian Serbs, and the Catholic Croatians.

In 1992, the Bosnia-Herzegovina Parliament voted in favor of independence in opposition to the stand taken by the Serb population of Bosnia, and in response, a short time later, the Yugoslavian Federal Army (under Serb control) placed a siege on Sarajevo. In the course of the bloody civil war that unfolded in Bosnia, the Serb militias perpetrated ethnic cleansing and massacres among the Muslims, while the latter also carried out massacres among the Serb population. U.S. intervention and the Serbs' bombardment by NATO ended in a peace agreement in 1995. In consequence, Bosnia-Herzegovina was divided up between the Serbs, the Muslims and the Croatians. The state is currently divided into two political entities (the Serb Republic and the Muslim-Croatian Republic), and a large international force maintains peace in the region.

## Alija (Ali) Izetbegović [1]

Alija (Ali) Izetbegović was born in 1925 in Bosanki Samać, North Bosnia, to a prosperous Muslim family. Up until 1868, his family resided in Belgrade. During that year most of the Muslim residents left for Boasnaski Samać, as did his family. His grandfather served as the city's mayor. As mayor, the grandfather saved the lives of forty Serbs in his city in 1914, after Gavrilo Princip assassinated Crown Prince Franz Ferdinand in Sarajevo.

Izetbegović's family moved to Sarajevo in 1930. During World War II, Alija was caught by General Draža Mihailović's forces, which fought the Nazis, but was released thanks to his grandfather's deeds.

Following the Nazi invasion of Yugoslavia, an independent country was established which included Croatia and Bosnia-Herzegovina.

Despite his young age, at that time Izetbegović founded a youth organization named "Al Hidayya" (The Muslim Youth Movement) which was a radical offshoot of the "Young Muslims" youth movement. The movement was influenced by the ideas of Bosnian students who had studied Islam at the al Azhar University in Cairo, and regarded Islam not only as a religion, but rather a "comprehensive" ideology that covers all of the lifestyles of the individual and the state.

From 1943, Izetbegović encouraged Bosnian Muslims to volunteer for the SS Divisions established with the backing of Mufti Hajj Amin al Husseini. During World War II, the Muslim Divisions of the SS were involved in crimes against the Jews and Serbs in Yugoslavia.

Izetbegović was placed on trial in 1946 for his actions during World War II and he was sentenced to five years of imprisonment for crimes against the Yugoslavian people and state.[2] When he finished serving his sentence, Izetbegović was released from prison. He studied Law at Sarajevo University and continued to be active in the promotion of the status of Islam in Bosnia-Herzegovina.

Izetbegović published his most famous book called The Islamic Declaration in 1970. The latter reflects his worldview and vision regarding Islam and its role in the Balkans and throughout the world (see subsequent elaboration on this issue).

In 1983, the Communist regime in Yugoslavia arrested Izetbegović and twelve of his colleagues under the suspicion that they had been conspiring with Iran to establish a religious Islamic state in the Balkans.

The prosecutor at the trial maintained that in his book, The Islamic Declaration, Izetbegović had already presented his vision regarding the establishment of a religious Islamic state that would cover Bosnia-Herzegovina, Kosovo, and additional areas with Muslim populations in the Balkans. The prosecutor also claimed that the book calls for a religious Islamic uprising to be followed by a political revolt.

Izetbegović was sentenced to twelve years of imprisonment, while some of his colleagues received lighter sentences.[3]

In 1989, Izetbegović was pardoned following the collapse of the Communist regime in Yugoslavia and he was released.

While serving his sentence Izetbegović wrote an additional book, Islam between East and West. The latter was smuggled out of prison and published in the United States. In the book, Izetbegović reviews the history of Islam and analyzes its sad state in the 1980s.

In his book, Izetbegović claims that there are three basic worldviews: religious, materialistic, and Islamic. The latter is preferable to the others. Izetbegović's slogan, in the spirit of Khomeinism, was: "Neither East, nor West. Islam is the solution." [4]

Izetbegović wrote two autobiographical books, My Escape to Freedom, and his final book, Memories.

Following the dismantling of the Yugoslavian Federation, Izetbegović founded the first ethnic-national party in Bosnia-Herzegovina, the Democratic Action Party (SDA). In actual fact, the SDA was a Muslim party that conspired to establish an independent state in Bosnia-Herzegovina under Muslim dominance, in which the Serbs and Croatians would be a minority (though at the time they constituted the majority).

In November 1990, the SDA won the elections and the three ethnic parties (that represented the Muslims, the Croatians, and the Serbs) reached an agreement regarding the distribution of the political power as follows:

- Izetbegović, the Muslim, was chosen to head a presidium numbering seven members.
- A Croatian served as prime minister.
- A Serb served as the head of Parliament.

According to the agreement there was to be rotation of the various roles.

The SDA's election campaign was headed by Fikret Abdić, a secular Muslim who was chosen for the role due to the desire to diminish the radical Islamic character of the movement (Izetbegović appeared only as the SDA's number two candidate). Abdić advocated a moderate and pragmatic approach and aspired to come to agreements with the Serbs and Croatians in Bosnia-Herzegovina.

Abdić opposed the war in Bosnia-Herzegovina and upon its outbreak tried to obtain an agreement among all the parties, the Serbs, Izetbegović's Muslims, and the UN, in order to keep the Bihać Pocket in northern Bosnia outside of the warfare. Abdić's "independent" policy led him into a direct confrontation with Izetbegović, who had the upper hand.

On February 27, 1991, Izetbegović declared in the Bosnian Parliament that "he was willing to sacrifice the peace in exchange for a sovereign Bosnia-Herzegovina, but he was unwilling to sacrifice the sovereignty of Bosnia-Herzegovina in exchange for peace."

On June 3, 1991, Izetbegović and Macedonian President Galigorov published a proposal to establish a wobbly federation of sovereign countries in the Balkan (a proposal which was rejected by the Serbs).

Several days later Slovenia and Croatia declared their secession from the Yugoslavian Federation and the foundation of independent states, a step that triggered the outbreak of the Serb-Croatian War that began in July 1991 and ended in January 1992. Bosnia-Herzegovina declared its neutrality during the war.

In 1991, Izetbegović set up the Bosnian Muslim National Council (MNC) that acted to promote the concept of a Muslim state in the Balkans and establish a Muslim military power.

In October 1991 the Council published its political platform which stated the following: "The day of the declaration of the Islamic Republic of Bosnia-Herzegovina is approaching, a day awaited by all Muslims—this day has been set on December 31, 1991."

The document also warned the Serbs against taking any kind of violent measures vis-à-vis this act and promised severe collective punishment if the Serbs resolved to resort to violence.

On October 14-15, 1991, Izetbegović initiated a referendum in Bosnia-Herzegovina regarding secession from Yugoslavia.

The Serbs in Bosnia opposed this initiative but nevertheless a referendum was held on February 9, 1992, and the Muslims and Croatians (who together constituted the majority) voted in favor of independence for Bosnia-Herzegovina.

The Bosnia-Herzegovina declaration instigated a confrontation between the Serbs and the Muslims in the state as well as the intervention of the Serb army on behalf of the Serbs in Bosnia.

Under Izetbegović's influence, the presidency of the Association of the Islamic Clergy (Ilmia) of Bosnia and Herzegovina[5] published a document that contributed to the inculcation of the radical Islamic worldview among the Muslim population in the Republic.

One of the chapters in the document deals with the issue of the inherent nature of Jihad. This matter is addressed as follows in the document: [6]

> The Jihad in Islam is not just a war in Allah's name. In reality, Islam is a revolutionary ideology whose goal is to change world social order according to the laws of Islam. Islam aspires to destroy all of the countries and regimes that are opposed to Islamic ways. The goal of Islam is to establish a state based on Islamic law and principles, and it is irrelevant which regimes or societies are destroyed while realizing this goal.

The war in Bosnia-Herzegovina ended in 1995 with the signing of the Dayton Accords which brought about the partition of the country into two states—the Serb Republic and the Muslim Croatian Republic headed by Izetbegović.

Izetbegović stepped down from the presidency in the year 2000 due to health problems and died in Sarajevo on October 19, 2003 at the age of seventy-eight. He was interred in the Shahids' Cemetery in the city.

Following Izetbegović's retirement, Suleyman Tihić was elected to head the country's Presidium. Up to the time of Izetbegović's demise, many regarded Tihić as a "puppet" who did as he was bid by the charismatic leader Izetbegović. In a speech delivered after Izetbegović's demise, Tihić stated:

> Izetbegović signed the Dayton Accords in 1995 under duress and was forced to agree to the establishment of the Serb Republic (SRPSKA) as part of the Bosnia-Herzegovina Federation. Tihić added that "the Bosnian Muslims aspire to alter this arrangement which was established in the Dayton Accords," implying that the aim was to dismantle the SRPSKA Serb Republic.

This aggressive declaration attests to the fact that even after Izetbegović's death, the Islamic aspirations that he instilled continue to beat in the hearts of his successors. As Dr, Elfatih Hassanein, Izetbegović's fellow fighter and friend, so aptly summarized this worldview: [7]

> In the end, Bosnia must be Muslim. If that does not happen, the entire war was meaningless and was fought for no reason.

## Izetbegović's Worldview—The Islamic Declaration

The Islamic Declaration deals with the history of Islam in the Balkans and discusses the background leading to the inferiority and backwardness of the Muslim people in comparison to those in Western nations.

Izetbegović negates the stand taken by modernists which states that Islam is only a religion and claims that Islam is an all-encompassing system which fuses all of the beliefs and lifestyles of the faithful Muslim, "religion and information, tradition and politics, ideal and interests." The document repudiates the Western lifestyle adopted by modernist circles that, according to the author, causes corruption and social degeneration.

As an example of such failure, Izetbegović offers Turkey's modernist approach under the rule of Kamal Attaturk. Izetbegović minimizes the value of Kamal Attaturk's achievements when establishing modern Turkey. As a counterpoint, he uses the example of Japan, which he claims succeeded in incorporating its culture with modernism, thus becoming a superpower, while Turkey, which denied its Islamic tradition and strived to adopt Western culture, remained a Third World country.

According to Izetbegović, history indicates that all of the malaise and failures of the Muslims have stemmed from refuting Islam. Therefore, the key to re-establishing the status of the Muslim nations is by returning to their roots and obeying religious commandments.

The documents call on the faithful to abandon their everyday lives to take action, and even sacrifice themselves, on behalf of Islam. The author expresses his reservations regarding nationalism and secularism which he alleges the West exploits to ensure that, "the Muslim nations will remain spiritually weak and dependent on the West from the materialistic and political aspects."

He calls for the establishment of a universal Islamic community of believers (the Umma) that will unify all of the Muslims from Morocco to Indonesia. According to Izetbegović, these concepts should be introduced in Bosnia where the Muslim Bosnians are faced with the choice of "taking action in order to rejuvenate Islam and its political application least they be fated to atrophy and degenerate into stagnation."

In order to realize this vision, the Muslims must fight for a new Islamic order in their country. Izetbegović believes that "there is no possibility of peace or coexistence between the Islamic faith and non-Islamic political and social institutions."

This statement implies that the Muslims in Bosnia must refuse to accept non-Islamic rule and which they must aspire to establish an Islamic regime to replace the existing one.

Izetbegović's Islamic Declaration grants minorities religious freedom and protection on the condition that they are faithful to the Islamic regime. This approach is compatible with the Muslim tradition of providing protection to those who claim shelter in the shade of Islam.

The Islamic Declaration extols the importance of the "Dawa"—education and preaching, whose goal is to attain the support of the Islamic public as a prerequisite for the establishment of an Islamic order. To quote Izetbegović: "We must first be preachers and become soldiers later." According to Izetbegović, Islam will use force only when "Islam is sufficiently strong from the point of view of morality and numbers."

Izetbegović asserts that "history is not only the story of incessant changes, but also the perpetual realization of the impossible and unexpected."

Izetbegović distinguishes between Judaism and Zionism. He praises the period when Jews lived under Islamic rule, but completely negates the Jewish demand for independence and a national status. Thus, Izetbegović accepts the Jews when they are submissive and stateless, and relegated to the status of protected residents ("Demis") of the Islamic state that he envisions. The demand for independence, and the taking of a stand vis-à-vis the Muslim world, are to be considered unforgivable actions. Izetbegović claims that Jerusalem is not only a Palestinian city, but it is first and foremost a Muslim city. He argues that the Jews are the ones who triggered the conflict with Arab and Muslim regimes, which will fight a continuous war until every centimeter of the conquered land is freed.

In summary, Izetbegović's The Islamic Declaration, which is based on the Koran and the resurgence of Islam, addresses the universal community of Muslims with the aim of establishing an Islamic world order. Izetbegović opposes the concept of nationalism and prefers the Islamic community of the faithful, which he believes is the only entity that can meet the challenges of the modern world and restore Islam's "Golden Era."

## Muslims in the Balkans and in the Muslim World

The Islamization process of the Muslims in the Balkans and in the Muslim world, primarily in Bosnia, was influenced by several central factors:

- The history of Islam in the Balkans and the historical opportunity that arose to restore the Islamic political entity and identity following the dismantling of Yugoslavia.
- The figure and leadership of Alija Izetbegović (see above).
- The radicalization of Islam in the aftermath of the Mujahidin victory in the Jihad in Afghanistan and the collapse of the Soviet Union.

The Muslim struggle for independence in Bosnia raised a considerable degree of interest among Muslims worldwide and stimulated the mobilization of countries, organizations, and individual volunteers.

There were three main channels of assistance used by the Muslim world on behalf of the Muslims in Bosnia:

- Humanitarian aid, mainly through Islamic charities.
- Humanitarian and military aid sent by Muslim countries.
- The aid of terror organizations and Islamic volunteers (Mujahidin).

The war in Bosnia-Herzegovina, and subsequently in Kosovo, and the ethnic cleansing that the Serbs perpetrated among the Muslims, triggered a mass exodus of Muslim residents who became refugees, and the populations that remained suffered from wartime shortages and hardship. (It is noteworthy that the Serb population also suffered extreme hardship and many became refugees, but this study focuses only on the Islamic issue).

Against the background of the grave humanitarian problem in the Balkans, the Western world and the Muslim world rose to the aid of the populations that were experiencing extreme hardship.

The aid from the Western world was mainly presented through international humanitarian organizations that dealt in the transfer of aid to needy populations. Another part was transferred in the form of financial aid to the Muslim government in Bosnia. However, a vast part of the funds sent by the Muslim world to the Balkans was funneled through official and independent Islamic charities.

Although the funds were designated solely for humanitarian needs, in actual fact much of the funding, which came from the Muslim world, found its way to guerilla and terror movements and strengthened the Balkan terror organizations during the war and in its aftermath.

Aid for the Muslims in the Balkans poured in from many Muslim countries: Iran, Turkey, the United Emirates, Egypt, Malaysia and others, but the most prominent was Saudi Arabia.

## Saudi Arabia and Charitiable Organizations

Saudi Arabia's prominent status as a central donor to the Muslims in Bosnia calls for a brief discussion of the exceptional complexity characterizing the relationship between the Saudi Arabian regime on the one hand, and radical Islam and terror on the other. Consequently, this chapter will discuss the activity of Saudi charities and analyze Saudi Arabia's policy.

Saudi Arabia's status, vis-à-vis the issue of Islamic terror, is unique and particularly complex as, on the one hand, Saudi Arabia is an American ally which opposes and fights Islamic terror endangering its regime while, on the other hand, Saudi Arabia supports and assists radical Islamic organizations in their activities in distant arenas.

The roots of the Saudi "Islamic dilemma" lie in the historical alliance between Muhammad Ibn Saud, founder of the Saudi dynasty, and Muhammad Ibn Abd Al Wahhab. The Saudi dynasty was granted religious legitimacy and, in exchange, promised to include the Wahhabian dynasty in the government and award legitimacy to the religious school of thought that it represents. However, there is a basic contradiction between the lifestyle and pro-Western policy of the Saudi monarchy, and the Puritanical, radical worldview of the Wahhabist school of thought.

Saudi Arabia constitutes the bastion and influential factor of the Wahhabist movement that acts to export the radical Islamic concepts of the Wahhabi school to Islamic focal points throughout the Muslim world (the Balkans, Chechnya, Afghanistan, the African continent, and more).

Saudi Arabia acts to disseminate radical Islam through charities and welfare organizations that serve radical Islamic organizations and entities with the authorities' knowledge. In this framework, Saudi Arabia openly aids Islamic terror organizations (based on the claim that these entities are supposedly not terror organizations, but rather legitimate liberation organizations).

Saudi Arabia was also one of only three countries in the world that recognized the Taliban regime in Afghanistan that sponsored Bin Laden and Al Qaida and even aided this regime until September 11, 2001.

Saudi Arabia enables wealthy "private" entities to aid and support radical Islamic entities. The support and "adoption" of these entities are sometimes accomplished as part of the internal power struggles within the Saudi Arabian royal family.

In the early-1980s, the Saudi regime praised the Saudi volunteers who joined the struggle in Afghanistan, including Osama Bin Laden. Even after the danger inherent to the "Afghani alumni" became apparent, the Saudi authorities allowed volunteers to set out for areas of conflict where Muslim populations were in dire straits, such as the Balkans and Chechnya.

Upon his return to Saudi Arabia after the Jihad in Afghanistan, Osama Bin Laden was given a hero's welcome by the Saudi public and the authorities as well, but his growing criticism against the stand that Saudi Arabia had taken during the Gulf War eventually prompted the Saudi authorities to deport him from the country and revoke his passport. Bin Laden's deportation from Saudi Arabia did not prevent widespread solidarity of radical circles with Bin Laden and his worldview, and many joined the ranks of Al Qaida and the terror infrastructures that he established worldwide. It is no coincidence that fifteen of the perpetrators of the September 11, 2001 terror attacks were Saudi citizens.

The Saudi royal family is threatened by opposition entities that are motivated by a combination of social, economic, ideological, and religious factors. The ostentatious and extravagant lifestyle of the Saudi royal family, the inequality in distributing resources, the country's opulence, and its "non-Islamic" behavior according to the view of Islamic parties, have contributed, over the years, to the development of extensive cadres of opposition entities that aspire to overthrow the regime and establish a "true" Islamic state in Saudi Arabia.

Threats against the regime have also been posed by external factors such as subversion by Iran and the latter's attempt to export the Khomeini revolution to Saudi Arabia, or the former Iraqi President Sadam Hussein's activity against the Saudi regime.

The threats that the Saudi regime faces, on the one hand, and its power bases that lean on Western support and power factors close to the throne, on the other, compel the regime to follow a careful and intricate policy vis-à-vis the handling of radical Islam and terror.

The Saudi regime takes all of the necessary measures against entities that constitute a threat to its stability, including executing terrorists, but it nevertheless allows radical Saudi entities to act outside of its borders almost without disruption, thus creating a modus vivendi with these forces.

Thanks to its "petrodollars," from the 1970s onward, Saudi Arabia set up an extensive system of charities that deal in the dissemination of Wahhabi Islam all over the world. Between the years 1990 and 2000, Saudi Arabia spent some $70 billion from government sources on humanitarian aid and dissemination of Islam worldwide.

A Saudi weekly reported that thanks to these funds, some 1,500 mosques, 210 Islamic centers, 202 Islamic colleges, and almost 2,000 schools were built all over the world.

Today, in addition to the official charities functioning in Saudi Arabia, there are some 240 private charities including about twenty that were founded by Saudi intelligence in order to support the Mujahidin all over the world. These funds raised between $3-4 billion annually. Some 10-20 percent of these funds were dispatched outside of Saudi Arabia's borders to charity branches all over the world.

The outbreak of the violent conflict in Bosnia-Herzegovina, and the call for Muslims all over the world to come to the aid of their brethren, constituted a "window of opportunity" for Saudi Arabia to assist a Muslim population in distress and at the same time promote the export of the Wahhabi school of thought.

Over the years, most of the Muslim charities were active in the Balkans mainly on behalf of the Muslims in Bosnia. According to reports published by the U.S. Embassy in Saudi Arabia, Saudi citizens donated about $150 million in 1994 alone to Islamic charities functioning in the Balkans.[8]

A CIA report[9] written in 1996 pointed out about fifty Islamic charities in the Balkans, a third of which were connected to Islamic terror organizations such as Al Qaida, the Egyptian Jamaah al Islamiyah, Algerian terror organizations, the Hamas and Hizballah.

The link between Saudi charities and the activities of terror activities was manifested in two ways:

- Charities transferred hundreds of millions of dollars to terror organizations that dealt in Jihad worldwide, including Al Qaida.
- The charities served as a logistic infrastructure and cover for the terrorists' activities through the provision of documentation, work places and flight tickets.

According to reports from sources in Bosnia, the Mujahidin that began to arrive in Bosnia as early as 1992 via Croatia, used documentation provided by humanitarian organizations. The most widespread usage was provided by the following organizations: The Saudi High Commission (SHC), Third World Relief Agency (TWRA), IGASSA (IIRO), Kuwaiti Rebirth of Islam Mission, and the Egyptian Humanitarian Relief Agency.

The charities coordinated activities through Coordination Councils located in Zagreb and Sarajevo. These Coordination Councils followed a similar pattern to that used in Peshawar, Pakistan and dealt in coordinating arms and military equipment shipments and organizing training camps, while also providing humanitarian aid for the Afghani refugees.

Since the September 11 attacks, Saudi Arabia has vehemently denied any link between itself and the terror organizations. This also applies to Shiite charities that were active in the Balkans and had contacts with Islamic terror organizations.

Prince Sultan Ibn Aziz, the Saudi Minister of Defense and a significant contributor to some of the charities, claimed that the organizations deal in humanitarian relief and that, in any event, the Saudi authorities could not supervise the activities of private charities.

Despite these claims, investigations conducted in the United States after September 11 indicated that princes from the Saudi royal family, as well as prosperous entrepreneurs, sat on the boards of directors of many of the large Saudi charities. Moreover, a significant part of the funds donated to these charities came from government sources and were the personal donations of members of the royal family.

In a raid carried out by the Bosnian police (at the request of the United States) in the offices of the Benevolence International Foundation (BIF) in Sarajevo, Bosnia, a document was found containing a list of the main donors to Al Qaida (see elaboration below). The list, which was dubbed "the Golden Chain," contained the names of twenty Saudi donors including businessmen, bankers, government officials, and members of the Bin Laden family.

In May 2003, under American pressure, Saudi Arabia informed all of the Saudi charities that they must suspend their activities outside of the country until further notice pending a security examination to ensure that they were uninvolved with, or linked to, terror organizations. Since that time, many charities have renewed their activities, including some that were revealed to have been involved in terror activity. In some cases, the organizations changed their names and the addresses of their offices, and in other instances the organizations' directors or employees, who were suspected of involvement in terror, were replaced after which the organization renewed its activities.

## Islamic Charities in the Balkans

Benevolence International Foundation (BIF).

The Saudi charity Lajnat al Bir al Islamiya (LBI) was founded in 1987 in Pakistan and Saudi Arabia by Sheikh Adel Batterjee, a highly influential businessman from Jeda, Saudi Arabia.

The organization was established as the branch of another more veteran charity called the "World Assembly for Muslim Youth" (WAMY) which was financed by the Saudi government. In the beginning of 1990, Adel Batterjee, LBI's founder, decided to expand LBI's ties and influence throughout the world.

As part of the efforts to expand activities, Batterjee founded another organization (which was identical to its predecessor) called the Benevolence International Foundation (BIF). The purpose of the change was to camouflage the organization's Islamic identity, thereby facilitating its international activities. In actual fact, the "two organizations" that he established continued to function simultaneously under his management,

**Saudi Arabia, Islamic Charities and the Terror Infrastructure in Bosnia-Herzegovina**

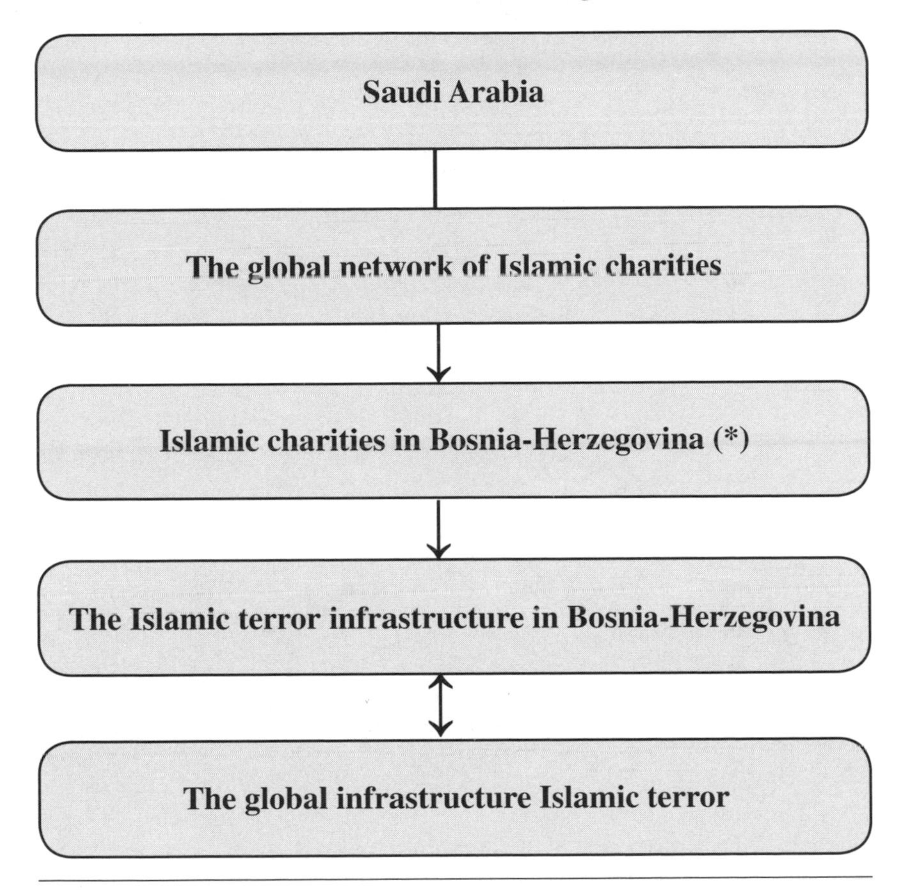


(*) Some fifty Islamic charities were active in Bosnia-Herzegovina and in the Balkans.

with LBI active in Saudi Arabia and Pakistan and BIF active in other places worldwide. In the first years of its existence, LBI dealt mainly in aiding the war of the Mujahidin in Afghanistan.

The LBI offices in Pakistan provided humanitarian relief for millions of Afghani refugees fleeing the wartime horrors in their country, and also organized and equipped Muslim fighters who were pouring into Pakistan and Afghanistan to join the Jihad.

After the end of the war in Afghanistan in 1992, the organization continued with its activities in that country while its parallel organization expanded its activities to other locatons where Muslim populations were confronting adversaries.

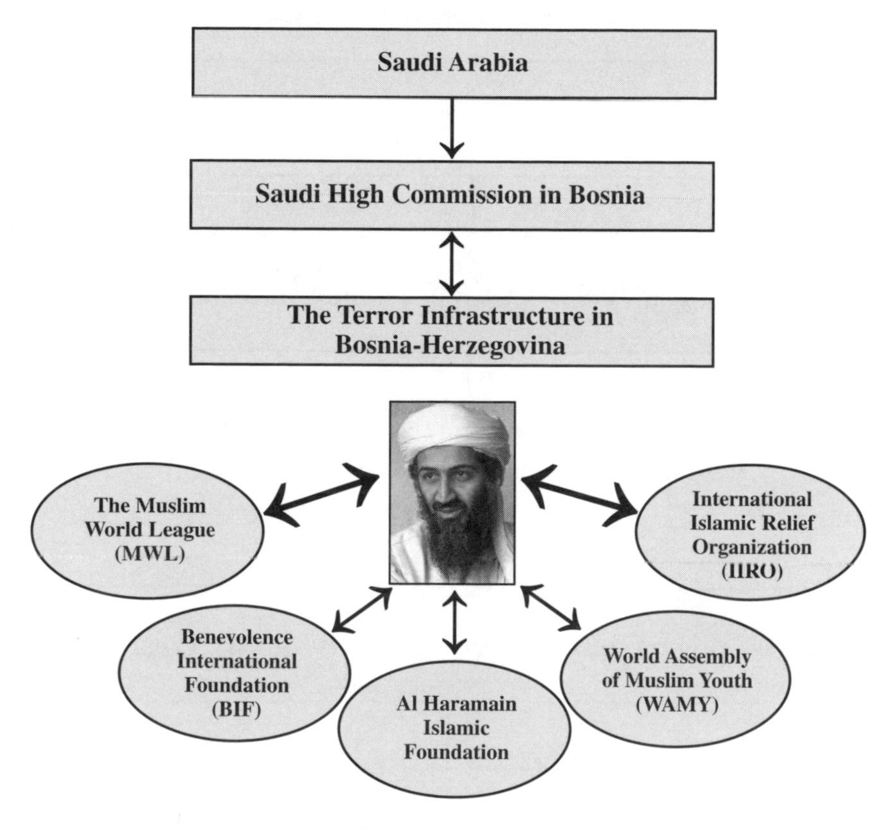


In 1992, Batterjee opened the first branch of BIF in the state of Illinois in the United States. In 1993, he handed over the leadership of the organization to a man named Enaam Arnaout who was also known as Abu Muhmmad Al Hamawi, and Abu Muhammad Al Suri. Enaam Arnaout had previously served in senior roles in the ranks of LBI in Afghanistan and had close work ties with Al Qaida and Bin Laden.

There is a "surprising congruence" between the establishment of Al Qaida's infrastructures in various locations worldwide and the opening of BIF offices at the same places (see list):

- In 1991, Al Qaida began transferring its headquarters and most of its activitists to Sudan, and that year a BIF office was opened in Khartoum, the Sudanese capital.
- In 1992, Al Qaida became involved in the Muslim conflict in Bosnia, and that year BIF offices were opened in this country as well.

**Reciprocal Ties and Links Between Al Qaida and BIF**

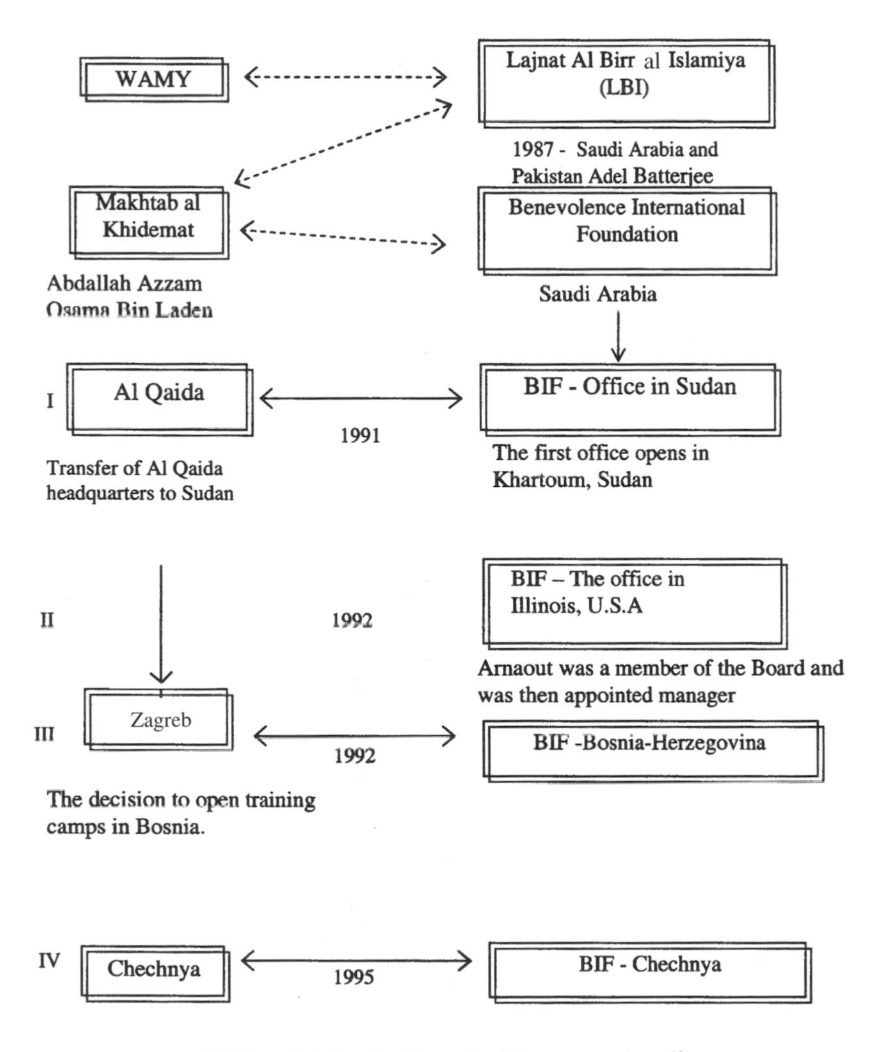


## BIF activities in Bosnia-Herzegovina.[10]

The BIF opened offices in many locations worldwide and, as stated earlier, was also very active in the Balkans, where it opened offices in Bosnia-Herzegovina, in Sarajevo, and in Zanitsa and Zagreb in Croatia. The organization's links with the Muslim Bosnian army and Islamic terror organizations were exposed after the September 11, 2001 attacks when the United States began investigating and taking action against Islamic charities in the U.S. that were suspected of maintaining ties with Al Qaida. Knuckling under American pressure, the Balkan authorities (in

Bosnia, Croatia, and Albania) also began investigating and raiding the offices of Islamic charities within their boundaries. Questioning of the charities' employees, and confiscated documents, provided the U.S. with an accurate perspective regarding the nature and scope of the charities' activities vis-à-vis terror.

One of these organizations, whose activities were exposed and subsequently banned, was the BIF. Enaam Arnaout, the organization's director in the U.S., was interrogated and brought to trial. His trial revealed the network of the organization's activities in the United States and worldwide. This book will provide excerpts from that trial which shed light on the BIF's activities in the Balkans. Among the documents confiscated at the BIF branches in Illinois in December 2001 (in the aftermath of the September 11 attacks), were handwritten documents in Arabic that attested to the organization's involvement in the Balkans. One of the documents stated:[11]

> The organization's headquarters in Croatia was established to provide humanitarian aid and assistance to the Jihad in Bosnia-Herzegovina … contribute to your brothers in order to block the Jewish-Crusader assault on Islamic soil.

Other confiscated documents attested to the assistance that the organization gave to the Mujahidin in Bosnia-Herzegovina:

- A receipt dated June 3, 1994 from the Muslim Army of Bosnia confirms the delivery of 2,000 uniforms, 2,000 pairs of shoes and radio equipment from the BIF.
- A receipt dated July 21, 1994 from the "Black Swans" (the commando unit of the Bosnian Muslims) confirms the delivery of 300 blankets and 200 pairs of shoes from the BIF.
- A Bosnian Muslim Army appeal sent to the BIF on December 31, 1994 requesting a military ambulance. (The ambulance was subsequently supplied in January 1995).
- A memorandum dated November 17, 1995, which was sent to the BIF Director Enaam Arnaout, describes the contribution of 200 tents to the Bosnian Muslim Army.

Two senior Al Qaida activists were employed at the BIF offices in the U.S.—Muhammad Loay Bayazid (known as Abu Rida al Suri), who was appointed BIF President in 1994, and Mamdouh Salim, who was known as Abu Hajjer al Iraqi.

Due to U.S. pressure, in March 2002 Bosnian security foes raided the BIF office in Sarajevo. A computer was found on the premises that contained many documents (some scanned) which attested to BIF links with Al Qaida.

One of the files found on the computer was called Osama's history (Tareek Osama). This file contained documents and pictures depicting the history of Bin Laden in Afghanistan and the establishment of Al Qaida.

Another computer file contained a scanned, handwritten document listing the main donors to the Mujahidin. This list was dubbed "The Golden Chain." [12] A quote from the Koran—"spend money for God's purposes"—tops the page. The list included twenty names alongside which were the names of the recipients of the donations.

Another file contained an article from Arab News featuring a picture of Osama Bin Laden and Enaam Arnaout, who is called "Abu Mahmud of Syria" in the caption. One file contained a letter from Bin Laden to Abu al Rida, whose real name, as stated, is Loay Bayazid.

In another letter sent by Bin Laden to Abu al Rida during the Jihad in Afghanistan, the former wrote that the time had come to attack the Russians. He ended the letter with a request to convey his regards to Abu Hassan al Medani, and expressed his hope that the latter would visit him after his visit to Saudi Arabia and bring him at least 500,000 Rupees (Pakistani money). Abu Hassan al Medani is a well-known Saudi businessman, also known as Wael Julaidam, who headed several Islamic charities that supported Bin Laden.

Another letter sent by Enaam Arnaout to Abu Hafez (Muhammad Attef al Matsri, an Al Qaida military commander killed in Afghanistan in 2001, states that "the organization loaned us (Al Qaida) a Howitzer cannon, and it must be returned so that it can be transferred to Kabul." Bin Laden's signature appears at the bottom of the page.[13] In another letter written by Bin Laden to Abu Rida, Bin Laden instructs him to pay Abu Obeid and Abu Hafez a monthly wage of 6,500 Saudi Riyals, just as they had been paid by "Makhtab al Kidmat." [14]

The "Tareek Osama" folder also contained a document called "A List of the Organization's Goals" which was apparently written towards the end of the war waged against the Soviets in Afghanistan. The document attributed considerable importance to the continued recruitment of donations for Al Qaida and mentions a number of chaities that could be incorporated in the raising of donations such as Rabita of the World Muslim League (WML).

The document calls for the establishment of a leadership committee and lists the preferred locations for its activity. In addition to the "Tareek Osama" folder from which sections are quoted above, two other large files were found on the computer:

- Tareek al Musadat – a file containing documents pertaining to the "al Musadat" camp in Afghanistan and individuals connected to the camp's activities.
- Al Jabel – The file deals mainly with the activities of the Afghani Mujahidin organization Hizbi Islami headed by Golbudin Hikmatiyar.[15]

The hundreds of documents found in the above-mentioned files, and in scores of other files, leave no doubt as to the ties and links between Al Qaida and its senior activists on the one hand, and the BIF charity on the other.

### Al Haramain Islamic Foundation in Bosnia.[16]

The Al Haramain Islamic Foundation is a Saudi charity that operated offices in forty-nine countries worldwide and annually raised some $30 million in donations in Middle Eastern countries as well as throughout the Muslim world.[17]

The Al Haramain Islamic Foundation had offices in the Balkans at the following locations: Zagreb, Rijeka, in Croatia, seven offices in Bosnia, as well as offices in Albania and Macedonia.[18]

According to American intelligence sources, the organization's offices in Somalia and Bosnia were directly involved in Al Qaida activities. As stated earlier, the Bosnian branch was involved in activity initiated by Al Qaida and by the Egyptian terror organization, Jamaah al Islamiyah. The director of the Al Haramain Islamic Foundation, Sheikh Aqeel al Aqeel, is currently being investigated by the Saudi authorities in connection to suspicions that additional worldwide offices affiliated with the organization (in Indonesia, Kenya, and other countries) were connected to Islamic organizations' terror activities.

The branch in Bosnia-Herzegovina was headed by Ibrahim Sati. This branch was in direct contact with the Internet website of Azzam Publications, one of the sites that Al Qaida used for Jihad related propaganda.

Russian intelligence (the FBS) claimed that the Al Haramain Islamic Foundation in Bosnia transferred one million dollars to the Muslim rebels in Chechnya and helped them to purchase artillery from the Taliban regime. Moreover, the Russians also intercepted conversations between the Chechnya terrorists and the leaders of the Al Haramain Islamic Foundation in Saudi Arabia, a fact that attests to links between these entities.

In March 2002, the Al Haramain Islamic Foundation was designated a terrorist entity by the U.S. authorities and all of its assets in the United States were frozen. Following the implementation of this step by the Americans, NATO forces raided seven of the organization's branches in Bosnia.

The raid on the organization's office in Sarajevo exposed documents connecting the charity to Al Qaida and also revealed letters calling for Jihad against NATO and U.S. forces.

In the framework of its investigations, the U.S. Treasury exposed links between the Al Haramain Islamic Foundation and the Egyptian terrorist organization Jamaah al Islamiyah (this organization had also been included in the U.S. list of terror organizations since November 2, 2001).

Intelligence investigations in Bosnia revealed that all of the financial records of the Al Haramain Islamic Foundation in Bosnia for the years 1994-1998 had been destroyed and that some $1.59 million out of the organization's funds had been withdrawn over the years 1999 to 2001 for unknown purposes. (These funds were apparently used to fund the activities of terror organizations in Bosnia).

In May 2003, a new charity named Wazir started to operate in the offices that had formerly belonged to the Al Haramain Islamic Foundation in Bosnia (which, as noted earlier, had been shut down by the authorities). The organization was headed by a man named Safet Durguti.

The identity of "the new organization" was quickly exposed and the UN declared that the Wazir organization was merely a new name for the Al Haramain Islamic Foundation whose activity had been banned. This organization was also included in the list of the terrorist entities whose activity was prohibited.

The Al Haramain Islamic Foundation was active not only in Bosnia but also in other locations in the Balkans. Its offices in Albania and Croatia were also linked to terror organizations and shut down by the authorities. In the wake of U.S. pressure, in October 2003 the Albanian delegation at the UN reported that the Albanian Treasury had frozen the organization's accounts in Albania.

### The Saudi Joint Relief Committee (SJRC).[19]

The SJRC Saudi charity served as the coordinator of several Saudi charities in the Balkans including the Saudi Red Crescent, IIRO, MWL, Al Haramain and others.

The organization acted on behalf of the Saudi authorities and transferred over $74 million to its offices in the Balkans during the years 1998 to 2000.[20] The organization was headed by Adel Muhammed Sadiq bin Kazim who was a senior activist in Al Qaida.

In June 1998, the CIA and Albanian security forces raided several offices and residences of SJRC members in Tirana, Albania. In July 1998, the director of SJRC was charged with using forged documents and possession of illegal weapons. During that year, additional employees were arrested under the suspicion that they were connected to the Al Qaida attacks perpetrated in Kenya and Tanzania[21] in August 1998.

The SJRC opened an office in Kosovo that served the organization's overt and covert activities. In April 2000, the multinational KFOR force raided the premises. One of the confiscated documents featured the names of Kazzim and Wael Hamza Julaidan,[22] identifying them as senior leaders in the organization. The two were also known to the U.S. authorities as senior activists in Al Qaida and it is evident that the SJRC also served as cover for the activities of terror entities and for the transfer of funds and organization activists to the Balkans.

### The Om al Qura Foundation[23]

The Om al Qura Foundation is a relatively small charity that operated offices in Bosnia-Herzegovina, Chechnya, Thailand, and Cambodia. This charity was involved in laundering money through orphanages and schools in Malaysia, and transferring it to terror organizations. The organization succeeded in enveloping itself in secrecy but, despite its efforts, from 2003 it, too, was included in the list of charities involved in the support of terror organizations. In Thailand and Cambodia some of the organization's employees were arrested due to suspicion of involvement in terror activity.

### Human Concern International (HCI)

The organization's headquarters was located in Canada and offices operated in Sweden, Pakistan, Lebanon, and in Zagreb in the Balkans. The HCI aided the Egyptian Jamaah al Islamiyah and the Algerian GIA terror organization.[24] According to press reports, members of the Jamaah al Islamiyah masqueraded in Peshawar, Pakistan as employees of the charity. The office manager in Pakistan was arrested under suspicion of involvement in the terror attack against the Egyptian Embassy in Islamabad, Pakistan. According to intelligence sources, the organization's branch in Sweden was involved in gunrunning.

### The International Islamic Relief Organization (IIRO)[25]

The IIRO was established in 1978 and its headquarters is located in Jeddah, Saudi Arabia. The IIRO is a critical component in the financial activity of the Muslim World League (MWL), which is financed by the Saudi government.[26]

According to the general auditor of the IIRO, the organization was the first to operate in Bosnia-Herzegovina at the very beginning of the war.[27]

The director of the MWL is appointed directly by the Saudi King Fahed, and he serves as chairman of the IIRO's board of trustees. The IIRO is one of the largest and most affluent Islamic charities, and it has offices in over ninety countries worldwide. According to Serb sources, the IIRO (also called IGASA in Bosnia) was operated by three individuals: [28]

- Abd al Aziz Zaher, also known as Abu Anas.
- Jamal al Jibouri, also known as Abu Mahmmoud al Iraqi.
- Djamel Lermani, also known as Abu Musab Djaziri.

In 1993, Abd al Aziz Zaher was deported from his home in Belgrade after the exposure of his links not only with the IIRO, but also with other charities suspected of ties with terror organizations. Terror training pamphlets written by the Palestinian Force 17 were discovered in a search of Zaher's home.[29]

Serb sources also reported that from 1992, Zaher's deputy Jibouri was personally involved in provision of logistic aid, weapons and ammunition to radical Islamic organizations in the Balkans.[30]

Moreover, according to a Serb Internet site,[31] Serb soldiers found documentation on the body of an Afghan Mujahid in Bosnia that indicated that he was employed by the IIRO in Peshawar, Pakistan.

According to "Compass Newswire," [32] the IIRO offices in Peshawar, Pakistan were headed by a senior Egyptian terrorist from the Jamaah al Islamiyah named Talaat Fuad Qassem who subsequently arrived in the Balkans. He was arrested in Croatia and extradited to Egypt where he was wanted for the perpetration of terror attacks.

In addition to its widespread humanitarian activities, the IIRO also aided the following terror organizations; Al Qaida, the Egyptian Jamaah al Islamiyah, Algerian terror organizations, the Hamas, and the terrorist who perpetrated the first attack at the World Trade Center in 1993.[33]

The organization has branches in the Balkans as follows: Zagreb, Sarajevo, Split, Lubliyana, and Tuzla. The organization also had offices in Vienna, Austria which supported its activities in the Balkans.

There are many examples that attest to the organization's involvement in aiding terror organizations. To present just a few:

- In April 1995, the Croatian authorities arrested the IIRO's regional bookkeeper, a citizen named Hussain Muawad Mohammad Hali, charging him with links to terror organizations.

- In March 1995, the Macedonian authorities shut down the organization's offices in Skoste, claiming that the organization was collaborating with Albanian Muslim isolationists and terrorists active in the country.
- The director of the IIRO in the Philippines, Mohammad Jamal Kalifa (Bin Laden's son-in-law), was charged with aiding terror organizations and involvement in a conspiracy to assassinate the Pope and detonate twelve American passenger planes in Southeast Asia.

## The Saudi High Commission (SHC)

The SHC was an official Saudi entity whose role was to coordinate the collection of donations and humanitarian relief, and distribute it to the needy Muslim population in the Balkans.

The organization operated offices in Zagreb, Sarajevo, and Tuzla and was also active in Zenica, Mustar, and Split. Due to its official capacity as coordinator for the Saudi government, the SHC maintained ties with other Saudi charities active in the Balkans. The SHC had links with the Hamas and Algerian terror organizations.[34] The organization's offices apparently employed activists from various terror organizations who acted under the guise and support of the Saudi charities.

In February 2002, British and American forces raided the SHC offices in cooperation with the Bosnian police. Computers, photographs, and forgery tools[35] were confiscated during the raid. Confiscated documents indicate that the SHC dealt in the provision of aid and support for terror organizations, even at the expense of the humanitarian relief that it was supposed to give Bosnian residents. Many documents on the premises consisted of letters from citizens and Muslim organizations complaining that funds raised by the SHC for humanitarian relief purposes had not reached their destination. Pictures of targets attacked by Al Qaida in the U.S. were also discovered in the offices including photographs of the Twin Towers, diagrams, photos of security facilities in the Balkans, and more.

Jane's Intelligence Review[36] wrote about the SHC:

> The Saudi High Commission is opaque; whether it is a Saudi government body, an NGO, or a private organization has never been made clear, although it is the focus of considerable interest among intelligence agencies.

Aside from Saudi charities, additional Islamic charities were active in the Balkans that were financed by countries such as Iran, Kuwait, and others. Here are several examples of such organizations:

## The Third World Relief Agency (TWRA)

The charity's headquarters operated from Sudan and an office operated in Istanbul, Turkey. In the Balkans, the organization had offices in

Zagreb, Tuzla, Sarajevo, and Split.[37] The organization aided the Mujahidin in Bosnia as well as the Egyptian Jamaah al Islamiyah. Here are several examples of its involvement in terror:

- The TWRA charity, which operated from its headquarters in Sudan, was mainly funded by donors from Saudi Arabia, and maintained close ties with radical Islamic entities in Sudan (the radical movement named the National Islamic Front which was established by the Sudanese leader Hassan al-Turabi), as well as Islamic terror organizations including Al Qaida whose headquarters was situated in Sudan during the years 1993-1996.

  The regional head of the TWRA, Dr. Muhammad Elfatih Hassanein, was a personal friend of the Bosnian leader Alija Izetbegović, who received assistance from the organization for the funding and the acquisition of combat means for the Muslims in Bosnia.[38]

  Izetbegović helped the TWRA to open a bank account in Austria through which funds were transferred for the funding of the organization's activities in Bosnia.

  Hassanein helped to employ Izetbegović's cohorts in key positions in the TWRA in Bosnia.

  Following the exposure of the TWRA's links with the transfer of money and combat means to Muslims in Bosnia, the organization was forced to shut its office in Zagreb and move its activity center to Sarajevo. (Its links with the CIRKL are specified below).

Here follow additional examples of the organization's involvement in terror:

- An employee of the TWRA (a member of the Egyptian Jamaah al Islamiyah) perpetrated a suicide attack at a police station in Reijka, Croatia in retaliation for the arrest of a senior member of the organization in Croatia.
- In August 1995, Hassanein sent his brother to Italy to assist a Jamaah al Islamiyah terror cell.

  The Italian police claimed that Hassanein had transferred funds (apparently via his brother) to organization members in Milan and Rome.

### The Islamic Relief Agency[39]

The organization's headquarters operated from Khartoum and maintained close ties with the Sudanese leader Hassan al-Turabi and his party, the NIF. The organization had branches in thirty countries. Offices operated in the Balkans at the following locations: Sarajevo, Zagreb, Tirana, Tuzla, Kalesija, Zvornik, Banovici, and Doboy East. The organization's office in Zagreb was involved in the transfer of combat means to the

Muslim Bosnian Army under the supervision of Hassan al-Turabi's people. It is to be noted that during the years 1991-1996 Bin Laden and the majority of senior Al Qaida members resided in Sudan and enjoyed the aid and patronage of Hassan al-Turabi.

### International Humanitarie Hifsorganization (IHH)[39]

This organization was established by a member of the Turkish Refah party. Its headquarters was located in Germany and branches were situated in Zagreb and Sarajevo. The charity was apparently linked with Algerian terror organizations and had ties with Iran.

### The Qatar Charitable Committee[40]

The organization's headquarters was located in Doha, Qatar and was financed by private businessmen. It operated offices in the Balkans at the following locations: Zagreb, Sarajevo, Tuzla, and Split. It would appear that the organization had links with the Hamas and Algerian terror organizations. Members of these terror organizations were apparently employed by the charity.

### Red Crescent Iran[41]

This charity was sponsored by the Iranian government. Alongside its humanitarian activities, it served as cover for Iranian intelligence activity and for the shipment of combat means to Iranian volunteers who were active within the ranks of the Muslim Bosnian army. The organization had offices in Sarajevo, Split, and Tuzla, and maintained ties with another Iranian organization named Merhamet that was active in Croatia.

### Kuwaiti Joint Relief Committee (KJRC)[42]

The KJRC was a charity that acted for the Kuwaiti government and was responsible for the allocation of funds to other charities.

The organization's headquarters was located in Kuwait, and it offices in Zagreb, Sarajevo and Lubliana. The organization was suspected of maintaining links with the Hamas, the Egyptian Jamaah al Islamiyah, and Algerian terror organizations.[43]

### The Maktab al Kidmat Charity[44]

The organization's headquarters operated from Peshawar, Pakistan and its main activity focused on assisting the Jihad in Afghanistan. In the Balkans, the organization had offices in Sarajevo and Zagreb. In its Balkan offices, the organization employed activists from Al Qaida, Algerian terror organizations, and the Egyptian Jamaah al Islamiyah.

Several of the senior employees of the organization's offices in Zagreb were arrested and charged with active involvement in terrorist activity.

### Human Relief International (HRI)

The organization was sponsored by the Muslim Brotherhood and was also linked to the Egyptian Medical Association. According to several sources, the HRI split up into two organizations, the initial one and the splinter group called the Human Relief Agency (HRA).[46] The HRI had ties with Islamic terror organizations including the Egyptian Jamaah al Islamiyah.[47]

The offices of the breakaway organization, the HRA, in Albania, were manned by activists of the Jamaah al Islamiyah, including the terrorist Anwar Shaaban, who was killed by security forces in Croatia in December 1993.

Shaaban's terror cell collected intelligence regarding the U.S. Embassy in Tirana, the Albanian capital, for the purposes of perpetrating a terror attack. The HRA offices in Albania were shut down due to U.S. pressure in April 1995.

### The CIRKL Organization as a Mechanism for Funding Terror Infrastructures in the Balkans[48]

In the early-1990s, Al Qaida (possibly in collaboration with the leader of the Egyptian Jamaah al Islamiyah Omar Abd al Rahman) established a secret organization called CIRKL whose role was to channel the contributed funds arriving for Muslims in Bosnia to terror organizations and the Mujahidin movements for the purpose of establishing terror infrastructures in the Balkans and Europe.

The CIRKL cooperated closely with the TWRA charity, which served as an overt and legitimate front to recruit and funnel funds to Muslims in Bosnia, while actually the routing of the funds was determined by the CIRKL. The headquarters of the TWRA and the senior leaders of the CIRKL were situated in Vienna due to Austria's liberal banking policies, which more or less enabled the Islamic organizations a free hand.

The organization included some 300-400 people including clergymen, military personnel, senior officials, and diplomats. The CIRKL fortified its influence through charities, the most prominent of which was the TWRA.

Muhammad El Fatih al Hassanein, who was a personal friend to Alija Izetbegović, was one of CIRKL's leaders. He also headed the TWRA and could thus synchronize the activities of the two organizations. According to the abovementioned document, he transferred some $2.5 million to Islamic terror organizations. Most of the funds were transferred via TWRA accounts.

After September 11, the U.S. succeeded in bringing about the shutdown and nationalization of the assets of charities involved in terror activity, but the CIRKL, which acted covertly, was not directly affected by this activity. Experts surmerize that the organization has continued its activities through the use of new cover organizations (usually by changing the name and address of an existing charity whose activities were banned).

## The Muslim Bosnian Army[49]

Details regarding the preparations of the Muslim Bosnians for the war, and arms running into Bosnia even prior to the war, were presented before a Yugoslavian court as early as September 1991, during the trial of Islamic activist Memic Seoad. He testified that Muslims in Bosnia transferred combat means to the Raska region, with the full knowledge of Izetbegović. These combat means were smuggled in from Croatia and included about 1,240 Kalashnikov rifles (AK47) made in Romania and M-56 machine guns.[50]

A senior member of the ruling party in Bosnia (SDA)[51] named Hassan Kengic was responsible for the acquisition of combat means. The weapons shipments were accompanied to the Raska region by a Libyan diplomatic car and camouflaged as a shipment of equipment for the Active Islamic Youth Movement. The weapon shipment was financed by a Libyan diplomat named Amer Musrati who served in his country's embassy in Belgrade.

At the same time, the Libyan Consul in Sarajevo also assisted another Bosnin organization headed by Rasem Kadić, which dealt in arms running to Bosnia and Kosovo. For this purpose, Kadić, and another Bosnian named Zekić Cefedin, visited Czechoslovakia several times in order to purchase weapons that were then smuggled into Bosnia and Kosovo.[52]

After the war broke out in Bosnia, Muslim fighters from other countries, called "Mujahidin," began to pour into Bosnia in addition to the arm shipments that already arrived there. Already in October 1992 a shooting incident was reported between a Mujahidin force of seven fighters and Serb forces combined with a UN unit in a Sarajevo suburb called Butmir, not far from the city's airport.

The incident was filmed in a videocassette used for propaganda and the recruitment of funds, and was distributed by the BIF "charity." The cassette features parts of the fighting and interviews with some of the fighters who survived the incident.[53] It tells the story of two fighters killed in the battle, one of who was Abu Zubair al Madani, also known as Mohammad al Habashi, a cousin of Bin Ladin's. Zubair was born in the city of Medina in Saudi Arabia, and at the age of seventeen he traveled to Afghanistan in 1985 to participate in the Jihad. Zubair participated in many battles including Host, Jaalabad, and Kabul. After the war in Afghanistan ended, he moved to Bosnia where he died in October 1992, apparently from the gunfire of UN forces.

The Mujahidin were placed in several types of fighting units within the Muslim Bosnian Army:

- The Mujahidin Brigades – Most of their commanders and fighters were foreign volunteers.
- Mixed Mujahidin Brigades – For the most part, the commanders were foreign volunteers and the fighters were Muslim Bosnians.
- Training units in which local and foreign fighters were trained by foreign volunteers with extensive combat experience from other combat arenas.

In 1993, just one Mujahidin brigade was active in Bosnia. By the end of the war, ten Mujahidin brigades and units had been established. One of the first brigades to be established in Bosnia was the Revolutionary Guards Brigade (No. 7) which was called a Mujahidin unit and was composed of members of the Iranian Revolutionary guards and Islamic volunteers, many of whom were Afghani "alumni" and members of Islamic terror organizations such as Al Qaida, the Egyptian Jamaah al Islamiyah, the Algerian GIA, and others. (See subsequent elaboration regarding Iranian involvement in Bosnia.) The 7th Brigade was subordinate to the Muslim Bosnian Army Fifth Corps and was based in Zenica.

As stated above, additional Mujahidin units were subsequently established as follows:

- The 9th Brigade (for Muslim liberation) of the Second Corps was based in Tuzla and its headquarters was in Trevnik.
- The 4th Brigade (for Muslim liberation) of the Fourth Corps whose headquarters was in Konjic.
- The 17th Light Brigade (for Muslim liberation) of the First Corps, based in Sarajevo.

In December 1995, the Muslims in Bosnia established new Mujahidin units that included many foreign fighters. However, most of the recruits were local Bosnians. Until the end of the war, ten of these units had been established throughout Bosnia-Herzegovina:

- The Muslim Liberation Brigade (No. 807) under Division 81, which was based in Gorazde.
- Brigade No. 117 "Dzemisetski Golubovi," based in Lukovac.
- Mujahidin Brigade No. 119 of the Special Forces, based in Banovici. This brigade was divided into two combat teams—Tigrici and Zelena Strela.
- Brigade No. 203 in Tesanj. This brigade was composed of three independent combat forces of Mujahidin.
- Light Brigade No. 204 "Citlovki Vukovi" based in Citluk.
- Muslim Brigade No. 115 whose forward headquarters was in Vogosc.
- Light Brigade No. 17 of the 14th Division of the First Corps whose headquarters was in Pazaric.
- Mechanized brigade No. 379 of the 37th Division based in Tesanj. This was an elite unit by Bosnian standards. Its headquarters was in Zenica.
- Operation Group with headquarters in Tuzla. This operation group included two combat teams named Janicari and Taut. This "Operation Group" was independent and was not connected to the other corps that was also based in Tuzla.

The overall number of foreign Mujahidin fighters in each of these ten units was somewhere between 750 and 1,000. These Mujahidin fighters constituted the hard core of the special forces and served as sappers and observers as well as playing other professional roles.

Foreign Mujahidin fighters also played an important role in training the army and special forces. They served as intelligence officers, military chaplains, and commanders of special forces. Commanders from the foreign Mujahidin ranks also served in these roles outside of the Mujahidin units. Examples can be observed in the following Bosnian units:

- The "First Bosniak," This brigade was considered very important and contained a group of commanders and military experts who arrived as volunteers from Turkey, Egypt, Afghanistan, Pakistan and Lebanon.
- "G Force" (the G is the first initial of Gazi'a which means revenge, retaliation and/or punishment in Arabic). This force was part of the Third Corps and dealt in the training of the foreign Mujahidin fighters and Muslim Bosnian fighters.

## Mujahidin Forces in the Bihać Region[54]

Large Mujahidin forces were deployed in the Bihać region during the war, and some remained in the vicinity even after the war ended.

The Muslim Bosnian government sent Mujahidin forces to this area due to the importance attributed to it, and against the background of the internal struggle within the Muslim camp vis-à-vis entities that refused

**The Muslim Bosnian Army**
**Mujahidin Brigades – Muslim Liberation Brigades – (MLB)**

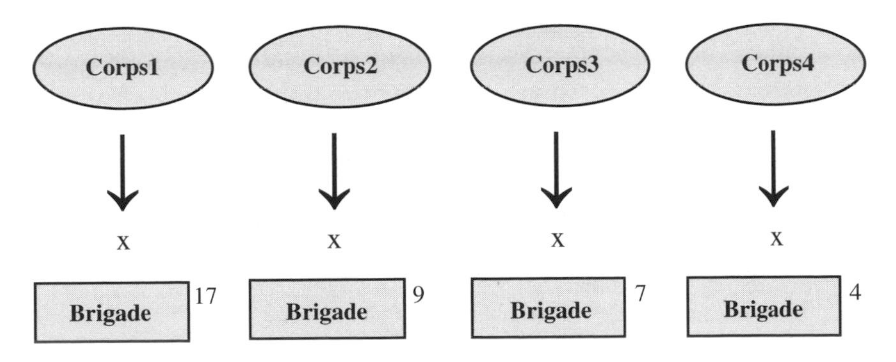


**"Mixed" Brigades in the Bihac Area**

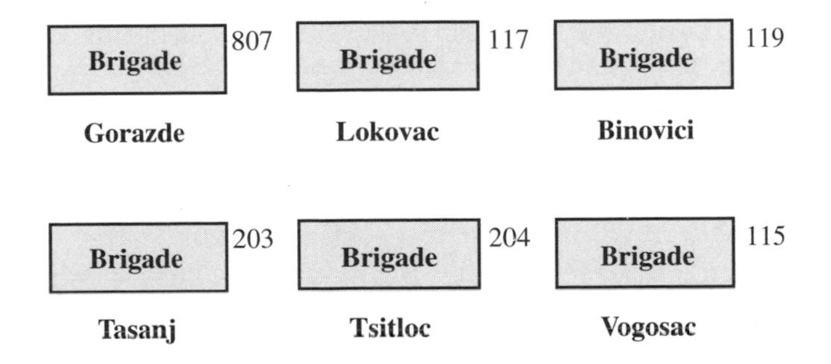


to accept the authority of the Muslim Bosnian government such as Fikret Abdić's militia. Thus, the role of the Mujahidin forces was to defend the Bihać region not only against the Serb forces but also against Muslim adversaries.

The Mujahidin infiltrated the area secretly through Muslim and international charities.

Large Mujahidin forces were incorporated under the No. 5 Corps' Command and deployed in the Bihać region as follows:

- Mountain Brigade No. 501 IDG.
- Mountain Brigade No. 503 IDG.
- Mountain Brigade No. 505 IDG.
- Light Brigade No. 511.

Each of the brigades contained between 1,200-1,500 foreign Mujahidin fighters. (It is important to note that these brigades were not established according to uniform standards, and their power and quality varied. The Bosnians identified "large" units with the letters IDG, while smaller units were marked FDC although they were all defined as brigades.

In mid-1993 a divisionary structure named "Handzar" was established in Sarajevo. It served as a presidential guard and also guarded additional senior members of the Muslim Bosnian government. The division was composed of two main sub-units as follows:

- The Sarajevo "Handzar" unit which contained between 2,500 and 3,000 elite fighters according to the standards of the Muslim Bosnian Army at that time.
- A reserve force based in Fojnica that included 6,000-7,000 fighters. The soldiers in this division were mainly Muslim Albanians, many of whom were from Kosovo-Metohia. For the most part, the force's commanders were Mujahidin fighters from Afghanistan and Pakistan who had considerable combat experience.

(See an elaboration about the "Handzar" Divisions during World War II in Section One.)

Muslim volunteers with expertise in the area of artillery, logistics, air defense and other areas also served in the framework of the Muslim Bosnian Army.

According to varying assessments, 4000-6000 professional volunteers fought in the ranks of the Muslim Bosnian Army, most of who arrived under the guise of workers for charities and welfare organizations.

The London Institute for International Strategic Studies (IISS) estimated that during all of the years of the Bosnian war the total number of foreign volunteers who served in the framework of the Muslim forces in Bosnia came to about 40,000 people.

**Foreign Mujahidin in the Bihać Enclave**

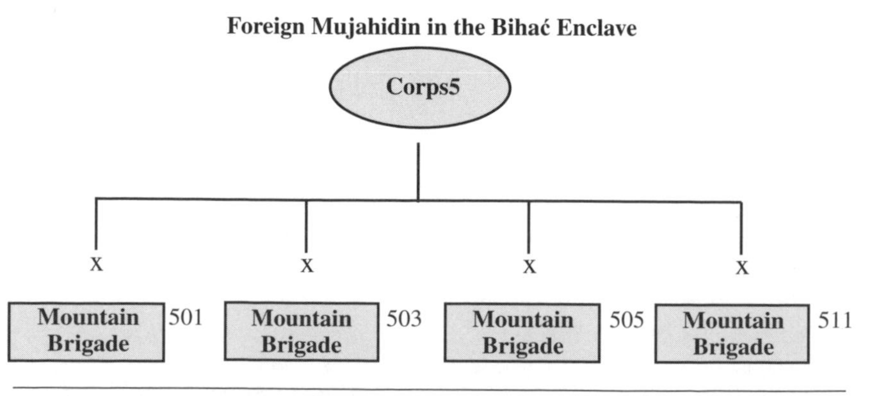


(*) Between 1200-1500 foreign Mujahidin in each brigade.

*The Mujahidin in Bosnia after the End of the War.* Following the signing of the Dayton Accords in 1995, the Muslim government in Bosnia needed to quickly reorganize the Islamic forces in the state. The Mujahidin fighters were either recognized as legal citizens following marriage to local women or were granted citizenship for their contribution to the Bosnian Muslim nation during the war. The granting of citizenship to the Mujahidin fighters was personally approved by the Bosnian leader Szetbegović. The assimilation of the Mujahidin in Bosnia was overseen by the assistant manager of AID (the Bosnian intelligence agency), who incorporated former Mujahidin fighters in senior positions within the Muslim Bosnian administration, the police, the legal system, and management.

Some of the Mujahidin that had arrived in Bosnia during the war, under the pretext of being charity employees, stayed and functioned in Bosnia in the framework of these organizations. In 1995-1996, the Muslim Bosnian Army initiated a program whose aim was to camouflage the continued presence of the Mujahidin fighters in the army units.

The Third Corps of the Muslim Bosnian Army was dismantled in January 1996 and was turned into a training unit in which many of the Mujahidin fighters were incorporated as instructors.

Reports published by Polish intelligence sources in the Multinational Force (SFOR) indicate that over 1000 Mujahidin remained in Bosnia after the war. These Mujahidin are located in Sarajevo, Tuzla and Zenica as well as ten villages. Since 1998, the largest group of Mujahidin has been situated in the Serb village Bocina Donja that was abandoned by its residents.[55] (See appendix).

Washington Post correspondent Jeffrey Smith wrote of the village Bocina Donja:[56] "At the entrance to the village there is a large sign that warns visitors 'Fear Allah.'" Smith recommends to take this warning seriously due to the fact that there are examples of strangers who dared to enter the village and were attacked, including two NATO generals who entered the site by mistake and an employee of a humanitarian relief organization who was attacked with an ax.

Some 100 Mujahidin families live in the village and maintain a strict Islamic lifestyle. This is reflected in the women and men's clothing and appearance (the women wear black and the men have beards), strict abstention from alcohol, the establishment of many religious schools, and regular prayers at the mosque.

Based on gathered testimony, Smith claims that the area is not controlled by the Bosnian government and NATO forces also refrain from entering whenever possible.

In the course of 1999-2000, several terror cells were discovered in the U.S. and Canada. Some of their members had lived in Bocina or were connected to radical Islamic entities that resided there.

Here follow several examples that were exposed regarding aid given to the Mujahidin by official Bosnian entities:[57]

- In the year 2000, charges were brought against a senior clerk of Islamic descent in the local government (police), who lived in the Sarajevo area. He was arrested for illegally issuing identity cards to foreign citizens. However, instead of being subjected to any type of legal procedure, he was promoted in the police force by the Muslim Bosnian government.
- According to Serb sources this action was taken due to pressures applied by the AID director, who was his cousin.
- Serb sources quote evidence attesting to the fact that a senior official, who was in charge of legal and administrative issues (an office affiliated with the Bosnian census registration), illegally signed citizenship papers for 103 foreign citizens (Mujahidin) of African and Asian origin on December 28, 1995. The employee was subsequently promoted to the position of police commissioner of the federal Ministry of Interior.
- Karim Sayid Atmani, a terrorist member of the Algerian "Group Islamique Armee" (GIA) was granted Bosnian citizenship in 1995. (He is currently imprisoned in France).
- Mehrez Aduni, a former fighter in a Mujahidin unit and one of Bin Laden's associates, was arrested in Turkey carrying a forged Bosnian passport.
- The last three members on this list received illegal Bosnian passports in 1994 from the Tealić police commander, a man named Semsudin Mehmedović.
- Mohammad Zuhair Handalla, one of the senior organizers of the booby-trapped car in Mostar in 1997.
- Ekrem Avdi of Kosovo, who established the local Mujahidin unit.
- The Mujahid Abubaker Sadeq who fought in Kosovo-Metohia.

With the help of the Muslim administration in Sarajevo, Iran reorganized its infrastructure in Bosnia. Following the signing of the Dayton Accords in December 1995, the Seventh Brigade of the Revolutionary Guards was officially disbanded, but many of the commanders and soldiers (some 150-200 people, or according to Serb sources 750-1,000 individuals) were subsequently incorporated in elite units and Bosnian army training bases. At the same time, several senior Iranian intelligence experts and commanders were stationed in the Iranian military attaché in Sarajevo. In addition, several dozen Iranian intelligence experts were annexed to the AID (the Muslim Bosnian intelligence organization) and continued to serve in its ranks in Bosnia. Some of the Iranian officers who fought in the Bosnian war returned to Iran and were stationed in training camps for Muslim fighters from all over the world, including the Balkans.

In the beginning of 1996 several hundred Muslim Bosnians were sent to attend military and intelligence training in Iran.

Iran also reorganized its "Charity Institutions" network in the cities Zenica, Mustar, Bihać, Visoko, and Sarajevo. In June 1996, Iran opened a large medical center in Bihać. Iran acted to maintain its long-term presence in Bosnia by investing in the construction of institutions in that country, based on the assumption that the peace preserving forces would leave Bosnia at some point and Iran would then claim a dominant status due to these infrastructures.

## Islamic Terror Activities in Bosnia-Herzegovina After the End of the War

Despite the end of the war and the presence of international forces in Bosnia-Herzegovina, it continues to serve as an activity arena for various terror organizations, some of which enjoy government patronage. The Muslims seem to be playing the West and the international forces on the one hand, against radical Islamic entities on the other.

Here follow several examples:

- On October 13, the Bosnian Border Guard in Bosnia-Herzegovina arrested an Algerian terrorist named Ais Benkhir whose name had appeared on the Interpol's wanted terrorists list. Benkhir was carrying a Bosnian passport granted in the framework of his work for the Kuwaiti charity "Kuwait General Committee for Help—Sarajevo." Benkhir was charged by the Interpol with participating in terror activities in Algeria in 1995, in which five civilians and an Algerian soldier were killed.[58]

  Several weeks before Benkhir's arrest, Border Guard forces in northern Bosnia-Herzegovina arrested Yusuf Amkad, an Egyptian citizen who was carrying a phony Belgian passport and a Bosnian passport.

  Amkad was charged with membership in the Egyptian terror organization Jamaah al Islamiyah and he is awaiting a decision whether he will be tried in Bosnia or extradited to Egypt (which requested his extradition).[59]
- In October 2001, the British and U.S. Embassies in Sarajevo closed due to the threat of attacks against these targets.[60]

  That month six individuals suspected of intending to perpetrate these attacks were arrested. The suspects were subsequently turned over to the American forces in Bosnia and were apparently transferred to the prison facility in Guantenamo.[61]

The Boston Globe claimed that one of those arrested was Sabir Lamar, who was employed by SHC.[62]

- On October 14, 2003, the international forces in Sarajevo (SFOR) raided a building that served the (Muslim-Croatian) Bosnian Intelligence Service. A SFOR spokesman claimed that the forces were searching for anti-Dayton Accord activities. NATO commander in Bosnia, General John Sylverstar stated in an interview with AP:[63] "In fact, there are international terrorist organizations which have individuals in Bosnia, including Al Qaida. What we have to determine is whether or not the individuals involved are here for the purpose of planning operations, or are here for the purpose of something else—being supported, being provided documentation, seeking respite or whatever."

These examples indicate the difficult and intricate reality of a widespread terrorist infrastructure which established itself in the Balkans during the war years in Bosnia and serves as a source of Islamization of the Muslim populations in the Balkans and as a subversive entity that encourages continued confrontations (Jihad) between the Muslims and their adversaries in this arena.

The supportive approach taken by the Muslim government in Bosnia under Izetbevgović's regime and the cooperation between terror organizations and the Muslim militias in the Balkans (in Bosnia, Kosovo, Macedonia and Albania) laid the foundations for the terror infrastructure with which the Balkan countries and the West are forced to contend.

The governments in Bosnia and Albania are currently situated between a rock and a hard place. On the one hand, the U.S. and Western European countries demand the cooperation of these governments in the global war on terror while on the other hand, the authorities and the public support the Mujahidin that stood by them in their past struggles.

This "dichotomy" is reflected in the relatively low scale government activity against the terror infrastructure in their countries, which is conducted mainly to satisfy the West and to avoid a crisis over the sensitive issue of the global war on terror. This activity, which is local and limited, does not deal with the problem in any depth nor does it uproot the terror infrastructures that have gained a foothold in the Balkans.

## Notes

1 This chapter is based on:
- Issa Special Reports, Balkan Strategic Studies, Alija Izetbegović: A retrospective look at his impact on Balkan stability, December 8, 2003.
- Biju Abdul Qadeer, Izetbegović passes away: The end of an era in the Balkans, Muslim Writers Society, December 29, 2003.

- Alija Izetbegović: His background and philosophies, A briefing paper for members of the 1992/1993 session of the Australian Parliament, December 21, 1992.
- Mustafa Ashour, Izetbegović—Muslim Freedom Fighter, Cairo, IslamOnline.net.

2. Supreme Yugoslav Military Court (566/46, June 15, 1946).
3. Izetbegović was sentenced to twelve years in prison on March 14 1983, under the guarantee of clauses 135 and 136 of the Yugoslav Republic's Penal Code.
4. Bosnian Muslim Leader Launches Book on Civil War, Sarajevo, IslamOnline.net.
5. The Association of the Islamic Clergy (Ilmia) of Bosnia and Herzegovina.
6. What is actually a Jihad? The Takvim, 1992, pp. 67-68.
7. Balkan Wars and Terrorist Ties, The Center for Peace in the Balkans, March 2, 2000.
8. Declassified 1996 CIA report regarding involvement of Islamic charities in sponsorship of terrorism.
9. Ibid.
10. This chapter is mainly based on the trial records of Enaam Arnaout in the United States.
11. Ibid.
12. "Glenner Simpson," List of Early Al Qaida Donors Points to Saudi Elite Charities," *Wall Street Journal*, March 18, 2003.
13. In the documents Bin Laden is referred to by his alias Abu al Qaaqaa.
14. "Makhtab al Kidmat" was the name of an office run by Bin Laden in Peshawar, Pakistan which dealt in the provision of funding and the recruitment of volunteers for the Jihad in Afghanistan.
15. Hizbi Islami is the Afghani Mujahidin organization headed by Golbudin Hikmatiyar.
16. This section is based on the document: Islamic Fundamentalists' Global Network—Modus Operandi—Model: Bosnia, Documentation Center of the Republic of SRPSKA, Banja Luka, September 2002. The organization's Arabic name is Mu'assasat al Haramain al Kharyry and it is also known as The Charitable Establishment of the Two Holy Mosques.
17. Based on the organization's website.
18. Declassified 1996 CIA report regarding involvement of Islamic Charities in terrorism.
19. Also known as the Saudi Joint Relief Committee for Kosovo and Chechnya.
20. Written testimony of Jeans Charles Brisard before the committee on banking, housing and urban affairs, October 22, 2003.
21. Declassified 1996 CIA report regarding involvement of Islamic charities in terrorism.
22. As stated above, Wael Hamza Julaidan headed a series of Saudi charities.
23. Memo on shutting down terror financing in Southeast Asia, Project for the New American Century, October 1, 2003.
24. Zacharya Abuza "Funding Terrorism" in Southeast Asia: The Financial Network of Al Qaida and Jamaah al Islamiyah. The National Bureau of Asia Research, NBR, Arablysis, Volume 14, November 5, December 2003.
25. Declassified 1996 CIA report regarding involvement of Islamic charities in terrorism.
26. The organization is also called The International Humanitary Relief Organization. The organization operated in the Balkans under the name Haya'at al Ighata al Islamiyva.

27. "IIRO-Welcome" http:/www.arab.net/ iiro.
28. Moneyclips "Counter Anti-Islam Propaganda," says MWL, May 6, 1995.
29. Ibid.
30. Moneyclips, "IIRO Saves forty Thousand Bosnians from Starvation," July 4, 1993.
31. Vecernje Novosti (Belgrade), "Bombs in the Name of the Almighty: Part II," September 27, 2001.
32. Compass Newswire, November 1, 1995.
33. United Nations Security Council Committee concerning Al Qaida and Taliban report of December 2, 2003.
34. Written testimony of Jean Charles Brisard before the Committee on Banking, Housing and Urban Affairs, October 22, 2003.
35. Boston Globe, "Fighting Terror, A War on Many Fronts, Saudi Group: Charity's Files Hold U.S. Data, Bosnians Say," February 17, 2002.
36. Jane's Intelligence Review, "Islamist Groups Take Root in the Balkans," January 1, 2002.
37. Declassified 1996 CIA report regarding the involvement of Islamic charities in terrorism.
38. Declassified 1996 CIA report regarding the involvement of Islamic charities in terrorism.
39. Declassified 1996 CIA report regarding the involvement of Islamic charities in terrorism.
40. This organization is also known as IARA, TARA, the African Islamic Relief Agency.
41. Declassified 1996 CIA report regarding the involvement of Islamic charities in terrorism.
42. The organization is also known as Helal Ahmer (in Arabic) and the Iranian Red Crescent Society or the Iranian Humanitarian Aid Organization (in English).
43. Also known as The General Committee for Refugee Assitance.
44. Declassified 1996 CIA report regarding the involvement of Islamic charities in terrorism.
45. Also known as Al Kifah and the Human Services Office (HSO)
46. Declassified 1996 CIA report regarding the involvement of Islamic charities in terrorism.
47. Ibid
48. Bosnian Political Head is a Marionette of Islamic Terrorists, Tuzla Night Owl, Patriot Serbian Bi-monthly from Banja Luka, August 16, 2004.
49. Islamic Fundamentalists' Global Network Modus Operandi—Model Bosnia, Documentation Center of Republic SRPSKA Banja Luka, September, 2002.
50. Issa, special reports, Balkans Strategic Studies, Strong Warning Indicator for New Surge in European Islamist Terrorism, October 15, 2003.
51. People's Democratic Party (SDA in Serb).
52. Islamic Fundamentalists' Global Network Modus Operandi—Model Bosnia, Documentation Center of Republic SRPSKA, Banja Luka, September, 2002.
53. Segments of the tape also appeared on the BIF website.
54. This chapter is based on Islamic Fundamentalists' Global Network Modus Operandi—Model Bosnia, Documentation Center of Republic SRPSKA, Banja Luka, September 2002.
55. Press report on "Training of Mujahidin in Bosnia," Tanjug, December 16, 1997. Marek Popowsky, quoting Polish daily Warsaw Rzecspospolita.
56. Jeffrey Smith. A Bosnian village's terrorist ties linked to U.S. bomb plot arouse concern about enclave of Islamic guerillas, *Washington Post*, March 11, 2000.

57. Islamic Fundamentalists' Global Network, Modus Operandi—Model Bosnia Documentation Center of Republic SRPSKA, Banja Luka, September, 2002.
58. Ibid.
59. Ibid.
60. Ibid.
61. http://news.Bbc.co.uk/l/hi/world/europe/1767554.stm, accessed July 27, 2003.
62. Ibid.
63. Boston Globe, "Fighting Terror/Islam, Religious Conflict; Saudi "charity" Troubling to Bosnian Muslims," January 27, 2002.

# Section Four

## The War in Kosovo

# The Background of the War in Kosovo

Kosovo was an autonomous region in the southwestern part of Serbia. The region's area is 10,900 square miles. In 1989, when the last general census was conducted, the country's population was 1.9 million, of which 1.2 million were Albanians (mostly Muslims). The tension between the ethnic groups and religions, and the change in Serbia's approach to the region's autonomy (which was declared in 1974 and annulled in 1990) are the main reasons for the chain of events that led to the war. However, the problem's roots—like the roots of most problems in the Balkan Peninsula—are embedded farther back in the past.[1]

Tito was careful not to form homogenous national units in Yugoslavia in order to prevent secession for nationalist reasons.

In the framework of this policy, two principles prevailed:

- Inclusion of Serb populations within the boundaries of the Yugoslavian Federation (this was prominent in Croatia and Bosnia-Herzegovina).
- The granting of the status of an autonomous region rather than that of a republic to the Wivodena area (which borders on Hungary), together with the Hungarian majority in the northern part of the country, and to the Kosovo region with a Muslim/Albanian majority along the Albanian border.

The boundaries of the Kosovo region were delineated so that it included a population composed of 85 percent Albanians, 13.2 percent Serbs and 1.8 percent members of other nationalities. This method was repeated in other places as well. Thus, for example, the Albanians constituted some 20 percent of the Macedonian population and 5 percent of the Montenegro residents.

However, during the years of Tito's regime, the Albanian population in Kosovo grew rapidly, mainly thanks to the "Albanization" policy of the local authorities that encouraged emigration from Albania to the region while restricting the moves of the Serb population. As a result of these processes, the Muslim population constituted over 90 percent of Kosovo's population in 1990.[2]

The Muslim Albanian residents of Kosovo were granted cultural and social autonomy; the Albanian language was taught at schools, and until the collapse of Yugoslavia, life in the region generally ran undisturbed. In 1981, a national and religious Albanian awakening began in Kosovo resulting in the demand to recognize Kosovo as the seventh republic of the Yugoslavian Federation. The Albanian demonstrations and riots that followed were ruthlessly oppressed by the Yugoslavian authorities, and order was restored in the region. However, the tension continued.[3] As stated earlier, in 1989, when Yugoslavia began to crumble and split up into several independent countries, the Yugoslavian authorities (today only Serbia and Montenegro) aspired to turn the region into an integral part of Yugoslavia. They feared that the Albanian majority in Kosovo would also demand independence or annexation to Albania, which shared its border. This decision increased the tension in Kosovo, causing the formation of organizations for national liberation.[4]

In 1992, Ibrahim Rugova was elected president of Kosovo. Rugova headed a party named the Democratic League of Kosovo (DLK), which called for a non-violent struggle for Albanian autonomy, but the Serb authorities declared the elections illegal and persecuted Rugova and the members of his party.

In 1995-1996, the Kosovo Liberation Army (KLA)[5] was founded. This was a nationalist organization which perpetrated terror not only against the Serb government, but also against the moderate liberation movement led by Rugova who was elected president a second time in elections held in 1998.

In 1999 violence in Kosovo escalated, and following the unfruitful peace talks held in Paris, a war spearheaded by the KLA broke out between the Serbs and the isolationist Albanians.

NATO, led by the U.S., took the side of the Muslims in Kosovo and after Miloshevich refused to comply with NATO's demands, the latter launched an aerial attack against the Serb forces in Kosovo, and subsequently expanded the attack to cover all of Serbia until its capitulation. Upon Miloshevich's surrender and the end of the war in Kosovo, negotiations were launched between the Muslims and the Serbs to regulate the situation in Kosovo. In the resultant agreement, Kosovo was divided between the rival populations, and an international force enforced the agreement on both sides.

## The Kosovo Liberation Army (KLA)

The war in Bosnia that ended in the division of Bosnia-Herzegovina, and the establishment of an Muslim Bosnian autonomy, awakened the realization among the Kosovo Muslims that through an armed struggle it would be possible to promote the matter of Kosovo's independence.

The founders of the KLA, which was established in the late 1990s, had already begun their subversive political activities in the 1980s, for example in student demonstrations (held in Pristina in 1981) demanding the establishment of a republic in Kosovo. Many of the political dissidents were arrested by the Yugoslavian authorities. Others fled to various European countries (Switzerland, Germany, and Sweden),[6] and continued their subversive activities from there.

Following the collapse of Yugoslavia, the KLA was established at the initiative, and with the funding of, the Muslim "expatriates" in Europe and the U.S.. Most of the founders were members of the radical circles within the Muslim Albanian population in Kosovo and the Albanian community worldwide.

Prior to the organization's establishment, some of its founders had been affiliated with nationalist Albanian organizations such as:

- The National Kosovo Movement – NKM
- The Popular Movement for Kosovo Liberation – PMKL

The KLA's first armed group, led by Adam Jahsari and Donji Prekaz, was established in the Drenica region. Most of the group's members were recruited from among the founding members' families. Subsequently, the group was joined by commanders and soldiers of Albanian origin, who had previously served in the Yugoslavian Federal Army, as well as Muslim fighters who had participated in the fighting in Bosnia-Herzegovina.

The KLA's terror activities were launched in 1995. During this year, the organization carried out a series of attacks against Serb police stations in Kosovo, but at that stage the organization refrained from publicly claiming responsibility. In 1996, the organization first claimed responsibility for a series of attacks against policemen and police stations throughout Kosovo.

KLA members first appeared in public wearing ski masks and wielding arms at the funeral of a teacher and member of the organization who was killed by the Serbs in the village of Drenica in November 1997.[7]

The Serb authorities responded forcefully to the attacks by declaring the KLA a terror organization. Widespread arrests were conducted among its commanders and activists. Despite the Serb security activity, the organization succeeded in expanding its ranks and activities against Serb targets and Kosovo residents (including Muslims) suspected of collaborating with the Serbs.

The KLA relied on a well-trained operational nucleus that could be moved from place to place, and on broad infrastructures that included most of the organization's members who acted on a regional and local basis.[8]

At the beginning, the organization generally acted via small cells made up of three to five fighters, and refrained from activating large combat units due to their vulnerability. Some of the fighters and commanders who, as noted earlier, had served in the Yugoslavian army and intelligence, spoke the language and were acquainted with the Serbs' operational capabilities. This fact was helpful when dealing with the Serb security forces.

The KLA enjoyed the support of former Albanian President Sali Berisha, who regarded the war in Kosovo as a Jihad and issued a call to all Muslims to fight for the protection of their homeland. Berisha gave the KLA a ranch owned by his family in the Tropoje region in northern Albania so that it could serve them as a training base.[9]

The Serbs claimed that the new government in Albania, which replaced Berisha's regime, continued to help the KLA and enabled it to operate training camps on Albanian soil.

The Serbs maintained that these camps were sponsored by the Albanian army and police, and that they aided the KLA by providing combat and logistic means, as well as training fighters.

The KLA had two headquarters—one in Pristina and the other on Albanian soil. The organization controlled its men via radio contact and a messenger system that also dealt in the gathering of intelligence for the organization.

Initially, the KLA demanded that Kosovo be recognized as an independent republic in the Yugoslavian Federation, however, after Serbia had turned down these demands, the organization subsequently took a more radical stand and demanded the establishment of an independent Islamic state.

However, the organization had even more far-reaching goals: as stated, the KLA's declared goal in the initial stages was to establish an independent Muslim state in Kosovo, but its long-range objective was to bring about the establishment of an Islamic state covering all of the Balkans ("greater Albania"), which would include Albania, Kosovo, Macedonia, and Bosnia-Herzegovina.

The KLA spokesman Jakup Krasniki declared in July 1998: "We want more than independence—the reunification of all Albanians of the Balkans."

The KLA guerilla and terror activities led to a gradual deterioration of the security situation in Kosovo and to the escalation of the Serb forces' retaliations against the Muslim population. This led to a mass flight of the population and accusations that the Serb authorities had conducted massacres and "ethnic cleansing."

From 1998 onwards, KLA activities expanded and it began operating on a larger scale as a semi-military force. Its fighters began capturing territories from the Serb forces and holding on to them, such as the area between Pec and Djakovic, which was called "the liberated space."

The KLA's improved combat capabilities stemmed from three factors:

- Better quality combat means that were acquired by the organization.
- Training of the organization's members by Islamic and Western entities.
- The arrival of Islamic volunteers—Mujahidin—who became involved in the anti-Serb combat (see further details in the chapter discussing the Islamic Mujahidins' involvement in the fighting in Kosovo).

Up to March 1998, the KLA used mainly light weapons in its combat against the Serb forces, but from that time on the organization succeeded in improving and expanding its arsenal and, as a result, strengthened its combat capabilities. Weaponry that was at the organization's disposal from March 1998 included anti-tank missiles (RPG-7's and Armbrusts), recoilless guns, mortars, and anti-aircraft missiles. This weaponry reached the organization from several sources:

- The storehouses of the former Yugoslavian army after they were stolen or sold to the organization by criminal entities.
- Aid from Albania, Muslim countries and Islamic terror organizations.
- Loot formerly belonging to the Serb police and army.

According to the periodical "Jane's," during 1998 about 198 KLA members were killed, including about 130 in penetration attempts from Albania to Kosovo. During this period, 112 Serb policemen and fifty-one Serb soldiers were killed in skirmishes with the KLA, and 395 Serb policemen were wounded. The Serb army responded with extensive assaults that forced the KLA members to withdraw after sustaining a lethal blow from the Serbs.

Against the background of the escalated violence, the number of refugees in Kosovo in mid-1998 reached 300,000 people who were forced to flee their homes.[10] International pressure led to the declaration of a ceasefire in October 1998. The latter's aim was to enable the refugees to find sanctuary before the approaching winter.

At a conference of Islamic organizations held in Pakistan in October 1998, a resolution was passed according to which the struggle of Muslim Albanians for independence must be regarded as a Jihad, and the participants called for the Muslim world to "fight for the freedom of the occupied Muslim territories."

At the end of 1998, an investigative committee was dispatched by the Organization for Security and Cooperation in Europe (OSCE) in order to resolve the conflict in Kosovo. However, despite the international intermediation, the violence continued and even escalated during January 1999.[11]

In light of the escalation, Yugoslavian President Miloshevich decided to try to overpower the Muslims in Kosovo. He believed that the Muslim resistance and the KLA in Kosovo could be eradicated swiftly.

The civilian Muslim population in Kosovo sustained widespread destruction and heavy injuries which were defined by human rights organizations as "ethnic cleansing."

The violent acts against the civilian population, and the lessons learned from the conflict in Bosnia, spurred the European community and NATO to take determined action to put an end to the violence. In the beginning of March 1999, peace talks were launched in Paris between the Serbs and the Kosovo Muslims under the auspices of the European Community. These ended in dismal failure on March 19, 1999. A diplomat in Pristina was quoted as saying in this connection,[12] "The KLA is everywhere and nowhere, like any guerilla force. To attack them you have to attack the civilian population of which they are a part. The Serbs did that and killed a lot of civilians. NATO will not make that mistake."

Following the failure of the talks, and due to the fact that the European community blamed Miloshevich for this failure, NATO made preparations to carry out a military offensive that would force its demands on Serbia. When they decided to launch the military campaign, it was clear to the decision makers that the international communication front was no less critical, and perhaps even more important, than the battlefront in Kosovo.

Until the final weeks before NATO resolved to launch a military campaign against the Serb forces posted in the Kosovo region, the conflict in Kosovo had not claimed international headlines. The international communication blitz began when there was actually something to cover.

The massacres perpetrated by the Serb forces amongst the Albanian population were linked to the gross cruelty that the Serbs had demonstrated three years earlier in the war in Bosnia and Croatia.

For years, Serbian President Miloshevich had been portrayed by the Western media as the "villain of the Balkans," and there were journalists who compared him to Adolf Hitler. The atrocious pictures broadcasted from Kosovo which, showed rows of civilian bodies that had been shot by the special Serb police in Albanian villages, transmitted an urgent message: immediate action needed to be taken in order to prevent a bloodbath similar to the one that had been perpetrated in Bosnia. The Western information blitz was meant to form and stabilize local and global support for the initial military offensive to be launched by NATO.

The "Bosnian Pattern" repeated itself in Kosovo—here, too, an "unholy alliance" was foed between NATO, the United States, and Islamic volunteers that rose to the aid of the Muslims in Kosovo.[13]

The United States, which played a key role in the war in Kosovo, had a complex relationship with the KLA. Until 1998, the organization appeared on the U.S. State Department's list of terror organizations, but at the end of that year the U.S. removed it from the list, a fact that enabled the granting of legitimacy to the organization and aid in the war against the Serbs.

At the same time, the U.S. demanded that the KLA refrain from violence in Kosovo in particular and in the Balkans in general, and sever ties with the Mujahidin and Islamic terror.

Despite the fact that the KLA continued with its violent activities and maintained its ties with Islamic terror organizations, the U.S. preferred to ignore the fact and sustain its ties with the organization based on the assumption that it was preferable to have limited influence rather than condemn and repudiate the organization, thus pushing it into the arms of radical Islam.[14]

This U.S. and NATO policy enabled the training and supply of arms to Muslim forces from Kosovo in Albania through three British and American "security" companies.

As mentioned earlier, during the period preceding the American assault on Kosovo in 1999, the KLA underwent a rehabilitation process and was presented by the West as a legitimate organization acting to promote national liberation and democracy in Kosovo.

As part of the organization's image change, its name was altered to the Kosovo Protection Corps (KPC) and it was granted funding and aid by the UN and the United States. After Miloshevich's noted refusal to submit to the ultimatum issued in March 1999 by the NATO countries to cease Serb military actions in Kosovo, NATO decided to take forceful action against Serbia. On March 24, 1999, NATO launched an offensive from the air in Kosovo, with the United States playing the main role in this assault. The offensive first focused on Serb military targets in Kosovo, but as these attacks did not bring about the desired results, the aerial attack was gradually expanded to the area of Serbia until the latter's submission and acquiescence to obey the NATO and U.S. demands.

Under the cover of the NATO offensive, the KPC expanded its ranks (at the peak of the fighting it numbered 20,000 fighters) and its military activity as well as its control over Kosovo's area. As noted, during the war in Kosovo, the ranks of the KPC expanded and it was organized in regimental frameworks in seven operational areas.

Initially these regiments acted independently, almost without mutual coordination, until the appointment of Agim Ceku as the Chief of Staff. Ceku established a central command that controlled all of the forces and reorganized the forces within this framework. An operational area was also eliminated, leaving six areas of operation. Since the end of the fighting to date, the KPC has constituted the main Muslim military force in the areas under Muslim control in Kosovo.

In the aftermath of the ceasefire, and following the arrival of the international forces in Kosovo, the KLA/KPC was forced to disarm itself in October 1999, but in actual fact the organization did not relinquish its status as a main power component in the arena but simply changed its structure and organizational identity. Many of the organization's heads joined the leadership of political parties established in Kosovo:

- The Democratic Party of Kosovo (DPK) - The party, which was founded by Hashim Taci on October 14, 1999, was originally called "The Democratic Progress Party of Kosovo." On May 10, 2000, prior to the elections in Kosovo, the party's name was changed to "The Democratic Party of Kosovo."
- "The Alliance for the Future of Kosovo" (AFK) – The party was established on May 2, 2000 in order to promote the political goals of its founder, one of the senior KLA members, Ramoush Haradimali.

Commanders and soldiers who chose to continue with the violent struggle in the various conflict arenas in the Balkans preferred to join Albanian terror organizations that were established at that time as successors to the KLA (see subsequent elaboration).

## The KLA's Funding Sources

Prior to the establishment of the KLA, the Muslims in Kosovo operated two main entities that dealt in aiding the establishment of Muslim forces in Kosovo:[15]

- The first entity, headed by the exiled Prime Minister Dr. Bujar Bukoshi, which acted to establish the nucleus of the Armed Forces of the Republic of Kosovo (AFRK). This entity dealt in fund raising, and the recruitment of combat means, fighters and commanders. Bukoshi gathered together a group of officers of Albanian descent who had previously served in the Yugoslavian Army and subsequently in the Croatian Army (HV),[16] paid their salaries and dispatched them to Kosovo. Bukoshi appointed one of these officers—Ahmed Kraniski—Defense Minister of the government in exile. Kraniski was killed in the fall of 1998 in Tirana, Albania in unclear circumstances.
- The second entity was a volunteer body of "the Albanian Communities Worldwide" based in Croatia. This body established a fund called "Homeland Call" which dealt in raising funds for the Muslims in Kosovo.

  Already in its first year of existence (1998), "Homeland Call" succeeded in raising some 4 million German Marks in currency and goods in Croatia on behalf of the KLA.

After the establishment of the KLA, the two entities merged and acted to aid the former by raising funds to promote its objectives.

An important fundraising source for the KLA was the Albanian community in the United States. In 1999, 400,000 people of Albanian origin resided in the United States, most of whom were members of the blue-collar class. This community maintained close ties with their families who had stayed behind in Kosovo and other areas of the Balkans. For almost a decade, the Muslim Albanian community in the U.S. supported Rugova's policy, but following the incident in Drenica in 1997, during which about eighty Albanians were killed (see above), support for Rugova's passive approach waned in the Albanian community in the U.S., and was replaced by support for the active line advocated by the KLA in Kosovo.

The U.S. Albanian community opened a branch of the "Homeland Call" organization, which helped to raise funds for the KLA's struggle in Kosovo. In 1998, the organization raised some $10 million in the United States. It also purchased night vision equipment and bulletproof vests.[17] Aside from the funds acquired through donations made by Albanian communities worldwide, a significant part of the KLA funding came from criminal activity.

In his testimony before the U.S. Senate, Frank Cilluffo[18] of the Global Organized Crime Program, stated that a large part of the monies funding KLA activity came from drug dealing. He noted that Albania and Kosovo were located in the heart of the "Balkan Route" which served as a thoroughfare for drugs en route from Afghanistan, Pakistan, and the Middle East to Western Europe. The value of this market was estimated at an approximate $400 million annually. Similar testimony was given by Ralf Mutschke[19] of the Interpol.

## Involvement of Islamic Terror Organizations in Kosovo

The involvement of Islamic terror organizations in the Kosovo conflict began in 1998. The terror infrastructures of Al Qaida and additional terror organizations built in the Balkans (in Bosnia-Herzegovina and Albania) in the early 1990s against the background of the war in Bosnia constituted the basis for the involvement of these organizations in Kosovo.

The Islamic organizations acted through two main channels according to the model that we will examine and which was successfully applied in the Bosnian conflict:

- The establishment of a network of "charities" which served as logistic backup (financial support) and covered the penetration of Islamic activists into the Kosovo arena.
- Incorporation of terrorists in combat units alongside the KLA in independent frameworks and on training missions.

## Islamic Charities and Terror Organizations in Kosovo

The network of charities established during the war in Bosnia-Herzegovina played a central role in supporting Muslims during the conflict in Kosovo as well.

The Islamic organizations that acted in Bosnia were supplemented by other organizations, or branches of veteran organizations, that operated under different names in order to aid the Muslims in Kosovo. In this conflict, much like its predecessor, Islamic charities played two main roles:

- They served as a channel for transferring financial aid to the Muslims in Kosovo.
- They constituted a logistic infrastructure and served as a cover for terrorist activity (by using the papers of charity workers).

There were many Islamic charities active in Kosovo, but the involvement of the following organizations was particularly prominent:

- The Albanian branch of al Haramain.
- The United Saudi Aid for Kosovo.
- The Global Relief Foundation.
- Igassa—another name for the IIRO.
- The Humanitarian Islamic Foundation.
- The Islamic Salvation Front.

These organizations dealt in the provision of humanitarian relief to the Muslim population in Kosovo and at the same time aided the armed struggle fought by the terror organizations.

Information based on Serb sources indicates that already in the spring of 1998 the first "Islamic instructors" arrived in Kosovo, mainly from Bosnia-Herzegovina. This group of instructors included the following Mujahidin:

- Abu Abd al Rahman Eimani, a Syrian citizen who served as commander of a Mujahidin camp during the war in Bosnia.
- Camel Lermani, an Algerian citizen who served as the representative of the Igassa relief organization (see elaboration in Section Two which describes Igassa/IIRO).
- Hamza Husamedin, a Palestinian who provided logistic aid while transferring Mujahidin from Bosnia-Herzegovina to Kosovo.

In Kosovo, the three helped to train Islamic fighters and establish a fighting framework for the Mujahidin called the "Abubaker Sadeq Unit."[20]

The unit was established in May 1998 in the Drenica area. It included 210 fighters, many of who were Muslim volunteers from Albania, Macedonia, Bosnia-Herzegovina, and Saudi Arabia. The unit's commander, who was called "Abu Ismaili," had acquired combat experience during the Bosnian war, when he had served as the commander of a Mujahidin unit.

The acquisition of equipment and combat means for the "Abu Baker Sadeq Unit" was financed by Islamic charities from Zenica in Bosnia:

- The Islamic Balkan Center
- The Active Islamic Youth (AIY)

It is to be noted that these organizations were founded by Saudi Arabia.

The first skirmish with the Mujahidin forces in Kosovo took place on the night between July 18-19, 1998, when a group of fighters attempting to infiltrate Kosovo from Albania encountered a unit of the Yugoslavian (Serb) Border Guard.

In the course of the fighting in Kosovo, evidence indicated that members of various tcrror organizations, including Al Qaida, thc Islamic Army for the Liberation of Aden and Abyan (a Yemenite organization), the Egyptian Islamic Jihad, and others, participated in the fighting alongside the Muslim forces of Kosovo.

During the years of conflict in Kosovo and in their aftermath, evidence found in Macedonia also attested to the influx of foreign Mujahidin, as well as Bosnian and Albanian, volunteers who helped the separatist Islamic terror organizations in Macedonia.

**The Infrastructure of Islamic Terror in Kosovo**

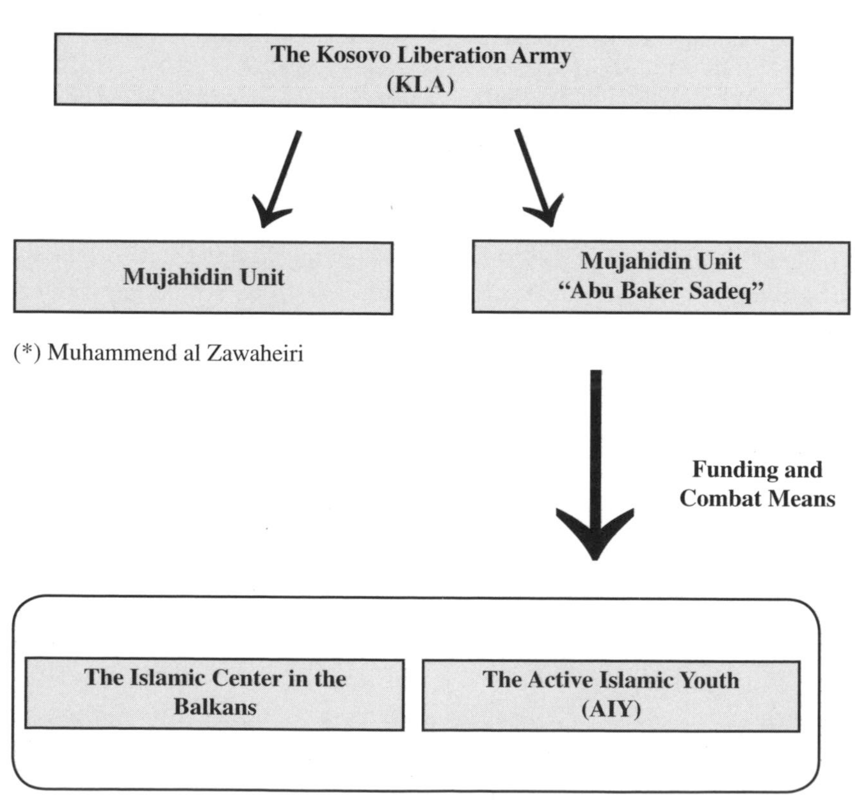


(*) Brother of Ayman al Zawaheiri, Bin Laden's deputy

## The Liberation Army of Presevo Medvedja and Bujanovac-LAPMB

The area of the Presevo Valley, which borders on Kosovo, is composed of three municipal authorities: Presevo Medvedja, and Bujanovac. Serbia attributes considerable importance to the region because the system of railways and roads that connects the central and southern parts of Kosovo, as well as the route connecting Serbia and Macedonia, pass through this valley.

Somc 70,000 Albanians residing in the Presevo Valley call the area "Eastern Kosovo."[21] The conflict in this region stemmed from power struggles between the local Albanians and the Serb population, and was also influenced by the fighting in Kosovo.

The agreement between Serbia and the NATO forces dictated the creation of a Ground Security Zone (GSZ) along the length of the boundaries of the Kosovo region. The Zone is 402 kilometers long and 5 kilometers wide, of which 139 kilometers run through the Presevo Valley.[22]

The withdrawal of the Serb forces from Kosovo and the restrictions applied to their activity in the GSZ, created relatively convenient conditions for the KLA and, subsequently, for the LAPMB to act in the "seam" area that lies between Kosovo and the Presevo Valley.

Most of the organization's money came from smuggling and the illegal sale of cigarettes and other goods, as wcll as drug traffiking throughout the Balkans.

After the LAPMB was dismantled due to pressure applied by the multinational force, many of its members transferred to the ranks of the NLA and the ANA.[23]

A group of the organization's commanders and soldiers established a new terror organization called the Liberation Army of East Kosovo (LAEK). Its declared goal was to continue the struggle of the LAPMB (which, as noted earlier, had been dismantled) to annex the Presevo, Medvedja, and Bujanovac regions to an independent Kosovo. However, LAEK failed to stimulate popular support and remained a less significant and smaller organization.

## Notes

1. Biger Gideon, Kosovo's Geographical History, Ma'archot, Issue 371, July 2000, p. 2. The Historical Geography of Kosovo.
2. Kosovo - Metohija: The Serbo-Albanian Conflict, Institute for Balkan Studies, Serbian Academy of Arts and Science, Belgrade, www.siri-us.com.
3. Ibid.
4. Michael Roman, Ethnicity and Territorialism in the Balkans, Ma'archot, Issue 371, July 2000, p. 7.
5. The KLA has several names: aside from the Kosovo Libertion Army including the Kosovo Protection Corps (KPC) and Ushtrija Clirimatre I Kosovo (UCK).
6. Marc Semo, "UCK at the Heart of Radicalization and Liberation," January 21, 1999.
7. Ibid.
8. Ibid.
9. Chris Hedges, "Kosovo Rebels and their New Friend," New York Times, June 9, 1998.
10. The Baltimore Sun, "Speculation Plentiful, Facts Few about Kosovo Separatist Group: KLA has Already Seized Region Near the Capital," March 6, 1998.
11. Farhan Haq's "Politics—Yugoslavia: UN efforts on Kosovo stalled," Inter Press Service, August 12, 1998.
12. Reuters, Pristina, Serbia, Analysis: "West has little leverage over Kosovo guerillas—the CNN factor," February 14, 1999.
13. Ibid.
14. Chris Stephen, "U.S. tackles Islamic militancy in Kosovo," *Scotsman*, November 30, 1998.
15. Sonya Hodak, "Some 300 former HV members fighting in Kosovo," Vecernji List, Zagreb, March 9, 1999.
16. HV – Croatian Army.
17. AFP, New York, Albanian Americans help fund the KLA, February, 1999.
18. U.S. Congress, Testimony of Frank J. Ciluffo, Deputy Director, Global Organized Crime, Program Director to the House Judiciary Committee, December 13, 2000.
19. U.S. Congress, Testimony of Ralf Mutschke of Interpol's Criminal Intelligence Division to the House Judicial Committee, December 13, 2000.
20. This unit was established in May 1998 by the Emum brothers, Muhammed and Akram Avdiu, together with Sapend Kopriva and the abovementioned Mujahidin.
21. "Terrorism and Ethnic Conflicts: Experience of the Western Balkans," *Forum, Magazine of FER*, Issue January-March 2003, p. 21.
22. Ibid.
23. The National Liberation Army and the Albanian National Army, two separatist Albanian organizations (see the chapter about Macedonia).

# Section Five

## Albania and Radical Islam

# Albania—Background

During the period of turmoil that the Balkans underwent prior to the Berlin Congress in 1878, as an ethnic group, the Albanians raised the idea of drawing under the wings of their national identity (which, at that time, was in its fledgling stages), all of the Albanians in the Balkans, even beyond the geographical borders of Albania itself. The concept of "a greater Albania" was first raised by the "Albanian League," which was established in Prizeren in 1878. However, this demand was never recognized by international powers and it thus remained a vision that could not be realized.

During most of the 1980s, under the Communist rule in Albania, the concept of "a greater Albania" was placed on hold, although Albania did support the demands of Albanians in Kosovo to recognize their national and religious identity. However, this issue did not have much impact nor was it given serious attention vis-à-vis Albanian-Yugoslavian relations.

In 1981, riots broke out in Kosovo when the Muslim Albanians demanded the status of a republic within the Yugoslavian Federation which, at that time, were six in number, (instead of the status of an autonomous district within Serbia). However, these riots did not serve to promote the goals of the Muslims in Kosovo. In 1991, after the downfall of Communism in Albania, the new Albanian regime recognized the independent Muslim Republic of Kosovo, and its leader Ibrahim Rugova opened an office in Tirana, the Albanian capital.

The collapse of Yugoslavia reawakened the old dreams regarding "a greater Albania," which was to include not only Kosovo but also sections of Macedonia, Greece, Serbia, and Montenegro, where Albanian populations had settled over the years. The reawakening of Islamic awareness in the Balkans, and the precedent of Bosnia, catalyzed the unification of all of the Albanians in the region under the banner of Albania and Islam, and increased the ethnic and religious tension in the Balkans. In 1992, under the leadership of Sali Berisha, the Democratic Party ascended to power in Albania, replacing Ramiz Alia's government. The change of government stirred great hopes in Albania regarding economic improvements and political stability, hopes that were quickly dashed.

In 1996-1997, Albania found itself embroiled in a serious economic crisis (the collapse of its banks) and political instability climaxed in riots that broke out in March 1997, bringing down the central government.

The events in Albania affected Albanian populations in other parts of the Balkans. For example, a split took place between Sali Berisha's supporters and his opponents in Albanian political organizations in Kosovo.

Dr. Ibrahim Rugova, who was prominent among the Albanian moderate leaders in Kosovo, sided with the opposition to Berisha while more radical entities supported Berisha. In any case, the crisis in Albania weakened its ability to support the Albanian communities in Kosovo as well as in other areas in the Balkans and to promote the concept of "a greater Albania."

The chaotic situation in Albania encouraged radical entities in Albanian society, both inside and outside the country's borders, and contributed to the strengthening of the KLA in Kosovo.[2]

The loss of military and police control in Albania led to the looting of arsenals and to the transfer of large quantities of weapons and combat means to citizens, crime organizations, and the KLA (see subsequent elaboration).

Even after the restoration of order and stability in the country, the basic problems plaguing Albania in the post-Communist era still remain:[3]

- It is a traditional society split on a tribal-family basis.
- The absence of a democratic and effective governmental establishment and tradition.
- Economic weakness and dependence on external aid.
- Backward infrastructure systems (transportation, energy, education, health, etc.)
- Political isolation in the Balkans and internationally.
- A developed "black market" based on strong crime organizations and a weak governmental system, as well as limited law enforcement capabilities.

One of the prominent characteristics of Albanian terror organizations, and organized crime, is a division into areas of activity based on tribal and familial affiliation.[4] Membership in these organizations is also primarily based on regional and extended familial affiliation (the term which is widely accepted in the Balkans is "fis" which means an extended family or tribe).

Familial and geographical distribution preserves the behavioral patterns and traditional social norms. The tribal Albanian society treats strangers with suspicion and maintains a clear and rigid internal hierarchy. The traditional Albanian society emphasizes family loyalty, and whoever deviates from this principle or harms it is punished severely.

Members of the organization are required to swear total obedience and loyalty to the organization and family. In exchange, the individual is granted its patronage and protection. Betrayal is punished by death.

## Albania and the Islamic Terror Infrastructure

When he ascended to power in 1992, President Sali Berisha acted to promote two main issues:

- The concept of "greater Albania."
- Restoring Albania's weak economy.

Berisha regarded the Muslim world as a natural ally when aspiring to promote these objectives. The war in Bosnia, the awakening of the Albanian and Muslim nationalism in Kosovo, and the mobilization of the Muslim world in aid of the Muslims in the Balkans, constituted the background that contributed to the close relationship between Albania with Berisha at its head, and radical Islam and the militant approach that he adopted in the matter of the conflict between the Muslims and the Serbs in the Balkans.

His point of view in this issue is reflected in his declaration that the war in Kosovo is a "Jihad," or a holy war, and in his call for all Albanians to rise to protect their homes.[5]

The widespread presence of Arab businessmen, Mujahidin (Afghanistan "alumni"), and Islamic charities in Albania, to a large extent, stem from Albania's economic collapse in the early 1990s and the policies advocated by President Berisha who tried to rehabilitate his country by appealing to Muslim and Arab states and by opening its gates to Islamic "investors."

Islamic terror organizations such as Al Qaida and the Egyptian Islamic Jihad leaped at the opportunity and, in exchange for relatively small financial investments, built up an economic and organizational infrastructure in Albania under the guise of commercial companies and charities that camouflaged a widespread terror infrastructure. The latter was earmarked to support the Mujahidin activities in Bosnia-Herzegovina and, subsequently, in Kosovo during the wars in the Balkans, and to serve as a forefront for the activation of terror infrastructures in Western

Europe. According to intelligence sources in Albania, Osama Bin Laden visited Albania in 1995 and met with the Albanian president at the time Sali Berisha, as well as with the director of Albanian intelligence, and other senior leaders.[6]

Following his meetings in Albania, an Al Qaida infrastructure was established in the country that was supported by a network of Islamic charities that had been active in the Balkans since the early 1990s. In the framework of establishing the organization's infrastructure in Albania, Mujahidin from various Muslim locations worldwide arrived in this country, and from there also moved on to Kosovo (with the KLA's assistance), where they aided the Muslims and organized terror cells designated to serve as a future infrastructure in the anti-West battle in the Balkans and Europe.[7]

As noted earlier, in the late 1990s Albania suffered from political and economic instability that peaked in 1997, when riots broke out due to the collapse of the Albanian economy. The regime lost its control over events for a period of time. During these riots tens of thousands of firearms, ammunition, and explosives were stolen from the police munitions stores, as well as 100,000 empty Albanian passports. Much of the weaponry and passports found their way to criminal and terrorist entities, including the KLA.[8] Albania is one of the thirty-four countries "marked" by the U.S. in the aftermath of the September 11, 2001 attacks as a country where Al Qaida maintains a terrorist infrastructure. Due to U.S. insistence that the Albanian government take steps against this infrastructure, the Albanian police raided the organization's offices and companies suspected of involvement in Al Qaida activities.[9]

One of the targets of these actions was a businessman named Yasin al-Qadi whose assets in the United States were frozen due to suspicions that he dealt in money laundering for Al Qaida.[10]

Al Qadi stood at the head of the Muwafaq Foundation Saudi charity through which, according to American allegations, he channeled millions of dollars worth of contributions donated to the Saudi organization to Al Qaida. During the years 1990-1992, Al Qadi established eight different companies in Albania that invested large sums of money in economic activities in Albania.

In the framework of the Albanian authorities' activities against Al Qaida infrastructures in their country, Al Qadi's assets, and those of at least nine other Saudi "businessmen," were frozen and 223 individuals were deported. While some of them were suspected of ties with Al Qaida, the official claim was that their entry permits had expired.

In 1998, an attempted attack against the U.S. Embassy in Tirana was thwarted. Under American pressure, the Albanian government, which was based on a socialist coalition, decided to act against Islamic terror organizations in the country. The Albanian government was offered U.S. aid and support (the FBI and CIA were involved in the activities). In several raids, twelve Egyptian terrorists, members of the Egyptian Islamic Jihad, were apprehended, arrested and extradited to Egypt (see the chapter entitled The Trials of the "Returnees from Albania" below).

That year, Albanian cooperation with the U.S. was also prominent in the issue of the Kosovo crisis when the U.S. and NATO supported the Muslim side in Kosovo.

Albania aided the KLA in various ways, from granting permits to establish training bases and commands in its territory to transferring combat means that arrived via various sources in Albania where it was handed over to the organization.

In 1998, against the background of the crisis in Kosovo, Albania made its position, vis-à-vis the conflict in that region, clear. In an interview with the Chinese news agency, the Albanian Prime Minister stated that Albanians in the Balkans must unite and organize a collective defense. The Prime Minister noted that the withdrawal of the Serb forces from Kosovo must be the first step to a resolution of the Kosovo crisis.

He warned that if the talks failed in France, and the violence in Kosovo continued, all Albanians living in Albania, Macedonia, Kosovo, and other areas of the Balkans would unite in the form of collective defense.

He also called on the U.S. and NATO not only to intervene diplomatically but to become involved on a military level and promised that Albania would join forces with this military intervention.[11]

According to Serb sources, not only did Albania help the KLA/KPC but the organization was actually placed under Albanian command (although the Albanian authorities never admitted this publicly). As proof of this claim, the Serbs point out Albania's ability to force the organization to come to the negotiation table at Rambouillt in contrast to the stand taken by some of its senior leaders.[12]

According to reports published in the Deutsche press Agentur,[13] part of the financial support for the KLA was channeled from Muslim countries, with the help of the former director of the Albanian National Intelligence Service (NIS),[14] who left Albania in 1998 and was arrested and questioned about his ties with terror organizations.[15]

The smuggling of combat means from Albania to Kosovo was also conducted as part of the "illegal" commercial system based in Albania that included the smuggling of combat means, drugs, and other merchandise, while circumventing the embargo imposed on the Balkans.

This phenomenon first began during the administration of Albanian President Sali Berisha, who "turned a blind eye" to the widespread smuggling that flourished in his country.

The crumbling of economies in the Balkans during the early 1990s, particularly the "reforms" in the Albanian economy that caused its collapse, created conditions for the development of a "black economy" which flourished during the years 1992-1997.

During those years, Albania became a focal point for the trafficking of drugs and women, as well as laundering money, sometimes taking the form of cooperation between Albanian crime organizations and foreign crime organizations such as the Italian Mafia and others. According to various reports, 75 percent of the drugs smuggled into Europe arrived via the Balkans (particularly Albania).

The main trafficking routes led to Albania's ports via the unsupervised mountainous passageways that lie between Albania, Kosovo and Macedonia. According to these reports, between four and six tons of heroin made their way to Western Europe[16] via the Balkans, and Albanian drug dealers constituted the dominant factor in the distribution of drugs in Western Europe.[17]

Western intelligence reports stated that senior members of the government and the Albanian secret service, were also involved in the drug trafficking, and that the money laundering processes in Albania were based on cooperation between organized crime and the banking system in that country. As noted earlier, since the mid-1990s and more intensely following the September 11, 2001 attacks, the U.S. has been pressuring the authorities in Tirana to take action against the terror infrastructures that struck roots in their country.

## Al Qaida's "Albanian Terror Network" [18]

The first public expression of the existence of an Al Qaida terror infrastructure in Albania came to light during the trial of a French citizen named Claude ben Abd al Kader who was charged with murdering an Albanian student during an argument. During the trial, Abd al Kader confessed that he was affiliated with the "Albanian Terror Network" of Al Qaida and stated that his role had been to recruit, arm, and train fighters for the KLA. Abd al Kader was found guilty and was sentenced in 1998 to twenty years of imprisonment.

This information was verified by the director of the Albanian intelligence service which stated that Bin Laden had dispatched Al Qaida fighters to help the Muslims in Kosovo.

Information regarding the existence of an "Albanian network" affiliated with Al Qaida was also found in a letter published in Bin Laden's name and signed by Sheikh Abdullah Abu al Farouk. In the letter, Al Qaida issued a call to all Muslims to join the Jihad on behalf of Allah against the enemies of Islam and not to turn their guns against their Muslim brethren.

The letter cites the achievements of the Mujahidin throughout the world "in Afghanistan, Palestine, Lebanon, Bosnia, Kosovo, Somalia, Hijaz (Saudi Arabia)" and other places.

## The Terror Infrastructures of the Egyptian Jihad in Albania

A short time after the consolidation of Al Qaida with the Egyptian Islamic Jihad under the leadership of Ayman al Zawaheiri, a senior activist of the Egyptian Islamic Jihad named Ahmad Ibrahim al Najjar was dispatched to Albania in order to establish terror infrastructures under the guise of his work in the Al Haramain organization (a Saudi charity – see above).

Al Najjar arrived in Albania with false papers and gathered a group of Egyptian Islamic Jihad members in this country. In 1999, in response to pressure applied on the Albanian authorities by the United States and Egypt, Al Najjar was arrested, together with the other members of the organization, and they were extradited to Egypt (see the list of the arrested organization members in the appendix).

The trials of the Egyptian Islamic Jihad members received a good deal of attention in the media and were dubbed "the trials of the returnees from Albania."

## The Trials of the "Returnees from Albania" [19]

In the largest trial in Egypt against radical Islam since 1981 (the trial of the assassins of President Anwar Sadat), the main defendants disclosed information regarding links between the Egyptian Islamic Jihad and Al Qaida. The Egyptian Islamic Jihad, much like Al Qaida, also set itself the goal of attacking American targets in the Middle East, Africa, and Southeast Asia.

In the course of the trial run by the Egyptian security organizations, over 2,000 pages were recorded, including detailed confessions made by the accused regarding subversive activities against the Egyptian government, violent activities inside Egypt, plans to undermine Egypt's stability, and intentions to perpetrate attacks all over the world.

The first lead in this investigation was the arrest of Ahmad Ibrahim al Najjar in Albania, where he had fled from the death sentence in Egypt after having been found guilty of attempting to perpetrate a terror attack in the Khan al Khalili market in Cairo in 1994. Following al Najjar's arrest, other members of the group were also apprehended.[20] Al Najjar revealed the names of many of his collaborators during the interrogation and disclosed information that he had received from the leaders of the Islamic Jihad, including Ayman al Zawaheiri, 'Adil' Abd al Majid and Tharwat Salah Shehatah. Al Najjar stated that the conflict with the U.S. presented a challenge for the entire Islamic nation and not just Ayman al Zawaheiri and Bin Laden. As stated above, Al Najjar was one of twelve individuals arrested for their affiliation with the Egyptian Islamic Jihad who were deported from Albania to Egypt in July 1999. Forty-three individuals were brought to trial and an additional sixty-four were tried in their absence. One was Ayman al Zawaheiri, Bin Laden's deputy.

In his confession Al Najjar spoke of his stand and his organization's approach to the American policy in the Balkans. Al Najjar argued that although the U.S. had supported the Muslims in Bosnia, it was not interested in the Jihad spreading to Europe because of the fear that the presence of Muslim forces in the Balkans would allow a repetition of the Afghani scenario.

*Non-Conventional Weapons.* The newest and most controversial information revealed in the confessions of the Albanian group was that entities connected to Bin Laden had succeeded in obtaining bacteria and viruses from factories in Eastern Europe and Indonesia that could serve for the development of biological warfare.

The interrogation of the group members indicates that Al Qaida, the Egyptian Islamic Jihad, and additional organizations such as the MILF and Abu Sayyaf in the Philippines had been involved in negotiations for the acquisition of bacteria for the development of biological weapons as follows; anthrax, botolinum, salmonella, and e-coli.

It is not clear from the investigation records whether these means reached Al Qaida and the other terror organizations or if these organizations succeeded in developing and manufacturing biological weapons.

*Modi Operandi of the Egyptian Islamic Jihad.* The investigations conducted by the Egyptian security agencies revealed changes in the modi operandi of the Islamic groups, which expanded their scope of targets and began attacking foreign targets, mainly belonging to the U.S. and France, and not only Arab and Egyptian targets.

According to the defendants, one of the reasons for the shift in the modus operandi was the involvement of these countries in the pursuit of the organization's members inside and outside their territories. The confession of the accused Sayyid Salameh indicated that these countries' targets were chosen in order to provide the organization with a media platform while proving its power and credibility. The interrogation of the Jihad members also indicated that the organization closely cooperated with "Jihad" organizations worldwide and that Al Qaida serves as a sort of "umbrella organization" for a range of additional radical Islamic organizations.

*Plans to Free the Jihad Prisoners with Gliders.* Legal sources in Egypt disclosed that Islamic Jihad entities under detention planned to perpetrate a rescue raid from the air in order to extricate some of the organization's leaders from the Turah Prison near Cairo. This information surfaced during the interrogation of one of the planners of the prison break, Khalid al-Dahab, who held both American and Egyptian passports.

He divulged that the heads of the organization, who lived in Afghanistan, had instructed him to plan an attack that would help release some of the Islamic Jihad leaders. He claimed that no date had been set for the attack and that the practical planning had not yet begun (prior to his arrest).

According to the plan, an explosive device was to have been dropped from an Adeltap glider, thus causing an explosion in the prison. The explosion was to have caused confusion and chaos, which would serve as a diversion when gliders landed near the prison cells of the organization's members and rescued them. Khalid al Dahab added that he had learned how to operate a glider in a civil aviation school in San Francisco during the early 1990s, and from there he had moved on to Afghanistan where he taught three of his associates how to operate the glider.

*Ahmad Ibrahim al Najjar's Confession.* The confession of Ahmad Ibrahim al Najjar, the first defendant in the trial against the "Albanian returnees," covered 143 pages.

Ahmad Ibrahim al Najjar divulged that he belonged to the second generation of the consolidation between the Egyptian Islamic Jihad and the Egyptian Jama'ah al-Islamiyah. This union was the result of the joint initiative of Aboud al-Zummar, Najih Ibrahim and Muhammad Abd-al-Salam Faraj, with the blessing of Sheikh Omar Abd-al-Rahman, who served as the spiritual leader of the two organizations after their consolidation. It is to be noted that the Jihad and the Jama'ah Al Islamiyah organizations assassinated Egyptian President Anwar al Sadat in 1981 during a parade in Cairo marking the "October victory."

He added that following the assassination he had been imprisoned for three years and was released at the end of 1984. After his release, he resumed his activities in the ranks of the Islamic Jihad and in 1988 recruited new members for the organization from the Nahiya area of the Al-Jiza district. The Egyptian security agencies exposed the activity and arrested the group, which was dubbed "the Islamic punishment" (al-ksas al-Islami). Ahmad Ibrahim al Najjar attempted to set up another group whose goal was to act against the Egyptian government, including through the planned attack at the Khan al Khalili market, which is an important tourist site in Egypt. However, the Egyptian intelligence agencies nipped the attack in the bud.

Ahmad Ibrahim al Najjar fled from Egypt to Yemen and lived for a short period in San'aa where he contacted another defendant, Yusuf al-Jundi, who was his collaborator in the planning of the Khan al Khalili attack. Al-Jundi was eventually apprehended by the Yemenite police and was deported to Egypt, where he was tried and sentenced in a military court. He is currently serving a life sentence with hard labor.

Following al-Jundi's arrest, al Najjar feared that his friend would reveal his whereabouts in Yemen to the Egyptian interrogators, and that the latter would demand his extradition to Egypt. He therefore decided to go to a European country and request political refuge like other senior members in the organization had done before him.

In his confession about the escape from Yemen al Najjar stated:

> I knew that the Yemenite government had adopted a policy of cooperation with the Egyptian authorities. Therefore, I decided to leave Yemen and go to some place in Eastern Europe or Latin America. At the time, I thought that one of the leaders of the Jihad, who had also been a fugitive for a long time (from the Egyptian authorities), would help me find refuge. I contacted "the brother" Adil Abd al Majid, who had been granted political asylum in Britain and lived in London. It was well known that Adil managed a printing press called "the Office for the Defense of the Egyptian People," where he printed flyers condemning the Egyptian administration. When I told Adil about my plight he helped me by sending me $1,500, and with the money I was able to flee Yemen. I left that country with a forged passport and arrived in Albania.

In Albania al Najjar tried to establish infrastructures for the Jihad organization. According to his testimony, he worked in Albania as an

Arabic and Islamic religion teacher at a school that was affiliated with the Muslim charity Al Haramain. He succeeded in earning the trust of the charity's managers and several months later became one of its managers.

At the same time al Najjar renewed his ties with leaders of the Egyptian Jihad in London as well as with Ayman al Zawaheiri, Bin Laden's deputy. Making contact with Adil Abd al Majid and Tharwat Salah Shehatah in London was a relatively simple matter, but it was harder to talk to al Zawaheiri. Contact was made with him via the Internet. Contacting al Zawaheiri became even more complicated when his hiding place in Geneva was exposed and he moved to another place that even al Najjar knew nothing about.

Al Najjar claimed that the leaders of the Jihad organization had not given up their ideas, and they believed that some day they would oust the Egyptian government and rise to power. He stated that the group had clung to this goal since 1981, despite the Egyptian government's success in inflicting considerable damage on the organization. In his confession, al Najjar recounted that al Zawaheiri became the organization's leader abroad, replacing Abbud al Zummar, the former leader of the Islamic Jihad, who is serving a life sentence for the assassination of President Sadat.

Al Najjar illuminated the reasons for the conflict between the organization's leaders sitting in jail and their associates abroad; the jailed leaders wished to cease the violent activities, while the leaders abroad rejected this initiative to stop the violence. Al Najjar explained that the organizational hierarchy of the Jihad is very complicated because the majority of the leaders live abroad, and the leaders residing in Egypt are unwilling to endanger themselves. He added that he was not personally acquainted with all of the organization's members and their roles, but he knew the role of Tharwat Salah Shehatah, a lawyer who had fled to London, and who, according to al Najjar, served as the head of internal security in the organization. As part of his role, he was responsible for the protection of the organization's members, information, and document security. Shehatah was apparently also responsible for the organization's security mechanism and its safety.

He claimed that Adil Abd-al-Majid, who also resided in London, was responsible for the "social committee" whose function was to take care of organization members inside and outside of Egypt. The committee also provided organization members with the money required to flee Egypt or for specific needs inside the country.

## Albania as an Arena for Islamic Terror Activity (2000-2004)

During the first half of August 2003, the continued activity of Islamic terror organizations in Albania became evident. Some 300 guerilla fighters, who had been trained in Albania (including about ten foreign Mujahidin), penetrated Kosovo from the Albanian border.

Most of them were incorporated into the semi-military framework of the KPC (which, as noted, is identical to the KLA), an entity that was purportedly dismantled after the war in Kosovo in 1999. The latter maintains close links with the ANA, which is active in Kosovo and Macedonia.[21]

In Albania, guerilla fighters were trained in three camps. These camps served for the training of guerilla fighters from Kosovo as well as other Mujahidin from 1999 onwards. The Albanian authorities gave these camps their blessing ansupported them.[22]

The fighters that infiltrated Kosovo in August 2003 brought large amounts of light weapons, mortars, and mines.

Some of the guerilla fighters initiated action a short time after their arrival in an area held by the Serbs in Kosovo, near the city of Gorazde and the Montenegro border. Serb sources point to at least four attacks perpetrated by these entities that resulted in the death of Serb civilians (including children).

Subsequently, some of the Mujahidin moved to Raska in Bosnia, while others were involved in laying mines and roadside explosive charges against the Serb forces along the border between Serbia and Kosovo. These instances serve as only a few examples that were exposed regarding guerilla and terror attacks launched from Albanian territory, which still serves as a rear base for radical Islamic entities in the framework of the ongoing conflict in various focal points of the Balkans (Bosnia, Kosovo, and Macedonia). In the matter of the links between Islamic terror and Albanian crime organizations, see the subsequent elaboration.

### Notes

1. Ramiz Alia replaced the previous ruler Enver Hoxa.
2. Dusan Janjic, "Kosovo between Conflict and Dialogues," Forum for Ethnic Relations, Belgrade, Center for Tolerance and Dialogue, Belgrade, 2003, pp. 36-37.
3. Ibid.
4. Tribal distribution to Tosks and Gegs.
5. Chris Hedges, "Kosovo rebels and their new friends," *New York Times*, June 9, 1998.
6. "Al Qaida hust heats up in Albania," AP Tirana, Albania, August 11, 2002.
7. Ibid.
8. Chris Hedges, "Kosovo rebels and their new friend," *New York Times*, June 9, 1998.

9. "Al Qaida hust heats up in Albania," A.P. Tirana, Albania, August 11, 2002.
10. Ibid.
11. Xinhua, Tirana, "Albania Calls for All Albanians Collective Defense," February 10, 1999.
12. Enton Abilekaj, "Albanian's Disclosure," Koha Jone, Tirana, February 1999 (translated from Albanian).
13. *Deutsche Press*—Agentur, March 13, 1998.
14. NIS—National Information Service.
15. *Daily News*, Ankara, March 5, 1997.
16. The report submitted by the German Federal Criminal Agency
17. Roger Boyes and Eska Wright, "Drugs Money Linked to the Kosovo Rebels," *The Times*, London, March 24, 1999.
18. A.P. Tirana, "Self-declared Bin Laden aide found guilty in Albanian slaying," November 14, 1998.
19. The Sharq al-Awsat newspaper reported about the trials. See also: "Egypt, Albanian returnee accused of membership in Islamic Jihad group," Arabnews.com, October 4, 1999.
20. Ibid.
21. ANA—Albanian National Army, a terror organization active in Macedonia.
22. Issa, special reports, Balkan Strategic Studies, "Strong warning indicators for new surge in Europian Islamic terrorism." October 15, 2003.

# Section Six

## Macedonia and Radical Islam

# Background—The Conflict in Macedonia[1]

Macedonia is situated in the western part of the ancient kingdom of Macedonia whose King Alexander the Great occupied large parts of Asia and the Middle East. Immediately after his death, the empire that he had founded began to crumble (in 323 B.C.). Macedonia was conquered by the Roman Empire in 168 B.C. In the sixth and seventh centuries Slavic tribes settled in the area, the forefathers of the modern Macedonians. During the Middle Ages the land served as an arena of struggle between the Byzantines, the Bulgarians, and the Serbs. In 1371 it was conquered by the Ottomans.

Macedonia is a mountainous, landlocked country in the heart of the Balkans. Its area is estimated to be 25,333 square kilometers and most of its inhabitants are Macedonians of Slavic descent who have no connection to the ancient Macedonians.

Macedonia's current population is about 2.2 million. It is composed of Macedonians, Albanians, Wallachs, Turks, gypsies, and others.[2]

The country's population is mainly divided between Muslim Albanians and descendants of the Serbs who converted to Islam during the days of the Ottoman rule (which constitute some 30 percent of the population) on the one hand, and Macedonian inhabitants, most of whom are Orthodox Christians, on the other.[3]

The question whether there actually exists such a thing as a Macedonian nationality is subject to controversy: The Serbs claim that the Macedonians are southern Serbs, the Greeks believe that they are Greek Slavs, while the Bulgarians claim that they are "related to the Bulgarians."

About half of Macedonia's population lives in cities, the largest of which is the capital Skopje, with 450,000 residents.

Macedonian national awakening began at the end of the nineteenth century, when at the end of the Balkans war, historic Macedonia was divided up between Greece, Bulgaria, and Yugoslavia. In 1941, Bulgaria invaded Yugoslavian Macedonia, and following World War II, it was returned to Yugoslavia and became one of the republics of the Yugoslavian Federation.[4]

During the 1980s, nationalism grew in the Republic. In 1991 Macedonia followed in the wake of Croatia and Slovania and declared its independence. Macedonia was not affected by the wars that shook the former Yugoslavia, and generally maintained a cautious neutrality while partially identifying with Serbia. Following the decision to break away from the Yugoslavian Federation, demonstrations and riots were instigated by the Serbs who opposed the secession on the one hand, alongside demonstrations held by Albanian nationalists who called for the establishment of an Albanian republic in Yugoslavia—Illyria [5]—on the other. The Macedonian authorities handled the riots firmly and restored order quickly. Another crisis in Macedonia's modern history took place on October 3 1995 when an assassination attempt was made against the President of Macedonia Kiro Gligorov through the use of a car bomb. The presdient survived but the assassination attempt shocked the country's political system.[6]

Macedonia attracted a certain amount of international attention during the presidential election campaign in 1995 and in the course of the elections for the municipalities in 2000, when there appeared signs of political instability and a surge of nationalist fervor was evident within the Albanian population on the one hand, and the Christian Macedonian population on the other.

The Macedonian economy is weak (the annual GDP is estimated at $13.8 billion), and the delicate ethnic balance is threatened by the Albanian refugees who arrived in the country during the Kosovo crisis, as well as by the Albanian minority's aspirations to achieve autonomy. In 2001 clashes broke out between the army and Albanian isolationists who demanded a special status in the constitution (see subsequent elaboration).

## Islamic Terror in Macedonia

Politicians and researchers regard the conflict in Macedonia as a spillover of the clashes in Kosovo, with clear links between the two situations.[7] However, it appears that the truth is that the conflict in Macedonia is fed by internal problems stemming from the ethnic and religious composition of the country, as well as the weakness of its political system, in addition to the significant impact of outside players such as Albania and the Muslims in Kosovo on events in the country.

Even during the conflict between the Muslims and Serbs in Kosovo, the Macedonian authorities feared that the conflict would spread to their country as well.

A first hint of future developments can be observed in the arrest of a "foreign" terrorist in 1999 (who served in the ranks of the Mujahidin) that attempted to detonate the police station in the heart of Skopje, Macedonia's capital. The latter was released subsequently due to pressure applied by one of the senior Muslim leaders in Macedonia.

The Macedonian Minister of Interior Georgievski claimed on March 8, 2001 that the international community could not ignore the fact that the Western democracies had created a new "Taliban" in Europe.

Three days later, the national security adviser to the Macedonian president declared in an interview for Newsweek that "Kosovo is a Balkan combination of Afghanistan and Columbia, as law, human rights and ethnic tolerance are non-existent there."

This message reflected the growing fears in Macedonia that the country would become another target for the Albanian narco-terrorism, particularly in the country's western areas where there is a marked Albanian Muslim majority.

Following the dismantling of the KLA and its conversion to the KPC (see below), due to the pressure of the NATO forces, many of the KLA commanders and fighters left the organization and helped to establish new guerilla and terror organizations in order to continue the struggle in new conflict arenas in the Balkans.[8]

The Albanian terror organizations established after the conversion of the KLA into the KPC were:

- The Liberation Army of Presevo, Medvedja, and Bujanovac.
- The National Liberation Army (NLA).
- The Albanian National Army (ANA).

These organizations, many of whose commanders and fighters had come from the ranks of the KLA, received support and aid from the KPC, which was considered a legitimate military force by the multinational forces in Kosovo and Macedonia.

The KPC served as these organizations' logistic support. It recruited fighters for them in Kosovo, trained them, and, subsequently, transferred them to these organizations' ranks.

Despite the fact that according to the agreement, the KLA/KPC was supposed to hand over all of its weapons to the multinational force, in actual fact a large part of these combat means was given to the NLA, LAPMB, and ANA.

Aside from these terror organizations, which were active in Kosovo, southern Serbia and Macedonia, about forty armed Albanian groups were active under the leadership of two commanders:

- Rustem Mustafa, whose was dubbed Remi.
- Fatmir Humoli.

These groups also cooperated with the Muslim intelligence service, which was established in Kosovo.

During 2001, Macedonia was dragged into the cycle of violence and for seven months fighting took place between the government forces and separatist Islamic terror organizations which were aided by terrorists from various Islamic terror organizations that had remained in the Balkans since the war in Bosnia. Scores of people were killed in the fighting and almost 100,000 were forced to leave their homes due to the clashes in the northern and western parts of the country.

During the months of conflict, the National Liberation Army (NLA) was the main entity to bear the burden of the fighting and when the conflict ended agreed to a ceasefire with the Macedonian authorities.[9]

The NLA was granted considerable assistance by the KPC and Albania, which enabled the passage of Mujahidin through its territory to the combat arena in Macedonia. According to various sources, the NLA ranks included some 150 Mujahidin from various countries who participated in the fighting (Albania, Bosnia, Turkey, Saudi Arabia, Afghanistan, and more). The "Albanian Al Haramain" charity played a central role in transferring the Mujahidin, weapons, and funding from Albania to Macedonia.

Part of this information was revealed following the arrest of an NLA fighter named Sedula Murati who served in a unit called Esmet Jashar, which was active in the Kumanovo and Lipkovo regions.

Another charity called the United Saudi Aid for Kosovo helped to supply arms and ammunition for the ANA Macedonian terror organization.

The charity's involvement in aiding terror was revealed following the arrest of eleven of the organization's employees by the international force KFOR under the suspicion that they were members of Al Qaida. It is to be noted that during the fighting and in its aftermath, additional Islamic terror organizations were active in Macedonia that do not yield to the authority of the NLA, although they are complying with the ceasefire, at least for the time being.

In the framework of the ceasefire, it was agreed that the international force in Macedonia would assemble the arms in the hands of the Islamic separatists and steps were taken to collect weapons (about 3,000 units were confiscated), but today it is clear that only a small part of the weapons in the possession of these organizations was handed over to the international forces.

## The Albanian National Army-ANA[10]

The Albanian National Army (ANA) was founded at the end of 1999 on the basis of a nucleus of commanders and fighters from the ranks of the KLA who were determined to continue their violent struggle in Kosovo and at other focal points in the Balkans. The organization adopted the ideology, modi operandi, and financing methods of the KLA.

The ANA is the military arm of a political movement called the Front for National Unity of Albanians (FNUA). The movement has an organizational structure including political leadership, a military branch, an intelligence mechanism (Albanian National Security—ANS), and a financial entity that deals in the financing of the organization's activities (Albanian National Fund—ANF). The ANA accumulated most of its power after the agreement signed in Macedonia to disassemble the NLA and confiscate its weapons. The extremist factors in the organization that aspired to continue the violent struggle transferred from the ranks of the NLA to the ANA.

At the time of its foundation, the organization was initially named "the National Committee for the Liberation of Occupied Territories" (NCLOT). Its name was changed to FNUA in mid-July 2002, while the intelligence and financial departments were established only in the beginning of 2003.

The organization was established by the members of a radical party in Albania called the "Revolutionary Party of Albanians of Tirana."

- The organization's leadership includes several individuals from Albania.
- The ANA is organized in the form of "divisions." Its main command is called the "Adem Jahari" Division. This command is responsible for Kosovo and Southern Serbia.
- The "Skenderbeu" Division is responsible for Western Macedonia (Iliriya).
- The "Mallsia" division is responsible for an area that shares the same name in Montenegro.
- The "Camerid" division is responsible for south Albania and Greece.

Most of the ANA organization's commanders previously commanded KLA, NLA, and LAPMB units. Commanders who left the Albanian army also serve in the organization's ranks.

The overall number of ANA members is estimated at two to three thousand fighters. The organizations in Kosovo and south Serbia have some 650 fighters at their disposal.

## Macedonia—Trends in the Activities of Islamic Terror Organizations

It appears that most of the Islamic organizations are determined to continue the struggle until achieving autonomy for the Muslims in Macedonia, as part of the concept of founding an Islamic state in the Balkans, and it is evident that their intention is also to strike out at Western targets which they perceive as obstacles to the realization of their goals.

According to Western intelligence entities, the Islamic terror organizations in Macedonia received combat means valued at over $3 million during 2002. In this framework, the organizations acquired SA7 and SA18 anti-aircraft missiles. The financing for the purchase of combat means apparently came from Albanian criminal entities interested in the continuation of violence and instability in the Balkans, a situation that enables them freedom to deal in the trafficking of guns, drugs, and women (the latter for the purpose of prostitution).

For a relatively prolonged period, reports regarding subversive activities and terror attacks perpetrated by Albanian Muslim separatists against the Macedonian population in areas with Muslim majorities were suppressed and covered up.

These reports were suppressed by the international community, particularly by NATO and Western Europe, because this would constitute an admission of failure to collect the weaponry in the hands of the separatist Muslims and reflect the inability of the international community to enforce the ceasefire agreement on the Islamic terror organizations.

The Western communities preferred to bury their heads in the sand because recognition of the gravity of the situation would force the European countries to take military action that they preferred to avoid.

This policy is exploited by the various Islamic organizations to consolidate their status in the field, and to expand their control in areas with Muslim majorities, while constantly attacking the Macedonian population and perpetrating sporadic terror attacks against the Macedonian security forces.

The presence of armed Muslims, not just in the periphery but also in the suburbs of Skopje the capital, is a common sight for all of the parties, including the international force whose role is to enforce the implementation of the ceasefire agreement. [11]

In February 2002, the Albanian National Army (ANA) declared its intention to continue its struggle against the Macedonian authorities, and the organization claimed responsibility for a series of attacks perpetrated in 2001. (Among other incidents, the organization claimed responsibility for the murder of three Macedonian policemen on November 12, 2001.)

The activity of the ANA in Kosovo and Macedonia (FYROM) reflects the organization's aspiration to instigate an escalation that will trigger extreme reactions followed by international intervention. The organization's leaders believe that the latter situation will serve their purpose. To their mind, restriction of the government's steps, and expansion of international control, will consolidate the status of the organization, which enjoys the support of Albania and the Muslim forces in Kosovo (the Kosovo Protection Corps-KPC). In the framework of the struggle against Islamic terror organizations, since March 2002 Macedonian security agencies have arrested four members of a terror cell, including two Jordanians and two Muslim Bosnians who studied in Germany.

During a search conducted in the house where they lived, a computer was confiscated which contained many files dealing with the wars in Kosovo and Macedonia, as well as plans for the perpetration of attacks against government institutions in Macedonia and foreign embassies. It appears that the arrest of these cell members subsequently led to the apprehension of another cell with seven members.

The Macedonian authorities handed over the confiscated material, and the four detainees, to the United States. Among other activities, they had planned to perpetrate attacks against American targets. According to Macedonian sources, the United States transferred the detainees to the detention facility in Guantanamu, Cuba where the Al Qaida and Taliban prisoners are being held.[12]

In March 2002, seven Islamic terrorists of various nationalities (Jordanian, Pakistani, Albanians, and Bosnians) were killed in clashes with the police force in Skopje, the capital of Macedonia. A large quantity of combat means and NLA uniforms were found in their possession. This was additional proof of the continued efforts made by local and foreign Islamic terror organizations to establish terror infrastructures in Macedonia.

The Macedonian Minister of Interior claimed that the clash had occurred in a suburb of Skopje inhabited by an Albanian Muslim population, and that the terrorists' intention had been to perpetrate attacks against the British, U.S., and German embassies.[13]

A splinter faction that broke away from the NLA terror organization, called "The Real Albanian National Liberation Army," declared in March 2002 that if the Macedonian authorities failed to introduce additional amendments into the constitution in favor of the Albanian Muslim minority, it would resume the armed struggle.

The NLA maintains close links with local Islamic terror organizations (in the Balkans) as well as with Mujahidin and foreign terror organizations.

The NLA commander, Ali Ahmet, and several Islamic clerics who preached on behalf of Jihad in the Balkans, were involved in the consolidation of these ties and traveled to Saudi Arabia from where they returned with volunteers who took part in the fighting in Kosovo and subsequently in Macedonia as well.[14]

The fragile ceasefire agreement that was achieved under the auspices of NATO and the European countries faces grave challenges posed by the Islamic terror organizations which do not comply with the agreement and continue with their terror activities (although sporadically at this time) against civilian and security targets in Macedonia.

In the framework of the noted wave of terror activity currently underway in Macedonia, Islamic Albanian terrorists set fire to an American-Macedonian textile factory (a joint economic project) in the Tetovo area. The presence of the armed terrorists in the area prevented the Macedonian firefighters from reaching the site and the factory burned to the ground.[15]

This represented a new peak in the activities of the Islamic terror organizations in this area, whose goal was to undermine stability and harm village populations that are not Muslim.[16]

On November 8, 2004 a general referendum was initiated by the opposition parties with the aim of repealing legislation granting autonomy to the Albanian minority in the country. The referendum was initiated by the nationalist Macedonian opposition leaders who oppose the peace agreement that put an end to the uprising of the Albanian minority in 2001. The Macedonian government, and the international community, appealed to Macedonian citizens to boycott the referendum and claimed that Macedonia's assimilation in Europe would be disrupted if the Albanian autonomy were to be annulled in the country. The referendum was actually forced on the Macedonian government by the Macedonian nationalists who had collected the required number of signatures. However, for a referendum to be valid, at least 50 percent of eligible voters in Macedonia, that is some 800,000 individuals, had to participate. The entire Albanian population, which constitutes a quarter of the country's population, was expected to abstain from voting. The main issue to be resolved through the referendum was the law that would alter the boundaries of the local government in Macedonia in such a way that concentrations of the Albanian minority, including the city Struga, would be granted greater administrative control. The law, which was passed by the Parliament in August 2004, reduced the number of local authorities from 123 to eighty-four and transferred sixteen authorities to the control of the Albanian minority. In addition, in some areas, including Skopje, the capital, the Albanian language was to be recognized as the country's second official language. Nationalist Macedonians regarded these changes as a de facto territorial division of the country on an ethnic basis.[17]

The results of the referendum will undoubtedly affect the current delicate balance between the Christian Macedonian majority and the Muslim Albanian minority. Exacerbation of the ethnic and religious tension could also influence the level of violence in the country in the near future.

## Notes

1. "Terrorism and Ethnic Conflicts: Experience of the Western Balkans," *Forum, the Magazine of FER*, Issue 3, January March 2003, p. 21.
2. Albanian Islamic World, Kruja@yahoo.com.
3. Ibid.
4. Today some countries, including Greece, call Macedonia the Former Yugoslav Republic of Macedonia (FYROM).
5. The Republic of Albania in Yugoslavia— Illirya.
6. Neither the identities of the assassins nor the reason for the assassination has ever been published.
7. Terrorism and Ethnic Conflicts: Experience of the Western Balkans, *Forum, the Magazine of FER*, Issue 3, January–March, 2003, p. 21.
8. "ANA threatens again," Reality Macedonia (January 14, 2002); "Unknown Persons Invisible to International Community," Reality Macedonia, February 17, 2002.
9. Ibid.
10. Ibid.
11. Christian Jenings, "Fear over Islamic terror groups using Macedonia as a base," *Scotsman*, March 4, 2002.
12. Ibid.
13. Albanian National Liberation Army—(ANLA)
14. Peter Finn, "Suspects in Macedonia turned over to U.S.," *Washington Post*, March 7, 2002. See also: Paul Anderson, "Security has been stepped up in Skopje," BBC, March 3, 2002.
15. "Mujahidin fight for NLA," Reality Macedonia, Skopje, September 18, 2001.
16. "Albanian terrorists target American citizens of Macedonian origin," Reality Macedonia, Skopje, August 10, 2001.
17. "Albanian terrorists burned the Macedonian-American textile industry, Mateks," Reality Macedonia, Tetovo, August 14, 2001.

# Section Seven

## The Infrastructure of Islamic Terror in the Balkans

# The Balkans as a Springboard for Iranian Terror in Europe

The initial penetration of Islamic influences in Yugoslavia in general, and Bosnia-Herzegovina in particular, stems from the pro-Arab and pro-Muslim policies adopted by Tito's regime during the 1960s, which favored the Muslims and militant Arab organizations. The latter were granted approval by the Belgrade government to conduct propaganda activity in Yugoslavia. In the 1960s and the 1970s, Yugoslavian citizens were granted official permission to join Palestinian terror organizations such as the PLO. As part of its pro-Arab policy, Yugoslavia also supplied military equipment, experts, and technicians (many of whom were Muslim) to Arab states in the Middle East.

Under the influence of Tito's pro-Islamic foreign policy, a "forbearing" approach towards Islam was advocated internally. This was reflected during the 1980s, which witnessed a significant increase in the number of mosques built and operated in Bosnia-Herzegovina.

Following this Islamic revival, many young people were sent to various countries in the Middle East to attend advanced studies, particularly religious seminaries in Iran (where approximately 250 Bosnian students attended studies annually).

It would appear that during the 1980s, security entities in Yugoslavia began to issue warnings regarding the danger of Islamic militancy (particularly, the type advocated by the Khomeini school in Iran), but the steps taken were partial and limited, and they failed to prevent the seeds of misfortune from sprouting several years later.

Iran grasped the potential inherent to the Balkans and acted to tighten its links with the local Muslims. As noted above, during the 1980s hundreds of Muslims from the Balkans underwent training and indoctrination in Iran. Upon their return, they acted to disseminate Islamic ideals in their communities. However, while Iran was interested in establishing Islamic infrastructures that would serve as a springboard to Western Europe, most of the activities of the Iranian "recruits" focused on the local arena and the struggles between the Muslims and the Serbs and Croatians due to the tension between the Muslim Bosnians and other ethnic groups in the Balkan.

Iran's most important political ally in the Balkans was Alija Izetbegovi (who later became the Bosnian president).[1]

As early as the 1960s, when Khomeini went into exile and settled in Iraq and subsequently in France, Izetbegović expressed his solidarity with Khomeini's struggle to establish an Islamic regime in Iran.

The Islamic revolution that took place in Iran in 1979 served as a source of inspiration for Izetbegović who began to act vigorously for the establishment of an Islamic political infrastructure in his own country, and he was imprisoned for this reason.

In early May 1991, after the collapse of Yugoslavia, Alija Izetbegović paid an official visit to Iran where he described his vision regarding the Islamic future of his country to his hosts. In Teheran, Izetbegović was described as a "faithful Muslim" who stood at the head of the strongest political organization in Bosnia-Herzegovina, and who recruited Yugoslavian Muslims on behalf of Islam.[2] During his visit, Izetbegović emphasized the deep Islamic roots in Bosnia-Herzegovina and claimed that Bosnia was interested in expanding its strong and diversified links with Iran. His Iranian hosts welcomed this appeal and promised massive economic aid in order to strengthen Bosnia's economy. In addition to the economic aspects, the intensification of religious and cultural ties was also discussed, including expansion of the training offered to Yugoslavian Muslims in Iranian schools, and the translation of important Islamic texts, including basic Shiite literature, into Bosnian.[3]

Subsequently, in the summer of 1991, Izetbegović also visited Libya, seeking political and economic aid. In an interview during the visit Izetbegović stated: "I do not ask for weapons from our Muslim brothers, but only for political support. But if the civil war in our country endangers our Muslim brothers many things may happen."

In light of the fighting in Bosnia-Herzegovina, and mainly due to the tightening of the Serbian siege on Sarejevo, Izetbegović reached the conclusion that he must take drastic steps to change the situation. Iran and other Muslim countries had already offered military aid to the Muslims in Bosnia, but Western legitimization was required in order to enable a significant flow of weapons, ammunition, and volunteers while circumventing the UN embargo against weapon shipments to the partoes of the Bosnian conflict.

The Iranians clarified the importance of acquiring international legitimization for the Muslims' steps to Izetbegovic and emphasized the need to present the Muslim side as a victim that required the intervention of the Islamic world and the international community in order to survive.

However, despite the heavy damage caused to the population in Sarajevo, and the extensive media coverage, the U.S. and the Western European countries were unwilling to take action at that time to put a stop to the Serbian offensive. Thus, following these failed efforts, and in light of the grave situation at the battlefront opposite the Serbs, Izetbegovic decided to appeal to Iran for aid.[4]

The Iranians welcomed the appeal made by the Muslim Bosnians and significantly increased their involvement in the events in Bosnia-Herzegovina. From the beginning of the conflict in Bosnia-Herzegovina, Iran claimed that the adversity faced by the Muslims in Bosnia was an issue that affected the entire Muslim world. Therefore, the governments of Islamic countries were obligated to rush to the aid of the Bosnian Muslims and take steps to prevent what they referred to as the genocide of Muslims in Europe.

The Iranians argued that despite the fact that the West recognized the gravity of the situation in Sarajevo, and understood the need for military intervention, it preferred to refrain from active involvement in the events. The Iranians further claimed: "It would appear that the Muslims have no other choice but to take practical steps in order to withstand the brutal Serbs and to compensate for the criminal indifference of the West." Iran warned that "if the Muslims do not rise up today in order to take preventive measures, the Serbs may continue with their crimes against Muslims in other places in Europe."

Iran's perception of the challenges to be faced was presented by its spiritual leader Ayatollah Ali Khamenei in a speech delivered on July 29, 1992. Khamenei claimed that Iran and the Muslim world were balanced on the brink of a fateful conflict with the West, a clash that might well bring about the expansion of the Muslim world beyond its current boundaries. Khamenei emphasized the distress of the Muslims in Bosnia-Herzegovia. He added that their oppression was part of the general policy advocated by the Christian world under U.S. leadership opposing Islamic reawakening worldwide. As the issue at stake was overall policy adopted by Christianity against Islam, the Muslim world, led by Iran, must rush to the aid of the Muslims living in Yugoslavia. He stated that the West sought the complete annihilation of Muslims so that no Muslim entity would remain in Europe. Khamenei added that any Muslim entity in Europe—be it a national entity or a significant minority in a country—was perceived as a threat by the West. It is this perception that helped to formulate Western policy regarding the Bosnian conflict.

Khamenei declared that it was Iran's holy duty to come to the aid of the Muslims in Bosnia-Herzegovina, not only due to the mutual bond of Muslims worldwide, but also because of specific Iranian considerations:

> We are very concerned about the distress of the Muslims in Bosnia-Herzegovina. They are Muslims, our brothers. They are a helpless minority surrounded by a coalition of countries that oppose Islam. They face an armed community and a strong army equipped with the most modern and advanced weapons—these are the same people (referring to the Serbs) who for years equipped Iraq with weapons to use against us. Therefore, it is the duty of the Muslim world to rise to the aid of the European Muslims, and Iran will help in any way possible.

Bosnian Foreign Minister Haris Silajdzic, who visited Teheran in August 1992, lauded the strong Iranian stand and stated that the Islamic revolution was a source of inspiration for the Muslims fighting in Bosnia-Herzegovina.

During his meeting with the Bosnian Foreign Minister, Iranian President Hashemi Rafsanjani pledged the Islamic Republic's (Iran) willingness to support the Muslim residents of Bosnia in any way possible. He promised that Iran would provide Bosnia-Herzegovina with all the fuel it required. The Iranians noted that experience indicated that international organizations never act on behalf of the Muslims and that the Muslims must help themselves.

During this visit, a senior Iranian official stated:

> In the heart of Europe, the bosom of liberty and democracy, a new independent state is being crushed and its soldiers massacred in an asymmetric war. The West is not taking firm action to prevent this humanitarian tragedy. Once again our analyses come true—the Muslim residents of Bosnia must pay the price for the differences in religion and culture between them and the rest of the European family.[5]

Several days after the Bosnian Foreign Minister's visit to Iran, the Iranians intensified their accusations against the West. Iran no longer sufficed to accuse the West of inactivity, but charged it with being the main force behind the massacre perpetrated by the Serbs against the Muslims. "The Serb declaration that they are butchering the Muslims in order to prevent the establishment of a Muslim entity constitutes an official announcement to the West about their goals."

In response to "this reality," Iran appointed itself the leader of Islam to protect the Muslims in Bosnia-Herzegovina.

The Iranians proposed to set up "an army that will include volunteers from all over the Muslim world which will rush to the aid of the Muslims living in Bosnia-Herzegovina, and will prevent the massacre of innocent people whose only sin is their Muslim religion."

Iran claimed that despite the fact that the European states were purportedly guarantors for the safety of the civilian population in this part of the world, as long as the West refrained from taking action, the responsibility would fall on the shoulders of the Muslim world.

Moreover, Iran believed that the time left for the Muslims to help their brothers was running out, and demanded resolute and urgent action from Muslims worldwide. In order to promote the dispatch of forces in aid of the Muslims in Bosnia, Iran sent a senior delegation headed by Ahmad Janati to Sarajevo to investigate the situation. The delegation reached Sarajevo, visited the front lines, and gauged the Muslims' military needs. Upon his return from Sarajevo, Janati stopped in Vienna where he stated that the supply of weapons to the Bosnians for self-defense was at the top of Iran's priorities.[6]

> The reality is such that only weapon supplies will save the lives of the Bosnians. We have given this issue some thought and have called on the Muslim world to attend a summit that will be held in Teheran to discuss the issue of aid. If all of the countries come to an agreement, we (the Iranians) will be the first to offer aid, Janati pledged.[7]

Janati acted vigorously within the Iranian administration to promote military aid to Bosnia-Herzegovina. In an interview with Iran Radio, he claimed: "The residents of Bosnia-Herzegovina are in urgent need of arms in order to defend themselves and their property. The Islamic countries must help the Muslim residents of Bosnia by establishing an army of volunteers and by providing arms in order to prevent a humanitarian tragedy in the area. ... Their main need is for arms. They defend themselves with amazing courage. They are currently under tremendous pressure, but they lack weapons and fear for their future. If they do not receive aid they may lose the battle and collapse. Action must be taken, and the Islamic Republic must be the first to rush to their aid and meet their needs in any way possible. If the Islamic states unite and establish a dispatch army or alternatively send them joint supplies, the Bosnian will be able to stand strong."[8]

In a sermon delivered several days later, Janati warned that if the Muslims were defeated in this battle, they would initiate a guerilla war throughout Europe. He added that in most of his talks with Bosnian officials, their main request was for weapons. He noted that the violent struggle being fought against the Muslims in Bosnia was a central stage in the conflict developing between Islam and the rest of the world. He explained that when he spoke of the atrocities perpetrated by the Serbs against the Bosnians he was reminded of the Crusades, which he claimed were almost repeating themselves. He reiterated that the only solution was to establish a joint Muslim army as well as to ensure the joint supply of arms. He summarized, "If Islam is to emerge triumphant, there is no other way."

## Iran and the War in Bosnia-Herzegovina

The violent confrontation in Bosnia-Herzegovina between the rival ethnic groups quickly evolved from a local conflict of a humanitarian nature to a standoff between external forces striving to affect the outcome of the conflict through their local allies, thus influencing not only the boundaries of the Bosnia-Herzegovina Republic, but also all of the Balkans.

Islamic Iran, which since 1979 had made tremendous efforts to export the Khomeini revolution to the entire Muslim world, viewed the civil war in Bosnia-Herzegovina as an historical opportunity to establish a radical Islamic infrastructure in the very heart of Europe. The conflict in the Balkans came at a time when Iran's geopolitical status and power were on the rise, in the aftermath of the collapse of the Soviet Union and the Communist Bloc, as well as the Gulf War (1991), which resulted in the defeat of Iran's main opponent—Iraq.

Due to controversy and conflicting interests in the support of the adversaries in the Balkan confrontation (Serbia, Croatia, Muslims, etc.), the European states refrained from intervening actively in the conflict, thus leaving a strategic "vacuum" which Iran hastened to fill.

Iran exploited the humanitarian "lever" in order to win Islamic and international legitimacy with the aim of ostensibly assisting the Muslim population, which it claimed was subject to a cruel Serb attack.

Western Europe approved of the mobilization of the Arab world (headed by Iran and Saudi Arabia) on behalf of the Muslim population in Bosnia that was in urgent need of humanitarian aid. Western Europe, and mainly the United States, preferred to disregard the military components which were linked to, and camouflaged by, the Islamic "humanitarian aid." (See elaboration in the section entitled The U.S. "Green Light" Policy).

As early as August 1998, in the wake of Janati's recommendations, Iran established "the command for the aid of Bosnia-Herzegovina."

During 1992-1993, the command dispatched food and medication to the Muslim population in Bosnia, as well as donations amounting to some $20 million.[9]

As stated earlier, the U.S. administration and the NATO countries were aware of the weapon consignments and the arrival of Iranian "volunteers" in Bosnia, in violation of the embargo imposed on the parties by the United Nations.

The "West" sided with the Muslims in Bosnia because it regarded them as the victims of Serb aggression, and there was a fear that the Bosnians would collapse without military aid.

There was nothing new in this approach, as these events occurred shortly after the "coalition" (1979-1989) in Afghanistan, which represented an unholy alliance between Islam's most radical elements (such as Bin Laden) and the United States, as well as its allies in the Western and Arab world.

Against this strategic background, Iran acted to promote its strongholds in the Balkans, and through the latter to tighten its grasp on the European continent.

## Iranian Intelligence and Terror Mechanisms—Background[10]

Khomeini's revolutionary regime had to respond to several serious challenges that threatened its very existence.

- Dealing with those who opposed the revolutionary regime, including those loyal to the previous regime (the Shah), as well as some elements that participated in the revolution and subsequently turned against it. For example, the communist "Tuda" party, the Mujahidin Khalq and the Fedayeen Khalq.
- Dealing with the Iraqi invasion of Iran (in 1980).
- Dealing with the threat of foreign countries that had supported the Shah's regime and were unwilling to recognize the revolutionary regime in Iran (the United States, Britain, and others).

In addition to facing these grave challenges, the revolutionary regime was committed to its revolutionary ideology and the principle of "exporting the Khomeini revolution" to the entire Muslim nation. Therefore, the regime needed to develop intelligence agencies, operators, and propaganda within a short period of time. In the initial stages, the Islamic regime used the agencies that it operated during the struggle against the Shah's administration[11] and in the course of the revolution, such as the Hizballah and the Revolutionary Guard militias that bore the brunt of the battle against the Shah's regime.

In the aftermath of the successful revolution, their prime task was to eradicate the military and security power centers that supported the Shah's regime. After these entities had fled the country, been eliminated or imprisoned, the regime's efforts were then focused on opposition organizations (Khomeini's allies during the revolution). At the same time, the regime had to fend off the Iraqi invasion in a frontal military confrontation, and deal with Iraqi and Western aid provided to opposition circles acting against the revolutionary regime.[12]

As the army and intelligence agencies in Iran were identified with the Shah's government, Khomeini's regime was forced to establish new intelligence agencies based on those loyal to the revolutionary regime. The Khomeini revolution in 1979 thus brought about the dismantling of the intelligence service during the Shah's era —the SAVAK—that served as a central tool of support for the Shah's government and exterminated his enemies. During the revolution and in its aftermath, the heads of the SAVAK became prime targets of the revolutionary regime, and many of them were imprisoned and executed.

According to the Iranian constitution, the spiritual leader is the supreme commanding officer of Iran's military forces. In actual fact, there are several "armies" and semi-military forces that operate under the supervision of various power brokers within the Iranian establishment (see subsequent elaboration).

Already in 1979, Khomeini's regime established its own intelligence service called the SAVAMA, whose main roles focused on internal security (pursuing and eradicating the opposition) and gathering information about Iraq.[13] The first director of the SAVAMA was General Faradost (who was arrested in 1985 and was charged with espionage for the Soviet Union.). The SAVAMA acted simultaneously with the Hizballah's branches and the Revolutionary Guards, which handled missions that were identical to those of the intelligence service. In 1984, the SAVAMA underwent reorganization: Muhammad Rishari was appointed its director and its name was changed to VEVAK (the Ministry of Intelligence and Security).

### The Ministry of Intelligence and Security (VEVAK)[14]

The VEVAK inherited the SAVAMA's roles while expanding its intelligence activities vis-à-vis Iraq and other foreign targets, and incorporating this in "revolutionary export" missions.

It appears that during these years VEVAK renewed the intelligence infrastructure established in Iraq and in Arab countries during the reign of the Shah, and utilized the intelligence capabilities for the promotion of Iran's goals despite the difference in ideological approaches between the revolutionary intelligence service and its predecessor. In order to boost its operational capabilities, military intelligence service experts (from the Shah's time) and junior SAVAK agents who specialized in Iranian leftists and in the Iraqi and Arab arena, were called back to service.

Due to the allocation of generous funding and extensive personnel, within a short period of time the Ministry of Intelligence and Security became one of the most powerful and influential agencies in the Iranian regime. In 1988, Ali Falahian was appointed the Minister of Intelligence. Thanks to his qualifications, connections, and status in the regime, he succeeded in establishing work procedures and coordination mechanisms between the various security and intelligence entities, as well as founding and heading the supreme council for intelligence matters, which supervised and coordinated all of Iran's intelligence and subversive activities.

The Ministry of Intelligence and Security is officially subordinate to the president, but in practice the heads of the Ministry were appointed from among the close associates of the supreme leader and acted according to his instructions. The Ministry is composed of twelve departments that activate over 20,000 agents inside and outside of Iran.

### The Ministry of the Revolutionary Guards (Pasdaran).[15]

The aim of the activities of the Revolutionary Guards was mainly to defend the Iranian revolutionary regime against internal opposition. After the Iraqi invasion of Iran (in 1980), the Revolutionary Guards became a central nucleus of the Popular Military Forces, which bore the brunt of the combat against Iraq, due to the weakness of the Iranian army that underwent purges as a result of the revolution. The Revolutionary Guards numbers about 120,000 members, including independent land, sea, and air forces. The land forces are divided into thirteen regional commands and twenty divisions (a division of the Revolutionary Guards is parallel to a military division).

The Revolutionary Guards are deployed along the borders with Iraq and Afghanistan with the aim of defending the country, and in Iran's large cities for internal security missions. In addition, they are responsible for Iran's non-conventional combat means.

Parallel to their missions related to safeguarding the regime and protecting the Iranian homeland, the Revolutionary Guards also undertook tasks related to the "export of the revolution," mainly through the use of terror and aid to Islamic terror organizations worldwide.

The Revolutionary Guards Ministry, which was established in 1983, handles all areas of activity inside and outside of Iran. In all matters relating to activities outside of Iran, the Revolutionary Guards are based on two central entities: a) the committee for intelligence abroad; b) the committee for operations abroad. The activity of Revolutionary Guard members abroad is generally conducted under a diplomatic, cultural, or commercial guise. The Revolutionary Guards support the training, instruction, and indoctrination of activists in Islamic terror organizations worldwide. These activists undergo training in Iran, Sudan, Lebanon, or Afghanistan (during the period of the war that took place in this country). Revolutionary Guard members also assist in the establishment of Islamic terror organizations, such as the Hizballah in Lebanon, and support Islamic entities at conflict arenas worldwide such as Bosnia or Chechnya.

The "Al-Quds Force" ("Jerusalem Force") of the Revolutionary Guards, which has been deployed in Lebanon since 1983, is an Iranian entity that leads Iranian activity in the region and supports the Hizballah. This force deals with the provision of military aid and in directing terror activity against Israel, particularly that of the Hizballah, but also Islamic and secular Palestinian organizations.

In Iran several militia forces operate under the auspices of or in connection with the Revolutionary Guards:

- The Bassij – This militia constitutes a national guard and is charged with the supervision of law and order in the country, and handling disorderly conduct and threats against the regime. The militia is based on civilians who can be recruited as needed. The Bassij is subordinate to the Revolutionary Guards.
- Law enforcement forces – These forces are subordinate to the Ministry of Interior, but in practical terms are operated by the leaders of the religious establishment and serve as a kind of "religious police."

## The Iranian Terror System[16]

Terror activity, subversion, and the elimination of the regime's opponents abroad are subject to the approval of the top decision-makers in the Iranian regime, including the spiritual leader (Valiat Fakia). Ideas and initiatives in these areas are first raised for discussion and approval in principle within a small forum composed of the president and four ministers. Following their authorization, these proposals are transferred to the Supreme National Security Council, which processes the recommendations and prepares them for the approval of the spiritual leader.

After gaining the approval of the spiritual leader, they are then transferred to the Supreme Council for Intelligence, which ensures implementation via the relevant ministries and the executive branches.

The trial of Iranian agents in Germany, who were tried and convicted of murdering four Kurd émigrés in the "Mikonos" restaurant in Berlin, constitutes a prominent example of the Iranian decision-making chain, and the German court unequivocally indicated the responsibility of the Iranian government's top leaders for the terror activity. In his verdict, the German judge pointed to the personal and direct involvement of Iranian Intelligence Minister Falahian in the planning and implementation of the terror activity and issued an arrest warrant against him (in absentia).[17]

Since the early-1990s, the Supreme Council for Intelligence Matters and the Ministry of Intelligence and Security played a central role in initiating, planning, and conducting terror activity abroad. The Supreme Council for Intelligence Matters and its head are responsible for coordination between the relevant ministries in all matters related to the planning and perpetration of an operational activity.[18]

As stated earlier, the various agencies that deal in the export of the revolution and international terror recruit and activate terrorists all over the world, who undergo underground training in Iran or Lebanon. For example, terror activity against foreign targets was perpetrated by the Hizballah's "special security agency" in Lebanon and by various cells of Hizballah members abroad, based on Iranian diplomatic infrastructure.

Imad Muraniya heads the "Special Security Agency" and receives his instructions directly from Iran. The "Special Security Agency" was responsible for the hijacking of airplanes, the kidnapping of Western hostages in Lebanon, and terror attacks worldwide.

## The Iranian Intelligence and Terror System in the Balkans

The Iranian intelligence played a key role in the allocation of the aid offered by the Iranian government to Muslims in Bosnia and in the establishment of the Iranian terror infrastructure in the Balkans.

As the leading advocate for Islamic support of the Muslims in Bosnia, Iran gathered under its auspices volunteers from Islamic terror organizations including Al Qaida, and helped with their training and dispatch to Bosnia. Iranian aid for Bosnia began as early as 1992 (in the aftermath of Izetbegović's visit to Teheran), and culminated during 1994-1995.

The Iranian Revolutionary Guards Ministry was also involved in the support efforts for the Muslims in Bosnia and dispatched the 7th Revolutionary Guards Brigade (the 7th Pasdaran Brigade), which included 2,000 soldiers and was incorporated in the Bosnian Muslim Army.[19]

The Revolutionary Guards 7th Brigade, which was stationed in Zenica, played an active role in the fighting and trained Bosnian soldiers. In addition, some 400 Iranian intelligence agents from the VEVAK and the Revolutionary Guards' intelligence service served in Bosnia.[20]

Iran and Croatia established diplomatic relations on April 18, 1992 and Croatia appointed a Muslim Croatian named Osman Muftic its first ambassador to Iran. According to the Serbs, Croatia's consent to the transfer of fighters and weaponry to the Muslims in Bosnia via its territory was granted silent approval by the United States and the Western countries, despite the U.S. embargo imposed on arms consignments to the parties in Bosnia. The U.S. policy in this matter was investigated by a U.S. Senate sub-committee and was dubbed "Bosniagate" (see subsequent elaboration). In May 1994, a cooperation agreement was signed between Croatia and the Muslims in Bosnia against the Serbs, and the road was paved for the transfer of weaponry shipments to Bosnia via Croatia.

In May 1994, the Iranians appointed Mohammad Taherian the Iranian Ambassador to Bosnia. Taherian had previously served as Iran's Ambassador to Afghanistan where he had handled the transfer of military aid to the militias fighting the Soviets in Afghanistan.[21]

The Iranians flew arm shipments and ammunition to Zagreb in Croatia under the guise of emergency supplies related to "humanitarian relief." Larger arms shipments were shipped by sea to the Croatian ports of Split and Rijeka and from there in truck convoys to Bosnia. These arm shipments reached their destination in Bosnia thanks to the Croatian government's decision to turn a blind eye and enable the flow of arms to the Muslims in Bosnia. These arm shipments included rocket launchers and 107mm, 122mm, and 230mm rockets manufactured in China and Iran.[22]

The Croatian policy regarding weapons supply to the Muslims was inconsistent and was largely dependent on the "good will" of Mate Boban, commander-in-chief of the Croatian forces in Bosnia, whose people controlled the routes of the convoys to Bosnia. Only part of them ultimately reached the Muslims.[23] During the years 1994-1995 the Iranians transported at least sixty weapon shipments to the Muslims in Bosnia.[24]

Some of the Iranian intelligence agents acted under the guise of employees of Iranian charities such as the Iranian Red Crescent, and others operated under diplomatic protection.

In the early-1990s, Zagreb, Croatia served as the focal point for Iranian intelligence activity, which dealt in directing intelligence gathering in the

Balkans and in coordinating activities between the Iranian intelligence and Islamic terror organizations. Serb sources point to Mohammad Dzevad Azayes as an example of an Iranian intelligence agent who operated out of the Iranian Embassy in Zagreb.[25] According to the Serbs, the Iranian intelligence agencies developed strong ties with the Muslim Bosnian Agency for Information and Documentation (AID) which, to a large extent, operated as an Iranian sponsored organization. The overt and covert Iranian presence continued in Bosnia-Herzegovina even after the war.

In January 1995, Iran announced its willingness to send a force of 10,000 soldiers to Bosnia-Herzegovina in the framework of the UN peacekeeping force, an offer that was turned down by the UN.

In November 1995, Iran initiated a convention of the Organization of Islamic States (OIS) in order to take a stand vis-à-vis the Dayton Accords and present ways to aid the Muslims in Bosnia from economic and military points of view after the signing of the agreement.[26] Subsequently, Iran expressed its reservations regarding the Dayton Accords due to the clauses in the agreement that dictated the withdrawal of Iranian forces from Bosnia-Herzegovina.

In February 1996, the Croatian Police in Bosnia-Herzegovina arrested several Iranians, claiming that equipment used for espionage had been found in their possession. Iran protested the arrest and claimed that the Iranians who had been arrested had dealt in the teaching of Islam at the request of the Bosnian authorities.[27]

In March 1996, the UN spokesman in Bosnia, Marc Van Duke, accused Iran of violating the Dayton Accords, citing its continued training of the Muslim Army in Bosnia-Herzegovina and claiming that Iran constituted a terrorist threat against the International Force in Bosnia.[28]

Bosnian President Alija Izetbegović, who was questioned regarding the matter of the Iranian presence in his country, admitted that Iranians had remained in his country, but he claimed that their number did not exceed fifty to sixty individuals, and that they were fighters who had cast off their uniforms, married local women, and set up their homes and families in Bosnia-Herzegovina.

Evidence regarding the continued Iranian involvement in the training of the Bosnian forces and intelligence agencies was found during a raid conducted by the International Forces (IFOR) on a training camp in Fojnica.

In the raid, eleven Iranians who dealt in the training of the Muslim Bosnian fighters were arrested. Weapons, sabotage equipment, Islamic

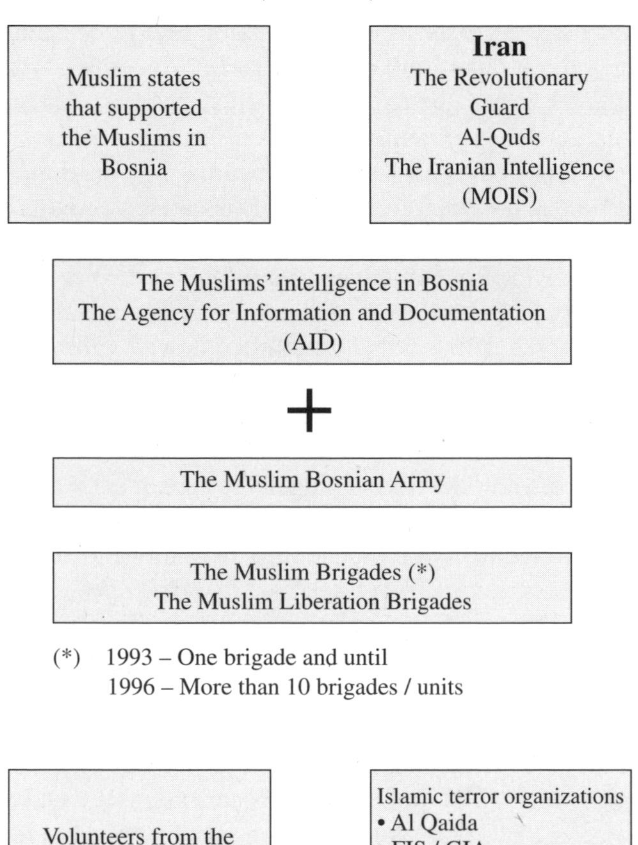


propaganda material, lists of Bosnian fighters who underwent training at the camp, and maps, as well as diagrams of the U.S. military headquarters in Sarajevo, were confiscated.[29]

In the aftermath of the raid that exposed the Iranian involvement, Ali Rezah Bayatta, who had been appointed director of the Balkans desk in the Iranian intelligence agency, was dismissed.[30]

In 1996, a terror cell (hit team) with five terrorists (four men and one woman) was arrested. The unit had been dispatched by the Bosnian Agency for Intelligence and Documentation (AID) and the Iranian intelligence (VEVAK) to assassinate Fikret Abdic, a Muslim Bosnian businessman and politician who had opposed the policy advocated by Bosnian President Alija Izetbegović during the war in Bosnia and in its aftermath.

## The U.S. "Green Light" Policy Regarding the Supply of Iranian Weapons to Muslims in Bosnia [31]

In 1996, two investigative committees of the U.S. Senate investigated U.S. policy in the matter of the Iranian shipments of combat means via Croatia to Muslims in Bosnia. The committees published their reports in October and November 1996, although sections were classified as confidential.

This chapter will not address the lapses in principle and procedure that the committees discovered in the conduct of the American administration, but rather will focus on the implications of the "green light" which Clinton's administration granted to the shipment of combat means from Iran via Croatia to the Muslim forces in Bosnia. This permission was given despite the fact that the U.S. had been a partner to the resolution passed by the UN Security Council (resolution no. 713, October 1991) to impose an arms embargo on Yugoslavia and the republics that broke away from it, including Bosnia-Herzegovina. As early as 1992, Iranian attempts were made to transfer weapon shipments to the Muslims in Bosnia via Croatia. The Croatian authorities consulted with the United States in this matter (at the time under the Bush administration), and the latter responded with a clear message negating the shipment of Iranian arms to the Muslims in Bosnia.

The Croatian government accepted the American position and an arms shipment that arrived in Zagreb on an Iranian airplane was confiscated and handed over to the UN forces, and the aircraft returned to Iran.

The Teheran government refrained from dispatching arm shipments via the "semi-covert" route of Croatia for three years, although it is known that small arm shipments were smuggled by Iran into Bosnia during this period.

The U.S. policy regarding support for the Muslins in the Bosnian conflict underwent a change due to the ascent of the Clinton administration. The Clinton administration believed that the Muslim side should be supported due to its view that the Muslims were the victims, while the Serbs were the aggressors in the conflict. The United States preferred to abstain from direct intervention in the conflict but it signaled Croatia, and indirectly Iran, that it would not take action to prevent the transfer of Iranian arm shipments via Croatia to the Muslims in Bosnia.

The Senate investigative committees revealed that the Croatian government had consulted with the U.S. administration regarding its position in the issue of the shipment of Iranian combat means to the Muslims in Bosnia.

The response of the American Ambassador in Zagreb was that the U.S. administration "had no instructions in this matter," an answer which was interpreted by the Croatians as the flashing of a "green light" for the flow of Iranian combat means to the Muslims in Bosnia via the sea and airports of Croatia. In return for its consent to the transfer of combat means, Croatia received 50 percent of the weapons that passed through the country on the way to Bosnia.

Galbraith, the U.S. Ambassador to Croatia, was a key figure in the promotion of the American "green light" policy and served as the liaison between the U.S. administration and the Croatian authorities.

It appears that Ambassador Galbraith was also a partner to the Croatian-Iranian activities and he met with the Imam Sevko Omerbasic, a senior Muslim cleric in Croatia, who served as the connecting link between the Croatian government and Iran.

Between May 1994 and January 1996, the Iranians shipped by sea over 5,000 tons of military equipment including uniforms, light weapons, anti-tank weapons, and shoulder land-to-air missiles.

U.S. intelligence has estimated that the Iranians supplied about two-thirds of the total amount of arms and ammunition received by the Muslim forces in Bosnia. Representatives of the Iranian Revolutionary Guards that were posted at the Iranian Embassy in Zagreb, Croatia handled the military equipment upon its arrival in Croatia and sent it on to Bosnia.

As a rule, the American representatives in Croatia refrained from any direct involvement in the transfer of combat means from Iran to Bosnia, but the committee cited at least two instances in which American involvement was evident:

- In May 1994, special U.S. envoy Charles Redman intervened with senior government officials in Croatia in order to bring about the release of a convoy headed for Croatia, which was apparently transporting combat equipment. (When questioned by the committee, Redman claimed that he did not know what sort of freight was being transported in the convoy).
- In September 1995, the Croatian authorities notified the U.S. representatives about a shipment of Iranian missiles that they suspected contained chemical warheads. The U.S. sent military experts to examine the missiles and, after the experts had examined them and determined that they did not carry chemical warheads, permitted the transfer of the consignment to Bosnia.

The Senate sub-committee reached the conclusion that the administration's "green light" policy enabled Iran to fortify its status in Europe and this endangered, and continues to endanger, the lives of American citizens. The sub-committee also determined that the Iranian presence and influence in Bosnia rose significantly.

The sub-committee claimed that members of the Iranian Revolutionary Guards accompanied the arms shipments on their way to Bosnia and within a short period of time were incorporated in the Bosnian army on all levels. The Iranian Intelligence Agency (VEVAK) acted unhindered in Bosnian territory: It established a widespread terror infrastructure, recruited sleeping agents and developed close links with the local political establishment.

In actual fact, the Iranians succeeded in harnessing a large part of Bosnia's security system for the promotion of terror purposes. The Iranian Embassy expanded and those serving there were granted unrestricted access to all Bosnian government bodies.

The sub-committee noted that in order to comprehend how Clinton's "green light" policy led to such a pronounced boost in Iranian influence, it is important to realize that this policy came against the background of rising radical Islamic influences in Bosnia, and that the Iranians and other groups of militant Muslims had been active in Bosnia many years beforehand. The American "green light" served as an important signal to the Sarajevo government, and to the militant Muslims, that the U.S. was incapable or unwilling to put a stop to their activities, and that to a certain extent it was willing to cooperate with them.

In its summary, the sub-committee determined that the policy advocated by the U.S. administration in effect turned the it into a "collaborator" after the fact with governments and organizations whose goal was the export of the Iranian revolution to the Balkans and from there to Europe. The main players in this activity were primarily Iran, but also Saudi Arabia, Malaysia, Pakistan, Sudan (one of Iran's central allies), Turkey, and Islamic "charities and humanitarian relief organizations."

## Iranian Involvement in Kosovo

After the end of the war in Bosnia-Herzegovina, the Iranian embassies in Croatia and Sarajevo (Bosnia) served as logistic and operational bases for Muslim aid in the Balkans. An Iranian Embassy also opened in Tirana, Albania's capital, in February 1999.

In May 1998, Iran established a center for Muslim aid in Kosovo headed by Ayatollah Janati, who was one of the first Iranian "patrons" of the Muslims in Bosnia. On May 8, 1998 Janati stated: "The double-standard policy that the United States adopted during the war in Bosnia on the one hand, and Washington's support for Muslim independence in Kosovo on the other hand, encouraged the Serbs to attack the Muslims in Kosovo."[32]

In the summer of 1998, following increased Serb pressure imposed upon the Muslim population in Kosovo, Iran called for cooperation with the West in order to save the Muslims from the Serbs.

An editorial published in the Teheran Times dated June 16, 1998[33] called on NATO and the Organization of Islamic Conference (OIC) to take immediate action against Miloshevich and the Serb forces.

There are no data available regarding Iranian military aid provided to the Muslims in Kosovo, but it is clear that this possibility cannot be dismissed, and the possibility also exists that Iranian intelligence entities served as military consultants for the Muslims in Kosovo.

## Bin Laden, Zawaheiri, and Al Qaida Infrastructures in the Balkans

For Al Qaida and other terror organizations, the wars in the Balkan constituted an opportunity to consolidate the terror infrastructure on European soil. Members of terror organizations, and thousands of Islamic volunteers, were initially mobilized to aid their Muslim brothers in the Balkans in the wars against their adversaries and, after the end of the violent confrontations, they turned the Balkans into a forefront for the foundation of terror infrastructures in Europe and other focal points worldwide.

Bin Laden, his deputy Zawaheiri, and Al Qaida played a central role in the wars in the Balkans, both in Bosnia-Herzegovina and Kosovo.

In autumn of 1992, Bin Laden instructed leading Al Qaida activist Jamal Ahmed al Fadl[34] to travel to Zagreb, Croatia, meet with organization activists who were already active in Bosnia, and examine how it would be possible to establish an infrastructure for the organization in the Balkans. One of the activists with whom Fadl met was Zubair, who, as noted earlier, was killed in October of that year near the Sarajevo Airport.

At the meeting, the Al Qaida activists in Bosnia proposed setting up training camps for the organization, as well as an infrastructure of charities which would serve as logistic support for the organization's activities and recruits. From his headquarters in Sudan, Bin Laden wove an intricate network of humanitarian organizations through which he dispatched hundreds of Al Qaida activists (Afghan "alumni") and transferred funding for the foundation of a terror infrastructure on European soil.

Some of the organizations that were part of Bin Laden's infrastructure sometimes changed their names and identity in order to make it harder to identify them as organizations that supported terror (which is what happened in the aftermath of September 11, 2001).

During the 1990s, Bin Laden himself visited the Balkans (Bosnia and Albania) at least once in order to examine the terror network that he had established. A Washington Times article published in 2001 stated that Bin Laden had visited Albania in 1995 when he laid the foundations for the establishment of an Al Qaida infrastructure in that country.

During his visit to Albania he met with senior Albanian officials. Moreover, according to various reports, Osama Bin Laden used Bosnian and Albanian passports when traveling all over the world. Jürgen Elsässer, author of the book "How Jihad Came into Europe: Holy Warriors and Secret Services in the Balkans," offers evidence that Osama Bin Laden made use of a Bosnian passport:[35]

- The Muslim weekly DANI, which is published in Sarajevo, reported that Osama Bin Laden had a Bosnian passport (1999).
- Based on sources in the Interpol the Wochenzeitung magazine, which is published in Zurich, reported in 2001 that Bin Laden used a Bosnian passport.

It is to be noted that these reports were denied by the Muslim authorities in Bosnia.[36]

Ayman al Zawaheiri played a key role in building the terror infrastructure in the Balkans that included the dispatch of thousands of Afghan "alumni" to the fighting arena in Bosnia and their organization in the framework of Mujahidin units that fought alongside the Muslim forces in this country.

In 1995, following the signing of the Dayton Accords and in light of Zawaheiri's belief that the IFOR[37] intended to implement the agreement and demand the banishment of the Mujahidin from Bosnia, Zawaheiri decided to transfer the Al Qaida headquarters in the Balkans from Bosnia-Herzegovina to Sofia, Bulgaria.[38]

Under the cover name of "Mohammad Hassan Ali," Zawaheiri established the organization's headquarters in one of the suburbs of Sofia, the Bulgarian capital, leaving behind him in Bosnia a terror infrastructure that could act against American and Western targets.

A meeting of twenty-five senior commanders of radical Islamic organizations was held in 1995 in order to plan continued activities in the Balkans.[39]

The arrest of Tala'atFuad Kassem, one of the leaders of the Jama'a al-Islamiya and the Egyptian Islamic Jihad, came against the background of the conference.

On October 16, 1995, a suicide driver detonated himself in front of a police station in Rijeka, Croatia. Twenty-seven people were injured in the attack, and the police headquarters and nearby buildings were seriously damaged.

The Egyptian Jama'a al-Islamiyah terror organization claimed responsibility for the attack that was meant to warn the Croatian authorities to decease its activities against the organization and bring about the release of Tala'at Fuad Kassem. Despite the attack, Croatia extradited the latter to Egypt. On November 20, 1995 another attack was perpetrated against the Egyptian Embassy in Sofia.

The attack was meant to convey a double message, a threat against Egypt to refrain from harming Tala'at Fuad Kassem, and a threat aimed at the Bulgarian government to refrain from intervening in Al Qaida's activities.

Despite the attacks and threats, Tala'at Fuad Kassem stood trial in Egypt and was sentenced to death due to his responsibility for many attacks perpetrated by his men in Egypt.

In the beginning of 1996, after Zawaheiri believed that his infrastructure in Bulgaria was sufficiently safe and strong, he instructed forty terror activists of Egyptian descent to travel to Bulgaria and plan to perpetrate attacks against Western targets in the Balkans.[40]

Iranian terror infrastructures, Al Qaida, and additional Islamic terror organizations that were built up in the Balkans during the war in Bosnia, remained where they were and even developed at the end of the war under the auspices of the Muslim regime in Bosnia. During the period of Izetbegović's rule in Bosnia, the Bosnian authorities granted passports and Bosnian citizenship to thousands of Islamic Mujahidin including many Al Qaida activists as well as members of additional radical Islamic organizations. (See appendix).

According to the Balkan Institute for Strategic Studies (the Serb Research Institute), Alija Izetbegović met with Osama Bin Laden several times and hired the services of Mohammad Zawaheiri as commander of the special forces in Bosnia during the war.[41]

Aside from Bin Laden himself, who, as noted, made use of Bosnian passports, it is known that other senior activists in the organization used Bosnian passports including Abu-Zubeida, one of Bin Laden's deputies (currently under arrest in the U.S.), who was one of the initiators of the "millennium attacks" (see elaboration below), as well as two Al Qaida activists that were involved in an attempt to perpetrate these attacks, Ahmed Rasem (under arrest in the United States), and Sayyed Afmani (under arrest in France).

The Serb village Bocinja, which was abandoned by its Serb residents during the war in Bosnia, was populated by Mujahidin and their families who lead an Islamic community life according to the laws of the Sharia (see Section Two above).

This village, like other villages inhabited by the Mujahidin, are, in fact, ex-territorial, where the Bosnian and international forces have no control and state laws are not enforced.

It is to be noted that in the eyes of radical Islamic circles, the establishment of independent Islamic territory including Bosnia, Kosovo, and Albania along the Adriatic Coast, is one of the most prominent achievements of Islam since the siege on Vienna in 1683. Expressions in this spirit can be found in publications of radical Islamic circles under the title "the return to Europe."[42]

At the end of the war, the Al Qaida terror infrastructure, and the other Islamic terror organizations in the Balkans, began acting against U.S. and Western targets in this arena and in Western Europe.

This chapter will present exposure of Al Qaida terror infrastructures and additional Islamic terror organizations whose roots are in the Balkans or which used Bosnian papers in the course of their activities.

The Al Qaida command considers Europe an important and central arena vis-à-vis the promotion of a Global Jihad and the realization of the vision of an Islamic Caliphate throughout the world. Europe is perceived in the eyes of Bin Laden and his associates as "Dar al-Harb,"[43] which they envision will be turned into "Dar al-Islam"[43,44] through Jihad and added on to the global Islamic Caliphate. As an arena for the site of the struggle of the "International Islamic Front," Europe offers several clear advantages:

- The Muslim population in the Balkans, and the infrastructures of Al Qaida and other Islamic terror organizations that are deployed in this area due to the wars in Bosnia and Kosovo, constitute a forefront for the inculcation of Al Qaida and terrorist infrastructures in Western Europe and the United States, as well as other places in the world.
- The presence of large Muslim minorities (emigrants) in various European countries in which Islamic terror organization members may be assimilated and receive aid. The establishment of a traditional Islamic way of life, including mosques, cultural centers, and NGO's, creates optimal conditions for the management of a system to identify potential volunteers for recruitment into the ranks of the Islamic Jihad.

- In Europe "agents" of the Islamic Jihad act through these institutions to recruit new cadres and convince them to examine the path of a Global Jihad as an ideological alternative to the Western secular culture and as a solution to life's problems. The Islamic institutions also serve as an important source for the recruitment of funds and their transfer to active terror networks throughout the continent.
- The democratic-liberal and open way of life in Europe enables unrestricted movement and relatively easy transfer of terror activists, equipment, and means between the various countries and outside of the continent.
- The target population for recruitment into the ranks of the Global Jihad includes members of the first and second generation of veteran emigrants. Most of them were born in Europe and grew up as local citizens, but many suffer from the syndrome of emigrants' children who still carry the insult of their parents' absorption difficulties or the stigma of "foreigners who are the sons of foreigners." The feelings of degradation and discrimination turn them into easy prey to the attractive concepts of returning to their roots, which are presented as a lever for the resolutions of their problems. This is sometimes accompanied by the suggestion that revenge can be taken against their oppressors along with the indication that the Western way of life is a central cause for their suffering.
- Another resource for mobilization into the ranks of the Global Jihad is young men who have fallen to the margins of society and crime. In European prisons there are intensive "repentance" activities and conversion to Islam. Islam, in its radical and militant interpretation, serves as an attractive source of inspiration for this population.

Bin Laden and his men view these cadres as a vanguard that will inflame the spark of the Islamic revolution and be incorporated within the process of Global Jihad, among other ways, through terror. A reflection of this approach can be found in a conversation that was intercepted between two members of a terror cell in Italy as follows: "God loves us because Europe is in our hands. Now we are the emigrants fighting the Jihad. This is our role, our destiny, to fill it with honor. We must be like serpents, strike out at them and then hide."[45]

For the Afghan "alumni" and the Islamic terror organizations, Europe also serves as central logistic home front. The terror networks, particularly in North Africa and the Magreb, view Europe as an arena for acquisition activities to further the struggle that their comrades are fighting to topple the "infidel" regimes in their countries, and therefore the purchase of weaponry, supportive equipment, and fund raising constitute part of their routine tasks. This activity is intertwined with widespread criminal activity on the part of these network members who deal in counterfeit credit cards, the sale of forged papers, and drug trafficking. Part of the income is sent to their native countries to finance the activities of terror organizations. The shared and formative experience of camaraderie and, at times, joint fighting in Afghanistan, the Balkans, and other focal points of the Jihad, have forged a joint destiny and acquaintanceships that have expanded the circle of participants among terror activists in various places all over the world, with the concept of a Global Jihad serving as the "glue" that keeps them cohesive.

It is impossible to point out differences in goals and modi operandi adopted by the terror infrastructures in the various countries because the majority of them have adopted similar modi operandi in order to achieve similar goals.

Europe knew waves of terror attacks and thwarted attacks during the 1990s when arrests of terror cells in Italy, Belgium, Germany, and France exposed the tip of the iceberg vis-à-vis the activities of the Afghan "alumni" and Islamic terror organizations in Europe. To date, there have been relatively few terror attacks in Europe, mainly thanks to enforcement and thwarting activities initiated by the European security authorities.

The exposure of terror cells in Europe from the year 2000 and to date, reflects the dimensions of the threat. During this period, a series of arrests of Global Jihad members took place in Germany, Britain, Italy, France, Spain, Belgium, and Holland. Their goal was to realize the terror policy of the Bin Laden school of thought in order to cause instability and spread fear on the continent. This activity was to be part of a process designated to ignite the spark of Islamic revolution in Europe combined with terror activity to be perpetrated in North America, Asia, and the Middle East, and culminating in the attacks on September 11, 2001. The objective of the attacks in the U.S. was to cause a war of cultures which, according to Bin Laden's vision, would ultimately to lead to the collapse of the United States and to the establishment of an Islamic Caliphate worldwide.

## The September 11 Attacks and the Balkan Connection

On September 11, 2001 the most lethal terror offensive in the annals of international terror was perpetrated in the United States. It was directed against targets symbolizing the economic and military power of the United States and had a dramatic impact upon international relations.

Some 2,500 people from eighty countries worldwide were killed in this attack, most as a result of the intentional ramming of two passenger planes flown by suicide terrorists into the World Trade Center in New York City. Another target, which carries symbolic significance, the Pentagon in Washington, DC and symbol of U.S. military power, was also severely damaged by a third passenger plane flown by suicide pilots who rammed into the building. The intention of the hijackers of the fourth passenger plane was apparently to crash into the Capitol Building or the White House, but their plot was thwarted thanks to the heroic struggle of the plane's passengers.

In all four planes, 246 passengers and crewmembers were killed—these figures do not include the nineteen hijackers.

The terror offensive in the United States caused grave direct and indirect damage to the U.S. economy which came to hundreds of billions of dollars, and its traces are still noticeable in the U.S. economy in particular and world economy in general.

The terror campaign of September 11 started in the early hours of the morning, a short time after the four airplanes took off from three different airports on America's east coast. All of the hijacked aircraft were en route to distant airports on the west coast. The hijackers intentionally chose long flights in order to ensure that they would be carrying large amounts of fuel and would be less populated. The copious amount of fuel would enhance the effect of the explosion, while the relatively low number of passengers would ensure that it would be relatively easy to overwhelm them if any opposition were to arise on their part.

The four airplanes that crashed were hijacked by four trained teams of terrorists who were affiliated with the Al Qaida organization (a total of nineteen terrorists, four of whom were pilots). Fifteen of the assailants were of Saudi origin, one was Egyptian, another was Lebanese, and two were from the United Arab Emirates (UAE).

The investigation of the September 11, 2001 attacks revealed that at least two of the hijackers, and several of the collaborators, were linked to the Al Qaida infrastructure in the Balkans.

*Muhammad Haider Zamar.* Muhammad Haider Zamar, a German of Syrian origin, was an Al Qaida activist in Hamburg, Germany. Zamar met with Muhammad Atta, Ziad Jarah, and Marwan a-Sheikhi in the Al Quds mosque in Hamburg and convinced them to join the ranks of the Global Jihad and set out for training in Afghanistan. Therefore, Zamar can be accredited with the recruitment of the "Hamburg cell" whose members played a central role in the September 11 attacks (three of the cell's members were suicide pilots in the attacks).

Zamar began his activities in radical Islamic circles in the eighties. He set out for Afghanistan where he fought the Soviets and trained other recruits. After the end of the Jihad in Afghanistan, he set out for Bosnia where he trained Muslim fighters and participated in battles against the Serbs. During the years that he spent in Bosnia he traveled to Afghanistan several times in order to meet senior Al Qaida members.

Airplane Hijackers Nawaf Al-Hamzi and Khaled Al-Midhar.[46] These two terrorists were part of the team that hijacked American Airlines flight no. 77 on September 11, 2001. This passenger plane crashed into the Pentagon building in Washington, DC. Both men grew up and were educated in the Saudi Arabian city of Mecca. In the mid-1990s the two set out for Bosnia in order to help the Muslims in their war against the Serbs.

At the end of the war in Bosnia (apparently in 1998), they left for Afghanistan, officially joined Al Qaida, and made an oath of loyalty to Bin Laden.

In 1999, the two returned to Saudi Arabia and in April of that year were granted U.S. visas at the American Consulate in Jeddah, Saudi Arabia. The two used these visas in order to enter the United States and, as noted, play an active role in the September 11 attacks.

The September 11 attacks were funded via Al Qaida's widespread financial infrastructure. Some of its members were linked to the organization's infrastructure in the Balkans. The following are several examples that demonstrate this involvement:

Mamoun Darkanzali. (Dubbed Abu Elias.) Born in Damascus in 1958, Darkanzali arrived in Germany in 1940 and ran an import-export business that apparently served as a cover for his activity for Al Qaida. Draknazli had close ties with the members of the "Hamburg cell" and helped to fund their activities (during the years 1994-1998, $600,000 were transferred through his account to fund Al Qaida activities in Germany).[47]

Large sums of money were placed in his account by a Saudi company named TWAIK (see subsequent elaboration). Darkanzali also had links with the Al Qaida terror cell in Spain, which played a role in the organization of the September 11 attacks. Funds for the financing of the attacks came from this cell and a meeting of the "Hamburg cell" members headed by Muhammad Atta[48] was held in that country.

Khaled Sheikh Muhammad. Khaled Sheikh Muhammad was the main operational entity who stood behind the September 11 attacks and fought in the Mujahidin ranks in Bosnia. According to a Serb source, Khaled Sheikh Muhammad was granted Bosnian citizenship and a Bosnian passport during his stay there in 1994.[49]

The Twaik Group.[50] The TWAIK Group is a Saudi holding company whose annual turnover is estimated at some $100 million. According to The Chicago Tribune, the group transferred some $250,000 to Darkanzali's account during the years 1995-1998. During this period at least two of the company's directors were members of Al Qaida:

- Reda Seyam – in October 1997 he was appointed director of a car rental agency (under TWAIK's ownership) in Serbia. Reda Seyam was a senior activist in Al Qaida and after leaving Bosnia in 1999 he showed up in Southeast Asia (Indonesia) and was involved in the Al Qaida attack in Bali.
- Nabil Sayidi (see elaboration below).

The Global Relief Foundation (GRF).[51] Nabil Sayidi opened GRF offices in Albania whose declared goal was to provide humanitarian relief to Muslim refugees in Kosovo. Sayidi recruited a former employee of the TWAIK group named Osama Naem to run the office in Albania. Sayidi transferred about $150,000 to the office in Albania.

Less than a year after opening the office in Albania, Osama Naem and his brother were deported from Albania after being charged with involvement in the planning of an Al Qaida attack against the U.S. Embassy in Tirana.

## The "Millennium" Attacks

*The Terror Cell of Ahmed Rasem Exposed in Canada and the United States.*[52] On December 14, 1999, during a routine check by customs agents on the Canadian-U.S. border, Ahmed Rasem, a Canadian citizen of Algerian roots, was arrested while trying to cross the border between Vancouver, British Colombia and Seattle. A search of his car revealed some 50 kg. of explosives and improvised detonators. Rasem tried to escape, but was apprehended.

Investigations carried out after his arrest revealed that he was a member of an Algerian terror network that was active in several countries including Canada, the United States, Britain, and France. Rasem was wanted for questioning in France due to suspicions that he had collaborated with the Algerian GIA organization that perpetrated terror attacks in France during the years 1995-1996. The French authorities believed that Rasem was connected to the Roubaix Group, and a French court found him guilty in absentia of involvement in the group's terrorist and criminal activity. The French authorities also suspected Rasem of involvement in an attack in the Metro (Port Royal) in 1996 in which four people were killed and ninety-one were injured.[53]

The initial suspicion was that he had planned to perpetrate a mega attack at the Space Needle in Seattle, which was to host the millennium celebrations at the end of December 1999, but he subsequently confessed that his main target was to blow up the LAX airport in Los Angeles.

In July 2001, two other Algerians, Hawari and Maskini, were tried in New York for collaborating with Rasem.

Prior to his sentencing, and with the hope for leniency, Rasem decided to cooperate with his interrogators and divulged many details to his interrogators (despite his cooperation, Rasem was sentenced to 130 years of imprisonment).

Rasem described the course of his recruitment and training in the framework of the war in Bosnia, his training in Afghanistan, and his plans to perpetrate attacks in the United States. Rasem also talked about his ties with activists in other Islamic terror networks in Europe, particularly the GIA. This testimony joins a series of others that illustrate the action patterns of the "Global Jihad Front" that operated under the auspices of Bin Laden in Afghanistan.

Ahmed Rasem, who first arrived in Canada in 1994, was identified by Hanoushi, Imam of the mosque in Montreal, as a potential candidate for recruitment into the Global Jihad Movement. Hanoushi encouraged Rasem to go to Afghanistan and provided him with a letter of recommendation which he handed over to Abu-Zubeida, Bin Laden's deputy who was in charge of receiving the young Muslim men joining the Global Jihad and dispatching them for training in Bin Laden's camps. In the beginning of 1998, Rasem traveled to Afghanistan and met with Abu-Zubeida who gave him a pass to join the Khaldun camp for training.

Rasem stayed in Afghanistan for six months, during which time he underwent training in terror and guerilla warfare. He learned how to shoot light weapons, prepare explosive charges, operate covertly, professionally gather intelligence, and perpetrate attacks. He even underwent "advanced" training in sabotage at the Darunte camp, at the end of which he was given $12,000 to prepare an infrastructure for terror attacks.

At the Khaldun camp, he met some of his fellow collaborators in terror from among 100 young Muslims of different nationalities who participated in the training; Jordanians, Egyptians, Algerians, Yemenites,

Saudi Arabians, and Muslims from European countries like Germany, France, and Sweden. Rasem was instructed to organize a terror cell in Canada with other Algerians who had undergone training with him at the camp and to prepare an infrastructure for perpetrating terror attacks in the United States.

As the arrival of his peers was delayed, Rasem decided to organize a terror network based on alternative local aid. He appealed to Hawari, an acquaintance of Algerian origins who was involved in criminal activity, to help him obtain forged documentation. Hawari introduced Rasem to another collaborator named Maskini, who mainly helped to procure the forged documents.

This documentation was apparently provided by Karim Saayed Afmani who, like Rasem, had participated in the war in Bosnia as a fighter in the Mujahidin Brigade. At the end of the war, Afmani stayed in Bosnia and became an expert in forging papers, which he provided to members of terror networks. Autmani himself arrived in Canada and was deported back to Bosnia on October 18, 1998, although the Canadians were apparently unaware of his links to Islamic terror.[54] In his interrogation, Rasem said that he had been detained for over a year in an Algerian prison after being charged with aiding Algerian Islamic terror organizations. After his subsequent release he emigrated to the West in 1992.

In the framework of his preparations for the attacks, Rasem gathered intelligence information about three airports in the United States. On one of his journeys from the Los Angeles Airport he left a suitcase unsupervised in a trolley in order to test the alertness of the security staff. His choice of this airport as a central target stemmed from his understanding of its importance as a strategic, economic target and of the political repercussions if it were to be hit.

Among his partners in the planning already in Afghanistan were Dr. Haider, "Abu-Doha," and his deputy Mustafa Labasi. The two were at the camps in Afghanistan during his time there. Labasi actually stayed with him for a time in Canada before moving to London, while Abu-Doha served as a trainer at the Afghanistan camps before moving to London. (The two were senior members of the terror network subsequently apprehended in Britain at the beginning of 2001.) An extradition order to the United States is pending against Abu-Doha, who was involved in Rasem's plans to attack the LA Airport, for his part in the planning.

In his testimony, Rasem also exposed his link with Abu-Doha in Britain, against whom charges were brought on August 28, 2003 for his part in a conspiracy to bomb the airport in Los Angeles. Abu-Doha served as a liaison between Al Qaida and the Algerian terror cell, which was supposed to act in the United States. Rasem described Abu-Doha as one of the key figures in the planning of the LA attack and noted that he had received his instructions from the latter. It is noteworthy that at the time of his arrest, Rasem was carrying Abu-Doha's telephone number. The latter was in touch with a senior assistant at Bin Laden's headquarters named Abu-Ja'afer, who lived in Peshawar and transferred instructions to Abu-Doha, who was considered a senior entity in the European network.

Abu-Doha, who is suspected of being the mastermind behind the planned attack in LA, is being held at the March prison in Britain prior to his extradition to the United States.

*The Terror Network Arrested in Jordan on the Eve of the Millennium.*[55] On December 13, 1999, a thirteen-member terror network, mostly made up of Jordanians, Algerians, and Iraqis, was arrested in Jordan. According to the charges, this network had twenty-eight members, some of whom are still on the wanted list.

The network planned to perpetrate a series of attacks in Jordan during the millennium celebrations as part of a combined assault planned by the Al Qaida headquarters in Afghanistan.

The attack targets were:

1. The Radisson Moriah Hotel in Amman.
2. The pilgrimage location in Ma'ats that according to Christian tradition is the baptism site of Jesus in the Jordan River.
3. Tourists visiting Mount Nevo, which according to Jewish tradition is the burial site of Moses.
4. Israeli tourists at the Jordanian-Israeli border.

Some of the members of the terror network underwent indoctrination and training at Bin Laden's camps in Afghanistan, at the end of which they made their oath of loyalty to Bin Laden and to the ideal of the "Global Jihad," and then returned to Jordan. Others trained at camps in Lebanon with the help of Hizballah members and Iranian elements.

The cell was financed by "Abu-Katada the Palestinian" (Omar Ibn Omar), a Muslim cleric who was considered one of the most prominent radical indoctrinators in Europe. The cell was also instructed to finance its activities through criminal activity, for example robberies.

The terror network in Jordan was headed by Abu-Hushar, who had been arrested in the past in Jordan (1993) and charged with perpetrating attacks against the throne, but his sentence was mitigated by the King and he was released. Abu-Hushar, who also underwent training in Afghanistan and subsequently returned to Jordan, established the "Army of Muhammad" organization that was also made up of Afghan "alumni."

Another central activist alongside Abu-Hushar was Raed Hijazi, an American citizen of Pakistanti origins, who was subsequently arrested in Syria and extradited to Jordan where he was given the death sentence for his role in the operation.

The leaders of the Jordanian terror network were guided by Abu-Zubeida (Zain al Abadin, a thirty-one-year old Saudi of Palestinian origin who was a senior activist in Al Qaida; he was responsible for the activation of the two "millennium cells" in Jordan and in the United States). Abu-Zubeida was arrested about two years later in Pakistan on March 28, 2002, and he is one of the most senior terrorist activists in American hands.

Some of the members of the network apprehended in Jordan used Bosnian papers and were linked to Al Qaida activists in that country.

The Pakistani, Afghan, and Jordanian planners of the terror operation thwarted in Jordan had intended to cause multiple Israeli, American, and other casualties. Only thanks to the Jordanian security forces was this conspiracy nipped in the bud, before it could cause casualties, thus leaving no impact on public opinion in Israel and throughout the world.

In February 2000, The New York Times reported that in the course of the year 1999, Jordanian intelligence warned the CIA that Albanian terrorists in Bosnia intended to attack American targets in Europe.[56]

## France and its Connection to Balkan Terror

There is a large Muslim community in France whose origins are in the North African states. This community became a central focal point for the activities of the Algerian terror organizations, as well as other Islamic organizations, including some that had infrastructures and links with their associates in Bosnia.

During 1995-1996, terror attacks were perpetrated in France by terror cells of the Algerian terror organization, the GIA. These attacks were designated to express the organization's protest against France's support for the Algerian regime and "settle historical accounts" with the French invasion of Algeria (up to the 1960s). A splinter group called the GSPC intended to perpetrate attacks in France during the World Cup soccer championship in the summer of 1998. Subsequently, attacks aimed at striking out at Christian targets in Europe were also thwarted in addition to attacks that were to hit American targets on U.S. territory.

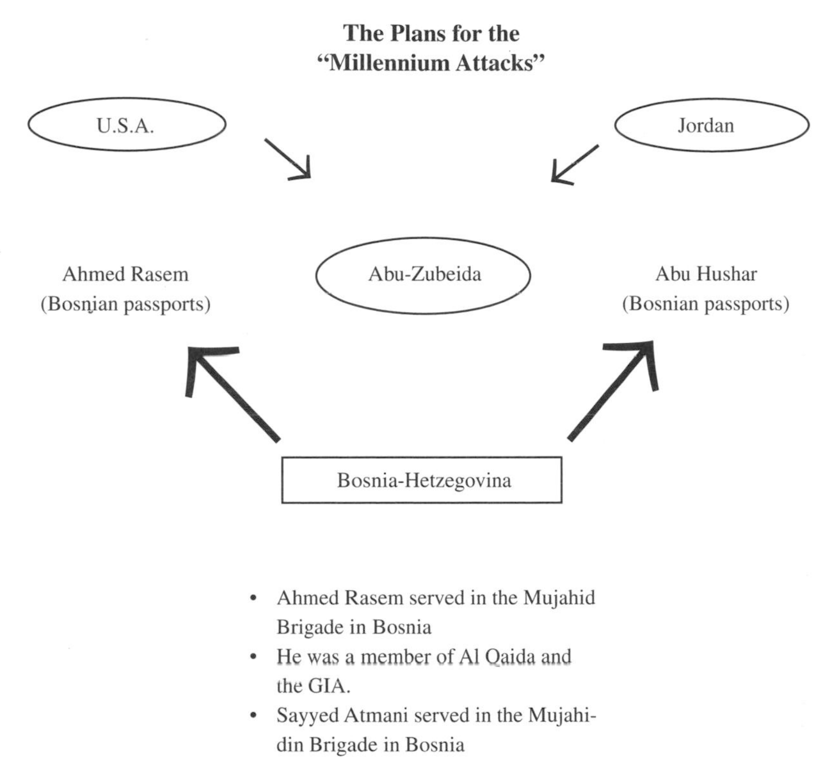


- Ahmed Rasem served in the Mujahid Brigade in Bosnia
- He was a member of Al Qaida and the GIA.
- Sayyed Atmani served in the Mujahidin Brigade in Bosnia
- Atmani was a forgery expert (passports).

As noted, the terror activity of these Al Qaida affiliated organizations in Europe was operative throughout the 1990s, but it took on considerable momentum in the latter half of the decade due to the consolidation of Bin Laden's headquarters in Afghanistan under the auspices of the Taliban, and thanks to the Al Qaida infrastructures in the Balkans.

*The Abu al Ma'ali Affair.*[57] Abd al Bakher Mukhtari (dubbed Abu al Ma'li), an Algerian national, was a senior activist in Al Qaida and served as the commander of the Mujahidin Brigade that fought alongside the Muslim Bosnians during the war in Bosnia.

In recognition of his contribution to Bosnia and due to his ties with Bosnian President Izetbegović, he was granted Bosnian citizenship and continued to act from this country in order to establish terror infrastructures in Western Europe.

*The Roubaix Group.* Abu al Ma'ali's name was linked to two medical students, Christophe Caze and Lionel Dumont, French citizens who had converted to Islam. In 1993, the two decided to travel to Bosnia in order to offer medical and humanitarian aid in this torn country.

The two men arrived in Bosnia but Abu al Ma'ali convinced them to join the ranks of the Mujahidin under his command rather than provide humanitarian aid.

At the end of the war, the two returned to France and, under Abu al Ma'ali's instruction, established an Islamic terror infrastructure in their country.

In 1995-1996, Caze operated the Roubaix Group, which included radical Muslim activists that underwent training in Bosnia. The group dealt in robberies in order to finance its activities and help radical Islam in its struggle in Algeria.

The group's activity was based in the city of Roubaix near the Belgian border, and its members did not hesitate to use firearms. On March 28, 1998 the group's members placed a car bomb loaded with explosives and gas balloons near the city's police station but the car was intercepted and the attack was thwarted.

After the discovery of the car bomb the police raided a building where the group's members were hiding. A shootout at the site caused ammunition to explode in the building, resulting in a fire. The remains of four bodies were found in the burnt out building. The other members of the group fled by car to Belgium. The fugitives were stopped at a police roadblock in Belgium. During the subsequent shootout one of the gang's members, Christophe Caze, was killed and another was injured and apprehended.

The interrogation of the captured terrorist, and Caza's electronic diary which was found in the car, indicated that the group had been in touch with terror activists in Bosnia, France, Canada, and England.

The weapons used by the group members were smuggled into France from Bosnia and it was proven that Caza was in contact with and operated by Abu al Ma'ali from his headquarters in Zenica, Bosnia.

Dumont returned to Bosnia after helping Caza to establish the terror cell in Roubaix. He was arrested in Bosnia, charged with murder, and sentenced by a Zenica court to twenty years of imprisonment. However, in 1999 he succeeded in breaking out of the Bosnian prison. Dumont went to Japan with a forged French passport in July 2002 and became a car dealer in the city of Nigata in northern Japan. During his stay in Japan, Dumont traveled to Europe several times ostensibly for business reasons. He ultimately left Japan in September 2003 and moved to Malaysia, never to return to the former.[58]

The Japanese authorities fear that during his stay in Japan, Dumont dealt in the establishment of a terror infrastructure and in gathering intelligence about targets for attack in that country.[59]

Dumont was arrested in Germany in December 2003 and was extradited to France in May 2004 where he had already been given a life sentence in absentia due to his involvement in robberies and terror as part of his activities in the Roubaix group.

*The Attempted Egyptian Jihad Attack.* In 1998, Abu al Ma'ali attempted to smuggle explosives from Bosnia for an Egyptian terror group (affiliated with the Egyptian Islamic Jihad), which planned to perpetrate attacks against American military targets in Germany. The shipment, which was intercepted by the CIA, included C-4 type explosives.

Due to Abu al Ma'ali's involvement in terror activity in Western Europe, the United States placed heavy pressure on the Muslim government in Bosnia to extradite Abu al Ma'ali, but the Bosnian government refused and enabled him to escape to Afghanistan in 1999.

*Jamal Begal's Terror Network in France, Holland, and Belgium.*[60] On July 28, 2001 Jamal Begal, a thirty-six-year old French citizen of Algerian descent, was arrested in Doha while en route from Afghanistan to Europe. In his interrogation he revealed the process of his recruitment into the ranks of the Global Jihad and his participation in the weekly sermons of Abu-Katada. After a preliminary "indoctrination" process in Britain, Begal traveled to Bin Laden's training camps in Afghanistan in November 2000, where he underwent basic training in combat and sabotage, combined with indoctrination lessons, and then pledged his loyalty oath to Bin Laden. At the end of his training, he was instructed by Abu-Zubeida, Bin Laden's senior deputy, to establish a terror network in Europe, which was to perpetrate terror attacks at the U.S. Embassy and Cultural Center in Paris at the end of 2000 and the beginning of 2001.

As a cover for his activities, Begal was instructed to open a business and Internet café, which would help him maintain e-mail contact with his operators in Afghanistan.

Begal, who was arrested with false documents on his way from Pakistan to France, was extradited to France in the beginning of October 2001.

Begal's network contained about twenty members and collaborators spread out in France, Holland, and Belgium. Some of the network members were alumni of the war in Bosnia-Herzegovina. Begal's arrest was kept under wraps, which enabled the security forces in these countries that were cooperating with each other, to place the cell members under surveillance and closely monitor their activities in order to thwart the attacks planned for Belgium and France. On September 13, 2001, about ten cell members were arrested in Belgium and Holland. In the possession of some of them were weapons, forged documentation, and Islamic incitement material.

The exposure of the arrests in the "Le Monde" newspaper and on French television forced the French security forces to bring the arrests of the remaining local cell members forward in order to prevent the destruction of incriminating evidence and their escape.

Prominent members of Begal's cell included: Nizar Terabelsi, a thirty-three-year old former professional soccer player who had converted to Islam and volunteered to drive a car bomb in a suicide mission at the U.S. Embassy in Paris. Nizar Terabelsi was also involved in the recruitment of Richard Reid and Sayyed Badat.

Kamal Daoudi, a twenty-seven-year old French student of Algerian descent, who was a computer expert. He underwent training in Afghanistan and lived in Begal's apartment in Paris. When the authorities came to arrest him, he eluded them and fled to Leicestershire, England where he was arrested on October 25, 2001 and was extradited to France.

*The Hadez Budela Affair.* Hadez Budela was a member of the GIA, the Algerian terror organization. He was also linked to the Jama'a al Islamiyah Egyptian terror organization. Budela came to Bosnia as an employee of the BIF charity and was registered as an employee of the organization's offices in Zenica.

During his stay in Bosnia he maintained contact with Abu al Ma'ali who served as the commander of the Mujahidin unit in Zenica. In the aftermath of the September 11, 2001 attacks, and as a result of the steps taken by the U.S. and the Coalition to locate and arrest terror activists connected to Al Qaida, Budela was detained along with five other terrorists in Sarajevo in October 2001.

Five of the detainees, including Budela, were of Algerian descent. The sixth was of Yeminte descent. It is to be noted that five of the detainees had Bosnian citizenship at the time of their arrest, and Budela himslef is marired to a Muslim Bosnian.

The six detainees were brought before a Bosnian court that ruled that they must be released due to lack of evidence. However, that same night the Bosnian security authorities handed the six over to the U.S. security

**Networks of Islamic Terror in France**

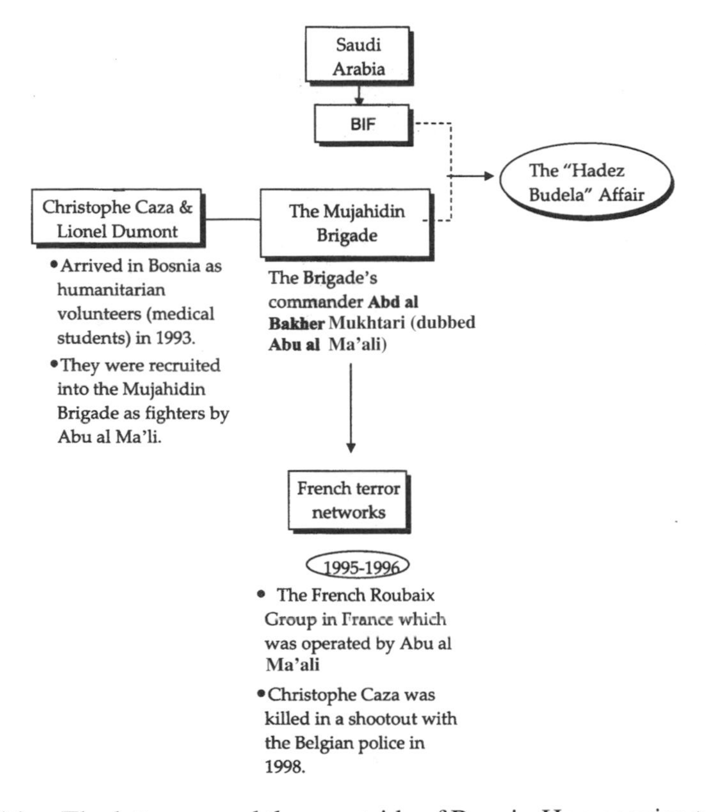


authorities. The latter moved them outside of Bosnia-Herzegovina to the detention camp for Al Qaida detainees in Guantenamo, Cuba.[61]

## Germany and its Connection to Balkan Terror

Germany also constituted a convenient base for the activities of radical Islam in Europe. In certain cities, such as Hamburg and Frankfurt, the members of the Islamic front acted out of a sense of security and made their preparations for the perpetration of terror outside of the country's boundaries. (The most prominent example is of course the "Hamburg Cell" which perpetrated the September 11, 2001 attacks in the United States.)

The freedom of movement in the country, the lack of intelligence and police surveillance in relationship to foreigners (particularly if the foreigners were students), in addition to Germany's geographical proximity to target states on the continent (mainly France and Italy), made it an attractive base for terrorists.

**The "Hadez Budela" Affair**

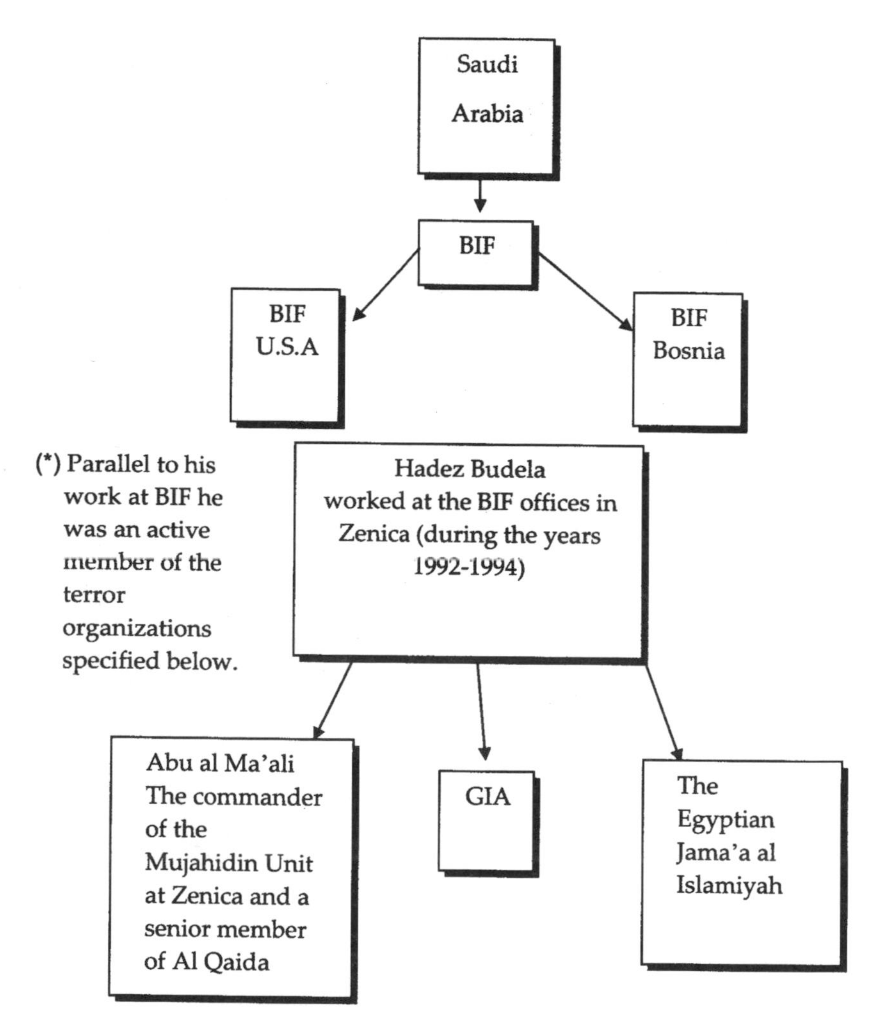


- Hadez Budela was arrested in Sarajevo in October 2001.
- He was extradited to the U.S.
- He is being detained at the detention camp in Guantenamo, Cuba.

The existence of a large Muslim community, the presence of mosques, cultural organizations, and Islamic charities enabled the Islamic terror entities to meet at these locations, recruit new individuals into their ranks, and mainly to continue with their underground activity under the guise of the religious and ritual freedom customary in that country. The presence of Muslim businessmen from all over the world in this country also helped them to raise funds without any government supervision. Thus, to date, Germany has not served as an arena for attacks, apparently due to the fear that this might damage the infrastructures in the country, which serves as a base for the activity of terror networks operating against other targets in Europe and the U.S.

It is no coincidence that a significant part of the Al Qaida infrastructure that subsequently perpetrated the September 11, 2001 attacks operated in Hamburg (the "Hamburg Cell" headed by Muhammad Atta).

*The Apprehension of a Terror Cell in Germany in 2001.*[62] On December 24, 2001, the Frankfurt police raided two safe houses in the city and arrested four individuals; two Iraqis, an Algerian, and a Frenchman who had in their possession weapons, forged documentation, and stolen credit cards. The weapons included rifles, grenades, 20 kgs. of improvised explosives, and homemade detonators. All four carried false papers under assumed names.

A videotape made in the framework of preparations prior to perpetrating attacks was found at the safe house. The tape described the planned targets including a cathedral and a Christmas market in Strasbourg, France.

One of the cell members named Muhammad Ben Zakaria, dubbed "Milliani," evaded arrest in Germany but was apprehended later in the Spanish city of Alhanta.

At the trial of the defendants held in Germany in April 2002, one of them claimed that a synagogue in Strasbourg was also among the targets. According to the charges brought against them, the terror cell was operated from Britain, from whence they received instructions and funding for attacks.

## Britain and its Connection to Balkan Terror

Britain has played a central role as the basis for an ideological infrastructure and as a site for propaganda activity and recruitment for Islamic terror organizations. Britain, which has a large community of about two million Muslims, has become a focus of Islamic radicalism in Europe due to, among other reasons, lenient emigration laws combined with a willingness to offer political asylum to entities claiming to be politically persecuted by the regimes in their countries of origin, and also strict adherence to individual rights and free speech.

The British liberalism ("Hyde Parkism") triggered a flourish of Islamic propaganda activity, hovering at the brink of incitement and even crossing the line from time to time. Britain has served as a central site for those requesting political asylum from among the Afghan "alumni," war veterans and many emigrants from North Africa who, at some point, were attracted to the concepts of the Global Jihad.

The activities of central mosques in British cities, headed by fanatic spiritual mentors, has turned them into an attractive focus for young people who have undergone "ideological indoctrination" and semi-military training that ultimately led them to Bin Laden's training camps in Afghanistan and, subsequently, to the Jihad arenas in the Balkans and Caucasia.

For years radical Islamic clerics have been active in Britain, openly and rabidly inciting their audiences against the West, and some of them are even suspected of involvement in terror attacks of the Afghan "alumni." The most prominent is Omar Abu Omar ("Abu Katada"), a forty-two-year old Jordanian of Palestinian origin who is considered a central figure among Muslim leaders in Europe. Abu-Katada is an Afghan "alumnus" who fought alongside the local Mujahidin during the 1980s. At the end of the war he was granted political asylum because he claimed that he was being politically persecuted. He served as the Imam of the Finsbury mosque and is considered the chief protagonist and instigator of the Global Jihad in Britain who expresses open support for all Islamic organizations that back the war against the United States and calls for a Jihad against Israel and Jordan.

In an interview that he granted to the "Confrontation" program on Al-Jazeera[63] television on March 9, 2000, Abu-Katada condemned the Arab states that prevent Muslims from fighting Israel. His ties with terror activists are extensive, and there is a death sentence pending against him for his part in aiding the millennium terror attacks in Jordan (at the end of 1999), because of his "fatwa" permitting the attacks planned there and his instructions to provide financial aid to this terror network. Incitement tapes and large amounts of money, which he claimed were designated for charity, were found at his home. Abu-Katada was arrested several times by the British, but was conditionally released until he finally "disappeared" in March 2002.

Another senior cleric is Mustafa Kamal Mustafa, dubbed "Abu-Hamza al Masri." Abu-Hamza heads a radical Idlamic organization called "Ansar al Shariya," (supporters of the Shariya).

Abu-Hamza participated in the fighting in Afghanistan and subsequently in Bosnia as well, where he lost his eye and one of his arms when an explosive device that he was preparing detonated. There are contradictory opinions regarding whether he was injured in Afghanistan or Bosnia.[64]

Abu-Hamza served as the Imam of the Finsbury Park mosque in London. He dealt in the recruitment of Muslim volunteers who were dispatched to training camps run by radical Islamic organizations including Al Qiada camps in Afghanistan and Bosnia-Herzegovina.[65] He also initiated the publication of a periodical on behalf of his movement that served as a mouthpiece for radical Islam.

Abu-Hamza publicly advocated the Jihad against the United States, supported attacks perpetrated by the Jama'a al Islamiyah against tourists in Egypt (the attack in Luxor in 1997), and was involved in attacks and the murder of western tourists in Yemen.

In October 2004, Abu-Hamza stood trial in Britain. The charge sheet included sixteen charges including abetting violence and murder.[66]

An important part of the evidence against abu-Hamza was audio and videotapes that he distributed in order to recruit Muslim volunteers.

One of the tapes describes the training of terrorists in house-to-house fighting in Bosnia, and includes a call to Muslims to be prepared to terrorize Allah's foes.

In another tape, Abu-Hamza advocates the perpetration of suicde attacks while offering religious justifications.

Abu-Hamza's link to Bosnia was reflected in a speech delivered at a conference of the Islamic Renewal Conference in Britain Abu Hamza stated:[67] "How is it that the UN and the U.S.A. can mobilize an army overnight to bomb Muslims in Iraq yet take years to mobilize an army in Bosnia and the answer is simple—Muslims must fight back for themselves."

Another radical Islamic cleric is Sheikh Omar Bakri of Syrian descent who emigrated to Britain after his deportation from Saudi Arabia. He heads the Mujahidin movement founded in 1996, and he also agitates for Global Jihad against the enemies of Islam, headed by the United States, Israel, and all of their supporters.

Against the background of the vitriolic Islamic incitement in Britain, it is not surprising that the latter has become a hothouse for the cultivation of activists who were directly involved in the perpetration of terror or in the planning of terror attacks. Among these is Zakaria Musawi, who was arrested in the United States in August 2001, and was thus prevented from participating as the twentieth hijacker in the September 11 attacks. Musawi's friend, Richard Colvin Reid, aspired to blow up an American Airlines flight on December 22, 2001 by igniting shoes loaded with explosives.

*The Apprehension of the Terror Cell in Britain—December 2001.* As a result of the investigation and findings confiscated upon the apprehension of the German cell in December 2000, the London police carried out a series of arrests in February 2001 of the terror cell members in England which played a central role in the activation of the terror networks in various European cities. The cell was led by Dr. Haider, also called Abu-Doha, and his deputy Mustafa Labasi. The thirty-six-year old Abu-Doha, of Algerian descent, was identified as a senior member of the terror networks active in Europe, and he was linked to several of them. He served as a trainer at the Khaldun camp in Afghanistan until 1999 when he moved to Britain and settled in London, apparently following the instructions of the Al Qaida headquarters. Labasi, his deputy, shared an apartment with Ahmad Rasem during his stay in Canada and, as noted earlier, was linked to terror infrastructures in Bosnia. Labasi is suspected of hosting some of the hijackers of the U.S. commercial airplanes in his home in London when they were en route to their suicide mission in the United States.

*The Richard Colvin Reid Incident ("the Man with the Explosive Shoes").*[68] On December 22, 2001, a suicide bomber named Richard Colvin Reid attempted to detonate American Airlines passenger flight 63, which was en route from Paris to Miami. His shoes were loaded with 100 to 200 grams of explosives that he attempted to ignite in order to blow up the aircraft along with its 196 passengers and crewmembers about two hours before the scheduled landing in Miami. Only thanks to the alertness of a flight attendant, who was summoned to Reid's seat by a suspicious passenger, and the terrorist's neutralization with the help of other passengers, was a grave disaster prevented.

In his interrogation, Reid claimed that he had acted independently but the investigation revealed that he was a member of a terror infrastructure that was active in various parts of Europe. In the course of the investigation another suspect was caught—Sayyed Badat—who confessed that he had also planned to perpetrate a suicide attack on a flight from Europe to the United States. Badat said that he had been affected by the massacre perpetrated among the Muslims in Bosnia-Herzegovina and that he had decided to join the Islamic struggle against its enemies. In 1998, he left Britain and went to Sarajevo in Bosnia-Herzegovina in order to help local Muslims.[69]

In January 1998, (at the age of nineteen) he went to Afghanistan and for two years underwent training in Al Qaida camps.

In September 2001, he returned to Europe and went to Amsterdam, Holland where he and Richard Reid met with terror activist Nizar Terabelsi who recruited them for a suicide mission. After the meeting with Terabelsi, Badat went back to Afghanistan in order to coordinate the attacks. In December 2001, Badat traveled to England and continued with the preparations for the attack.[70]

For various reasons Badat did not carry out the attack which he was supposed to perpetrate (perhaps because he had learned that Reid's attempt had failed).

Badat was arrested by the police in November 2003. He stood trial and in April 2005 was sentenced to thirteen years of imprisonment.[71]

His personal background indicates a familiar pattern of activity of recruiting British citizens who had converted to Islam into the ranks of Al Qaida and terror cells supported by the latter.

Reid was born in Britain. His father was of Jamaican roots and his mother was middle-class British. The father, a vagabond type who had also got entangled in crime, deserted his home and his pregnant wife. Reid was aware of the existence of his biological father, but he never met him before the age of twelve. Reid grew up in England as a child of a mixed marriage. According to his father and other family members who were interviewed after his terror attempt, Reid was "a confused, lost, restrained, and angry young man."

At the age of fifteen, Reid was sent to a juvenile detention center. In prison he was persuaded to convert to Islam and, upon his release, was attracted to radical religious Muslim circles in Britain and spent much of his time in mosques in the Brixton area.

The mosques served as centers for ideological indoctrination meetings that were targeted at persuading young Muslims throughout Europe to join the Global Jihad. After undergoing indoctrination in London, Reid traveled to Pakistan and, from there, to Bin Laden's camps in Afghanistan where he passed through the "melting pot" of the Afghan "alumni."

Reid's interrogators believe that he was among the supporters of Ali Shah Gilani who headed a radical Islamic group called "Jamaat al Fuqra" which dealt in the recruitment of volunteers for the Jihad at various focal points worldwide including Bosnia-Herzegovina.[72]

Sheikh Gilani himself visited Bosnia-Herzegovina at least once and dispatched volunteers from his organization to fight alongside the local Muslims.[73]

Another episode which is connected to Gilani is the kidnapping and murder of the journalist David Pearl in Pakistan. Pearl was trying to gather information and prepare an article about Sheikh Gilani and his organization. In the course of his efforts to reach Sheikh Gilani, he fell into a trap set by the head of a Pakistani terror organization, Omar Sheikh, who offered to arrange a meeting between him and Sheikh Gilani but actually kidnapped him and killed him.[74] Omar Sheikh headed the Harkat al Mujahidin terror organization.

Omar Sheikh has Pakistani and British citizenship. He joined the war in Bosnia-Herzegovina like hundreds of Pakistanis who responded to the call in the early 1990s to join the Jihad in the Balkans.[75]

At the end of the war in Bosnia, he continued with his terror activity in India. He was caught and imprisoned but was released in December 1999 due to the hijacking of an Indian aircraft by his associates. After his release he moved to Pakistan, which served as his base for the operation of his terror organization that cooperated closely with Al Qaida.[76]

Reid spent his time among the same radical circles in Britain that had produced notorious terrorists such as Zakaria Musawi, Jamal Begal, and Nizar Terabelsi. (As stated above, the latter recruited Reid and Badat for suicide missions).

The attempted attack by Reid serves as indisputable evidence that Al Qaida and its affiliated terror cells have not abandoned their intention to perpetrate additional deadly mega attacks. It testifies to the fact that, despite the heavy blow sustained in the onslaught of the international allied forces led by the U.S., Al Qaida's ability to persevere in the perpetration of painful terror attacks has not been impaired.

## Italy and its Connection to Balkan Terror

*Exposure of Plans to Assassinate the Pope.*[77] Yosef Bodanski claims that in 1997 Iran planned to assassinate the Pope through a joint Al Qaida terror infrastructure in Bosnia.

The assassination was supposed to take place at the end of December1997 through a terror group including twenty members with Bosnian, Croatian, Tunisian, and Moroccan citizenship. The venue for the attack would be Bologna, Italy.

It is to be noted that the terror cell members were all Mujahidin that had fought in Bosnia. The group was supported by the terror infrastructure in Bosnia that aided the Algerian GIA terror organization in Italy. The Italian police exposed the group prior to the attack and succeeded in apprehending fourteen of the terror cell's members.

*Exposure of the GSPC Terror Cell in Italy.*[78] In April 2001, members of the "The Salafi Group for Propaganda and Combat" (GSPC), were arrested in Italy. The cell was headed by a thirty-three-year old citizen of Tunisian descent named Sayyed Sami Ben Khamis. Together with his accomplices, he planned a suicide attack at the U.S. Embassy in Rome. The Italian security intercepted a telephone conversation between Khamis and his thirty-one-year-old Libyan partner, Lased Ben Hanni, in which they discussed a plan to introduce cyanide in the air-conditioning system of some target, thus causing the immediate death from asphyxiation of thousands of people, all in the name of the Islamic revolution in Europe. As noted, both of the attack plans were thwarted due to the arrest of the terror cell members.

*The Arrest of an Al Qaida Activist Connected to Bosnia in Italy.*[79] Bazaaoui Mondhar Iben Mohsen, a Tunisian suspected of being a central Al Qaida activist in Europe, was arrested on October 1, 2002 at the Italian port of Bari.

The thirty-five-year-old Bazaaoui fought in the ranks of the Mujahidin in Bosnia and, after the end of the war, moved to Italy where he set up a secret terror cell. Over the years he visited Bosnia in order to maintain ties with Al Qaida members in this country and recruit activists for the terror infrastructure that he had established in Italy.

Italian security entities stated that Bazaaoui was arrested upon his return from a visit in Bosnia, in the course of which he had recruited volunteers to perpetrate suicide attacks in the West.

Bazaaoui had been arrested earlier in 1998 in Bologna, Italy and charged with membership in a criminal association but was released. Bazaaoui was also tried in absentia in France and sentenced to six years in prison after having been charged with membership in a criminal association whose aim was to perpetrate terror attacks.

It is to be noted that Bazaaoui's arrest in Italy was part of a series of arrests in which thrity-five individuals were apprehended and charged with membership in Al Qaida.[80]

## Spain and its Connection to Balkan Terror

Several arrests of terror cells and activists connected to Al Qaida were carried out in Spain. As stated earlier, in June 2001 the head of the terror cell in Frankfurt called "Milliani" was arrested, but he succeeded in breaking out of detention in Germany in December 2000.

In July 2001, six members of an Algerian cell were arrested. They dealt mainly in logistic and criminal activity in aid of the "The Salafi Group for Propaganda and Combat" (GSPC). The group's members were experts in forging documents and carried out fraud with credit cards.[81]

On January 13, 2001, an additional cell with eight members was discovered in Spain. This cell was led by a Spanish citizen of Syrian origin named Imad a-din Barkat Yarkan, also known as "Abu-Dahdah." Some of the members had undergone training in Afghanistan and Bosnia, where they learned terror and guerilla warfare and pledged their loyalty to the Jihad. According to the charge sheet filed against the eight by the investigative Judge Garcon, they were also suspected of maintaining links with additional members of terror cells in Germany and France. The cell members worshipped at the central mosque in Madrid, and that is where they were involved in their secret activities. They were careful to maintain a routine middle-class lifestyle, but at the same time dealt in subversive activity, which included recruiting young men for the Global Jihad network, raising funds for the purchase of weapons and explosives, and the use of fake credit cards to finance their activities.

Abu-Dahdah maintained contact with the "Hamburg Cell" and its commander, Muhammad Atta, who visited Spain twice (in the framework of the preparations for the September 11 attacks). From 1997, Abu-Dahdah's telephone line was tapped. At this point it is not clear if any of the cell members had contact with Muhammad Atta (commander of the Hamburg Cell) during his two visits to Spain in 2000 and 2001. In the charge sheet there is mention of a coded telephone conversation between Abu-Dahdah and an activist named "Shoukour," in which they discussed activity suspected of being connected to aviation targets.[82]

In April 2002, three businessmen were arrested in Spain, headed by Muhammad Raleb a Zweidi (Abu-Talha) who, according to the charge sheet, led the Al Qaida financing network in Spain which operated under the cover of a construction company. Zweidi, a Spanish citizen of Syrian descent, gave a large sum of money to Abu-Dahdah and his group in Spain and also transferred money to Al Qaida members in various countries all over the world, including the U.S., Belgium, Turkey, Jordan, Syria, Saudi Arabia, and China.[83]

*The Balkan Connection to the Attacks in Madrid—March 11 2004.* On May 10, 2004, Dragomir Adnan, the commander of the police in Sofia, Bulgaria stated during a press conference that the terrorists who had perpetrated the attacks on Madrid trains had been trained in Al Qaida camps in Bosnia-Herzegovina and that eleven of the suspects had reached Spain via Sarajevo. He also claimed that the explosives used for the preparation of the bombs had been manufactured in Bosnia.[84]

Serb sources divulged that three terrorists, who had undergone training in the area of Zenica, left Bosnia-Herzegovina for Switzerland before the attacks in Madrid. From there they continued on to Madrid. The terrorists drove to Switzerland in a car in which they transported the explosives. In Switzerland they received help from radical Islamic entities from among the Bosnian refugees who live in that country.

From Switzerland, two of the cell members continued on to Spain, while the third went to Morocco in order to meet with members of the MCG[85] organization, which stood behind the attacks in Madrid.[86]

Jamal Zougam, a thirty-two-year-old Moroccan who is facing trial in Spain for involvement in the Madrid attacks, maintained contact with Abu Dahdah, the head of Al Qaida in Spain, (who is standing trial for his involvement in the September 11 attacks in the United States).

Zougam owns a cellular telephone store. He is suspected of providing cellular phones from his store to detonate the explosive devices in the Madrid attacks. The Spanish prosecution claims that he was also in contact with the Moroccan terrorist Salah-a-din Bin Yaish, "Abu-Muhin," an alumnus of the war in Bosnia who is under arrest in Morocco for his role in the attacks perpetrated in Casablanca on May 16, 2003.[87]

## The Terror Infrastructure in the Balkans and the Conflict Arena in Chechnya

From the mid-1990s, following the consolidation of Islamic "charities" and terror organizations in the Balkans, this region began to serve as a base for the transfer of military and humanitarian aid, as well as fighters, to the Chechnyan arena.

At the same time that the Afghan "alumni" arrived in the Jihad arena in Chechnya, the "Balkans" also began pouring into this arena (Islamic fighters, "alumni" of the war in Bosnia). The "Balkans" appeared in the ranks of the Chechnyan terror organizations, but also outside of Chechnya's borders in the area of Caucasia and the Crimean Peninsula.

## Trends in the Development of Islamic Terror in the Balkans

Money from Muslim states serves to fund the dissemination of Islam, mainly through educational frameworks. Some 100,000 Muslim Bosnian youths study in Islamic educational institutions today that advocate the extremist Wahhabi ideology.

Alongside the regular education in the educational institutions, Islamic organizations also operate summer camps and training camps for young Muslims attending the educational institutions. They undergo indoctrination and military training in these camps, which prepares them for recruitment into radical Islamic organizations inside and outside the Balkans.

Several organizations that actively operate these camps are al-Furqan, the Active Islamic Youth, and the Muslim Youth Council.[88]

Serb intelligence sources have detected several trends within Islamic terror identities in the Balkans:

- Escalation of the attacks against Serb civilians in the Kosovo region.
- Escalation of the attacks against civilian targets in southern Serbia and Montenegro, in cities with a Muslim majority (near the Albanian border).
- Increased activity on the part of the Albanian National Army (ANA)[89] in Kosovo and Macedonia under the auspices/aid of Albania.
- Escalation of the violence in Bosnia-Herzegovina in order to preserve the hostility and separation between the Muslim population on the one hand, and the Croatian and Serb populations on the other.
- Gaining control of the access routes between Albania-Montenegro and Bosnia, and isolating the Serb population in the Serb Republic in Bosnia-Herzegovina (no-go area for Serbs).

Researcher Yosef Bodansky believes that in light of the U.S. invasion of Iraq, the leaders of Al Qaida and the Global Jihad have decided to escalate the struggle against the West, and are basing this activity on infrastructures which they have established in the Balkans, among others.[90]

Bodansky claims that a senior Al Qaida member, named Emir Mussa Ayzi, was appointed the organization's coordinator vis-à-vis the Balkans and received instructions to recruit fighters and carry out operational activity.

Ayzi is an "alumnus" of the Jihad in Afghanistan and is closely associated with Bin Laden and the Taliban leadership. In August 2003, Ayzi began recruiting terrorists for the organization from among the Muslims in Bosnia and Russians who converted to Islam in Chechnya and in other areas of Caucasia. These new recruits have European facial features, a fact which is meant to aid their activities in the "West."[91]

In a letter, Ayzi wrote that he had succeeded in recruiting Slav volunteers (or persons of "Slav ethnicity") for the Jihad mission. He added that some of these "White Devils" had already undergone indoctrination and taken their oaths, and were ready to do their "work" in several cities in Europe and Israel. The preparation of additional cadres of Slavs for attacks in the United States is currently underway.[92]

According to Bodansky, Ayzi's recruitment and training sessions were conducted in the Balkans and Caucasia, mainly in Georgia.

The construction of the new infrastructures was carried out on the basis of instructions issued by Muhammed al Zawaheiri, brother to Ayman al Zawaheiri (Bin Laden's deputy), on Albanian land, in Kosovo, and in parts of Macedonia that are considered safe havens from which terrorists can penetrate Europe.

The training activity was carried out under the guise of the ANA (Albanian National Army) in Albania with the help of experienced instructors (former Mujahidin) that are affiliated with Al Qaida and came from Bosnia.

The link between the events in Iraq and the Balkan arena was reflected in the aftermath of the attack against the UN headquarters in Baghdad (August 14, 2003). An organization called the Abu Hafez al Masri Brigade (a cover name for Al Qaida) claimed responsibility for the attack and declared that the UN had ignored the massacre of women and children in Bosnia in 1992 and 1995. It also maintained that the UN was responsible for the bloodbath of 7,000 Muslims in Serbrenica in 1995 because it had advocated that a Muslim state must not be established in Europe.

On August 24, 2003, the al-Muhajiroun periodical, which appears in London, published an article in which it explained why the attack had been perpetrated against the UN headquarters in Baghdad:[93]

> Verily it was the UN soldiers in Bosnia who were recorded to have stood by when the barbaric Serbs massacred Muslims. The UN first decided to take away the weapons of the Muslims (fearing that they might actually defend themselves and establish Islamic rule) and thereby facilitated their massacre, and were then even photographed helping in the mass murder and gang rape of Muslim women and children. The wounds are still fresh.

According to Serb sources,[94] during the fighting in Faluja, Iraq the U.S. forces captured terrorists who had had come from Bosnia-Herzegovina and Kosovo. Additional reports quoted by Serb sources indicate the dispatch of combat means from the Balkans to the Mujahidin fighting against the Coalition forces in Iraq.[95]

Part of the Islamic terror activity is focused in some areas in south Serbia and Montenegro where there is a relatively large Muslim population, like the area of Novi Pazar.

The activity is marked in the following areas:

> The rural areas between the urban focal points (where there are relatively large Muslim populations) are generally populated by Serbs.

The Islamic entities strive to create territorial continuity that will provide them with control and freedom of movement. This is to be achieved via terror that will trigger the mass exodus of the Serb population from the relevant cities and regions.[96]

Similar activity is also noted in other areas with Muslim populations, in some areas of the Raska region.

Of all of the places mentioned above, Novi Pazar is the most important focal point for Islamic activity, which can be compared to Sarajevo in Bosnia or Pristina in Kosovo.

A new Islamic university was opened in the city that is based on the teachings of Wahhabi (radical) Islam and is financed by Saudi Arabia.

Grafitti all over the city testifies to solidarity with the SDA (Izetbegović's Islamic party), although it is a Bosnian party. Many of the city's inhabitants regard themselves as Islamic "Bosniaks" who aspire to be united with their brethren in Bosnia-Herzegovina within a Muslim community (the concept of a greater Albania).

Serb intelligence sources note that in October 2004, two terror cells with fourteen terrorists arrived in Croatia and Bosnia. The mission of the cells' members was to gather intelligence about the U.S. embassies in Sarajevo and Zagreb. These sources believe that the terror cells were dispatched by the Iranian intelligence.[97]

The examples offered above illustrate the ongoing activity of radical Islam in the Balkan arena on two levels: The level of the "Dawa" through educational, information, and humanitarian activity; and the terror level.

The terror infrastrucure and radical Islam in the Balkans pose a threat not only to stability in the Balkans, but constitute a danger of subversion and terror throughout the European continent and beyond it.

## Notes

1. See Section Three for further elaboration on Izetbegović's biography.
2. Ibrahim Al Marashi, "The Arab Bosnians. The Middle East and the security of the Balkans," http//www.rksg.harvard.edu.
3. Ibid.
4. The active European and American intervention began only in 1995 and eventually forced the Serbs to sign the Dayton Accords.
5. Ibrahim Al Marashi, The Arab Bosnians, The Middle East and the Security of the Balkans, http://www.ksg.harvard.edu.
6. Ibid.
7. Ibid.
8. Ibid.
9. Ibid.
10. This section is based on Shaul Shay, The Axis of Evil, Iran, Hizballah and the Palestinian Terror, Transaction Publishers, Rutgers University, State University at New Jersey, 2005, pp. 34-39. See also: Wilfried Buchta, "Who Rules Iran? The Structure of Power in the Islamic Republic," The Washington Institute for Near East Policy, 2002.
11. Edgar O'Balance, Islamic Fundamentalist Terrorism, 1979-1995, New York University Press, 1997, pp. 40-48.
12. Ibid.
13. Iran—A country study, Library of Congress, Federal Research Division, U.S., 1996.
14. James Bruce, "Iran's Cover Acts Proving Intolerance," Jane's Intelligence Review, August 1996. See also: Wilfried Buchta, "Who Rules Iran? The Structure of Power in the Islamic Republic," The Washington Institute for Near East Policy, 2002.
15. Ibid.
16. Ma'ariv, Tel Aviv, June 28, 1996.
17. Der Spiegel, April 9, 1997.
18. Ma'ariv, Tel Aviv, June 28, 1996.
19. Islamic Fundamentalists' Global Network-Modus Operandi—Bosnia Model, Documentation Center of the Republic of SRPSKA, Banja Luka, September 2002, p. 53.
20. Ibid.
21. "Teherann appointed ambassador to Bosnia," Teheran Islamic Republic News Agency, May 3, 1994.
22. Congressional press release, Republican Party Committee (RPC), U.S. Congress, Clinton-Approved Iranian Arms Transfers Help Turn Bosnia into Militant Islamic Base, January 16, 1997, available on the website of the Center of Reasearch on Globalization (CRG) at http://globalresearch.ca/articles/DCH109A.html. The original document is on the website of the U.S. Senate Republican Party Committee (Senator Larry Craig), at http://www.senate.gov/=rpc/releases/1997/iran.htm).
23. Ibid.
24. Peter Waldman, "Muslim Nations' Support for Bosnia Rises," *Wall Street Journal*, Aug. 11, 1995.
25. "Western Anxiety over the Presence of Islamic Forces in Bosnia," Echo of Islam, Teheran, Jan., 1995.
26. Documentation Center of Republic of SRPSKA, Banja Luka, September 2002, p. 54.
27. Kenneth Katzman, Julie Kim and Richard Best, "Bosnia-Herzegovina Support from Islamic Countries," CRS Report Congress.

28. Reuters, Feb. 22, 1996.
29. Documentation Center of Republic of SRPSKA, Banja Luka, September 2002, p.68.
30. Ibid, p.68.
31. This chapter is based on a report of the U.S. Senate investigative committee in this matter.
32. Cigar, Norman and Patrick Clawson, "The Arab World, Iran and the Kosovo Crisis," Special Policy Forum Report, Policywatch 391, The Washington Institute for Near East Policy, May 25, 1999.
33. Teheran Times, June 19, 1998.
34. Subsequently, Fadl collaborated with the United States and testified against Al Qaida activists that were arrested and brought to trial.
35. Bozinovich M., Bosnia and the Islamic Jihad in Europe, Serbian-com.html
36. Ibid.
37. IFOR—The international force stationed in Kosovo.
38. Yosef Bodansky, Bin Laden, the Man Who Declared War on America, Forum, Rosville Prima Publishing, California, 1999, pp. 155-156.
39. Ibid.
40. Ibid.
41. Mohammad's brother is Bin Laden's deputy Ayman al Zawaheiri.
42. ISSA Special Reports, Balkan Strategic Studies, "Interview highlights changing situation in Bosnia-Herzegovina and territorial escalation," October 7, 2003.
43. "Dar Al-Harb"—territory under the control of the infidels.
44. "Dar Al-Islam" —Islamic territory.
45. "Al Qaida terrorist related to the Bosnian government arrested in Italy," AP, October 1, 2002.
46. Testimony of the FBI director before a U.S. Congress investigative inquiry.
47. John Crewdson, "Suspect offers might on Al Aqaida finances, charged in Spain with 9/11 link, man is free in Germany," *Chicago Tribune*, October 5, 2003.
48. Ibid.
49. Ibid. See also: Defense and Foreign affairs Daily, September 17, 2003.
50. John Crewdson, "Suspect offers might on Al Aqaida finances, charged in Spain with 9/11 link, man is free in Germany," *Chicago Tribune*, October 5, 2003.
51. Ibid.
52. Yoram Schweitzer and Shaul Shay, "The Globalization of Terror," The Challenge of Al Qaida and the Response of the International Community, Transaction Publishers, Rutgers University, State University of New Jersey, 2003.
53. Yona Alexander and Michael S. Swetnam, Osama Bin Laden's Al Qaida: Profile of a Terrorist Network, Transnational Publishers, New York, 2001.
54. Mike Carter, "Feds Link Resam to Terror Camps," *Seattle Times*, March 9, 2001.
55. Yoram Schweitzer and Shaul Shay, "The Globalization of Terror," The Challenge of Al Qaida and the Response of the International Community, Transaction Publishers, Rutgers University, State University of New Jersey, 2003.
56. "Bin Laden's connections with the Balkans," the Balkans Peace Center, quoting the New York Times, February 6, 2000.
57. Darko Trifunovic, "Bosnia in network of Al Qaida terrorists," University of Belgrade, Faculty of Civil Defense, 2005. See also: *Los Angeles Times*, October 7, 2001.
58. AP Tokyo, "Terror suspect raises questions in Japan," May 21, 2004.
59. Kyoto News Service, May 18, 2004.
60. This chapter is based on the *Daily Telegraph*, Internet, September 23 2001, and *Time*, October 12, 2001.

61. "Bosnia suspects headed for Cuba," BBC News Europe. January 18, 2002.
62. Yoram Schweitzer and Shaul Shay, "The Globalization of Terror," Transaction Publishers, New Brunswick, NJ., 2003.
63. Al Jazeera, March 9, 2000.
64. BBC Monitoring, October 26, 2004.
65. Filr://websting links Hamza to terror camps, htm.
66. Ibid.
67. Daniel Simpson, "British Muslim Radicals Urge Islamic Fightback," Reuters, London, March 7, 1999.
68. Yoram Schweitzer, "The Case of the Shoe Bomber," January 4, 2002, www.ict.org.il .
69. The Guardian, "Former grammar student gets 13 years for shoe bomb plot," April 13, 2005.
70. Ibid.
71. Ibid.
72. The Center of Peace in the Balkans, Toronto, Canada, Analysis, July, 2003.
73. Ibid.
74. Raman, B., "The Blowback Continues," Muslim World Today, July 22, 2005.
75. Ibid.
76. Ibid.
77. "Bin Laden's connections with the Balkan," the Balkans Peace Center, www.balkanpeace.prg, September, 2001.
78. Ibid
79. "An Al Qaida terrorist related to Bosnian government arrested in Italy," AP, October 1, 2002.
80. Ibid.
81. An Algerian Islamic terror organization that sometimes cooperates with Al Qaida.
82. Ha'aretz, Tel Aviv, September 21, 2001
83. Al Hayat, Internet, April 28 2002.
84. Sofia News Agency, May 10, 2004.
85. MCG Moroccan Islamic Group.
86. Defense and Foreign Affairs Special Analysis, June 21, 2005.
87. *Morocco Times*, June 2, 2005.
88. http://www.Freesrpsk.org.
89. The Albanian National Army—A terror orgnization connected to the KLA in Kosovo
90. Yosef Bodansky, "Osama Bin Laden on the Balkans for the new wave of anti-Western terrorrism," ISSA, special report, Balkan Strategic Studies, August 29, 2003.
91. Ibid.
92. Ibid.
93. Al Muhajiroun, London, August, 2003.
94. BBC Monitoring, December 16 2004, Text report by Bosnian Serb news agency, SRNA.
95. Defense and Foreign Affairs Daily, Volume XXIII, No 33, March 5, 2005.
96. ISSA, Special Reports, Balkan Strategic Studies, "Strong Warning Indicators for New Surge in European Islamist Terrorism," October 15, 2003.
97. GIS, Islamic teams enter Bosnia and Croatia, targeting US embassies, October 14, 2002.

# Section Eight

## An Analysis of Theoretical Models and Summary

# Bin Laden's Islamic Terror as an Expression of the Confrontation Between Cultures

## Preface

The end of the twentieth century and the dawning of the twenty-first century are characterized by "the conflict between cultures," as defined by Professor Samuel Huntington, one of the fathers of this concept. He argues that the source of conflict in the world is first and foremost "cultural."

The conflict between cultures can be perceived and examined from a different angle, which classifies cultures into two main categories: The state-oriented, institutional, and territorial culture and philosophy; as compared to the nomadic culture and philosophy.

The philosophers Deleuze and Guattari also dwelled on the various aspects of the conflict between cultures. This section will focus on the way they discussed concepts such as "the conflict," "the war," and the "war machine" as expressed in the conflict between the nomadic culture and the state-oriented culture.

The global Jihad and Islamic terror, as reflected in the war in the Balkans, illustrate the conflict between cultures on two levels:

- The confrontation between the nomadic culture and the territorial, state-oriented culture.
- The confrontation between the Islamic culture and rival cultures—initially the Slavic culture and, subsequently, the Western culture.

## The Confrontation between Radical Islam and Western Culture

Professor Huntington states that the source of conflict in the world at the end of the twentieth century and at the onset of the twenty-first century is not rooted in ideological or economic reasons, but primarily in cultural ones.

If until the end of the "Cold War" the modern world was dominated by Western culture and most of the significant conflicts took place within the framework of this culture, or to quote his term of reference, "Western civil wars,"[1] at the end of this era the international political system was released from the framework of Western cultural dominance, and the center of gravity shifted to the reciprocal connections and conflicts between the West and non-Western cultures, and among the non-Western cultures themselves.

Nations and countries belonging to the non-Western civilization became active and dominant partners in the impetus and development of history. The classification of the political systems, and of the technological and economical development of the various countries according to categories (developed and underdeveloped countries, first-, second- and third-world countries, etc.), no longer applies, and the countries must be classified in terms of cultures or civilizations.

His definition of civilization is as follows:[2] "A civilization is the highest cultural grouping of people, and the broadest level of cultural identity people have short of that which distinguishes humans from others." Civilization is defined with objective components such as language, history, religion, customs, and institutions; and also via subjective components such as self-definition or the solidarity of the individual and a group. Thus, it is possible to say that the civilization with which an individual identifies is the one that, to him, constitutes the deepest and broadest level of solidarity. Huntington counts eight main cultures in the modern world—Western, Slavic, Chinese-Confucian, Japanese, Hindu, Latino-American, Islamic, and African—and states that the Islamic civilization is the most militant. The latter is embroiled in perpetual inherent conflict with Western culture and others.

A quick glance at the map of world conflicts supplies convincing support for Huntington's arguments: From Africa in the West to the Pacific Ocean Islands, Islam is involved in fault line wars or friction with other civilizations.

## The Wars in the Balkans as an Expression of the Conflict between Civilizations According to Huntington[3]

According to Huntington, at the end of the Cold War, and following the collapse of the Soviet Union, Yugoslavia crumbled as well, and the old order in the Balkans, which was based on ideological solidarity (Greece and Turkey were part of NATO, Bulgaria and Romania were affiliated with the Warsaw Alliance, Yugoslavia was non-aligned, while Albania was isolated and sometimes aligned itself with communist China), evolved into an order that corresponded to the roots of civilization—Islam and Christianity.

The Balkans became an arena of violent clashes between rival ethnic groups, or according to Huntington's terminology—a confontation arena between civilizations: Russia supported the Orthodox Slav Serbia, Germany sided with Catholic Croatia, and the Muslim countries aided the Muslims in Bosnia. The Serbs fought the Croatians, the Bosnian Muslims, and the Albanian Muslims, and the Balkan countries split up according to a religious and cultural partition: Catholic Slovania and Croatia; the partially Muslim Bosnia-Herzegovina; and the Orthodox Serbia, Montenegro, and Macedonia. Subsequently, there were secondary-level splits: Bosnia-Herzegovina split up during the war to three separate identities: Serbs, Muslims, and Croatians, and in Croatia the Serbs and Croatians fought each other.

Huntington defines the wars in the Balkans as fault line wars and points out their characteristics: The conflicts are of lengthy duration and are not given to resolution via negotiations and compromise; when agreements are reached they do not endure; the conflict is an "alternate war" igniting and subsiding by turns, and the identity conflagration and ethnic hatred are extinguished only rarely, unless genocide occurs; there are a large number of casualties and refugees (50,000 in Croatia, 50 to 200,000 in Bosnia); a high level of violence; the ideological beliefs of the rival parties are of marginal importance. Fault line wars, like other ethnic clashes, are characterized by the decisive importance attributed to the religious component. According to Huntington, as religion is the main defining characteristic of civilizations, fault line wars almost always occur between nations with different religions. Huntington views the demographic change that took place in Kosovo as the main reason for the outbreak of conflicts in the Balkans. The percentage of Albanian Muslims within Kosovo's population grew from 67 percent in 1961 to 90 percent in 1991. That year only 10 percent of its population was made up of Serbs who continued to view it as their "promised land" or "Jerusalem."

The Serb fears and Serb nationalism that awakened due to the growth in the number and strength of the Albanians increased even more as a result of demographic changes in Bosnia where the Muslim population grew between 1961-1991, thus becoming the majority.

Huntington states that the changes in the demographic balance were coupled with another factor—politics. After the collapse of the communist regime in Yugoslavia, its residents needed to define their new identity. In elections, which were held according to the old division into republics, the candidates placed emphasis on ethnic nationalism and attempted to promote the independence of their republics. This method proved to be effective and the distribution of the votes faithfully reflected the percentages of Muslims, Serbs, and Croatians in the population—each group voted for the party that raised the issue of nationalism on its banner and vowed to protect the national entity against other ethnic groups. Thus, due to considerations related to electoral rivalry, the country was drawn into a vortex of nationalist propaganda and fault line conflicts intensified to the level of fault line wars.

Huntington argues that the former Yugoslavia was the site of the most complex, confusing, and extreme system of fault line wars during the early-1990s. The conflict in Bosnia was unquestionably a war of civilizations. The three parties to that war came from different civilizations and adhered to different religions. Aside from one partial case, the participation of players on the second and third levels perfectly matched the model of the civilizations.

On the first level in Croatia, the Croatian government and the Croatians fought the Croatian Serbs, and in Bosnia-Herzegovina the Bosnian government fought the Bosnian Serbs who also fought each other.

On the second level, the Serb government acted to achieve a "greater Serbia" by aiding the Croatian and Bosnian Serbs, and the Croatian government aspired to achieve a "greater Croatia" by assisting the Bosnian Croatians.

On the third level there was a massive closing of ranks of civilizations behind the fighting forces: Germany, Austria, the Vatican, and other European Catholic groups, as well as the the U.S., emerged in Croatia's favor; Russia, Greece, and other Orthodox countries and groups closed ranks behind the Serbs; Iran, Saudi Arabia, Turkey, Libya, the "Islamic Internationale," and the Islamic countries in general backed the Bosnian Muslims.

The support of second and third parties was essential for the progression of the war, and the restrictions that they imposed were a crucial factor that brought about its end. The Croatian and Serb governments provided weapons, supplies, financing, refuge, and even military forces for their brethren who were fighting in the other republics. The Serbs, Croatians, and Muslims received considerable aid in the form of funding, weapons, supplies, volunteers, military training, and diplomatic support from their compatriots located outside of the former Yugoslvia.

The only exception to this uniform pattern of "a relation supports a relation," which acted in contrast to civilization links, was the United States which also supported the Bosnian Muslims.

Huntington poses the question as to why the United States was the only country that in the course of the war and in its aftermath chose to break away from the civilization mold in order to promote the interests of the Muslim Bosnians. He offers several explanations: It is possible that well thought out civilization power games were at play, through which the United States strived to mitigate the influence of radical Islamic states. Another possibility is that it gave in to the pressures of its Islamic allies—Turkey and Saudi Arabia—with the aim of preserving cordial relations with them. And finally, there is also the possibility that the United States's support was fed by its fundamental inclination, which was reinforced by media reports, to support what was conceived as the helpless underdog.

*The Support of the Muslim World for the Muslims in Bosnia.*[4] According to Huntington, the most massive and influential closing of ranks of any civilization was that of the Muslim world for the Bosnian Muslims. The Bosnian issue aroused widespread sympathy in the Muslim countries, and the aid poured in from various sources both public and private. Muslim regimes, the most prominent of which were Iran and Saudi Arabia, competed with each other in providing aid and in aspiring to wield consequent influence. Muslim societies, Sunni and Shiite, fundamentalist and secular, Arab and non-Arab, from Morocco to Malaysia, all rose to the call.

This closing of ranks had a great impact on the course of the war: It was essential to the survival of the Bosnian state and to its success in regaining territory after the Serbs' initial staggering triumphs. It also accelerated the Islamization of Bosnian society and the solidarity of the Muslim Bosnians with the world Islamic community, as well as serving as an impetus for the United States to express sympathy for the Bosnian needs.

Initially it was Iran that in 1992 declared itself leader of the camp supporting the Bosnian Muslims, describing the war as a religious conflict with the Christian Serbs who were intent on genocide. At Iran's urging, the "Islamic Conference" entered into the thick of things and established a group that lobbied the Bosnian issue at the UN. In June 1993, in the wake of intensive activity, they succeeded in obtaining the approval of the UN Committee for Human Rights vis-à-vis a resolution condemning the Serb and Croatian aggression. In August 1993, a delegation of the "Islamic Conference," led by the Turkish Foreign Minister, met with Warren Christopher and Boutros Boutros Ghali with the aim of convincing them to support immediate NATO air attacks which would protect the Bosnians against Serb attacks. The West's failure to protect the "safe areas" against Serb attacks in the summer of 1995 caused Turkey to approve military aid for Bosnia and train Bosnian soldiers, Malaysia to undertake the sale of weapons to Bosnia while violating the weapons embargo imposed by the UN, and the United Emirates to agree to finance military and humanitarian expenses in Bosnia.

The most crucial assistance that the Muslim world granted to the Bosnian Muslims was undoubtedly the military aid—weapons, money for purchasing weapons, military training, and volunteers. Immediately upon the outbreak of the war, the Bosnian government invited the Mujahidin that, as stated, included units of the Iranian Revolutionary Guards and many Islamic volunteers who had fought in Afghanistan. In autumn of that year, the Bosnian government used the Mujahidin in units fighting against the Serb forces, but these units often harassed the local population and caused the government other problems. The Dayton Accords had stipulated that all foreign fighters must leave Bosnia, but the Bosnian government offered citizenship to some of the fighters and enabled them to stay.

The rich countries of the "Muslim nation," led by Saudi Arabia and Iran, donated large sums of money for the development of the Bosnian military power. In all, between the years 1992-1995, the Saudi regime and private Saudi sources transferred over $1 billion in the form of aid for the Bosnians, half of which was for the purpose of purchasing weapons, and the rest ostensibly as humanitarian aid. Iran was also a central source of military aid, and American officials claim that it spent hundreds of millions of dollars annually on weapons for the Bosnians. The money, personnel, training, and weapons which poured in from Muslim countries enabled the Bosnians to tip the balance of military strength and turn what was considered an "army of riffraff" into a well-equipped, trained military force which emerged victorious in the battlefield and returned to Bosnia extensive areas that had been invaded by the Serbs, who were suffering due to the embargo.

It would appear that history attests to the truth of Huntington's arguments, as in 1999 a new war broke out in the Balkans, this time in Kosovo. The West once again sided with the Muslims, and following a massive air attack, Yugoslavia was forced to accept an autonomous entity in Kosovo under the auspices of the multinational force which ensured that the agreement was honored by the rival parties. Another violent clash took place in 2001 in Macedonia between separatist Muslims and the government.

It would appear that the struggles between civilizations in the Balkans are far from over and the tense calm is being preserved only thanks to the presence of the multinational force which, to date, has experienced partial success in preventing the next outburst.

## Reservations Regarding Huntington's Theory

Despite the corroboration which political reality seemingly grants to Huntington's overall theory, it behooves us to criticize his arguments and express our reservations vis-à-vis some of them. Huntington presents a sweeping approach that places all of the Muslim states in one Islamic cultural group, which is confronting Western culture as well as others.

A close scrutiny of the regimes in most Muslim countries indicates that the majority of them are secular regimes or governments with a pragmatic and moderate Islamic orientation which are not involved in any conflict with Western culture, in fact quite the contrary. They have adopted the "bandwagon" approach and joined the "modernization convoy," along with Western technology, values, and lifestyles. Not only have they adopted the patterns of Western culture, but they also rely on Western military, political, and economic aid in order to survive.

Huntington attempted to resolve the contradiction between the concept of the war between civilizations and U.S. support for the Muslims during the war in Bosnia, but his explanations are inadequate due to the fact that this U.S. policy repeated itself with even greater intensity in 1999 during the war in Kosovo.

Huntington does not distinguish between this mainstream in the Muslim world, and fundamentalist Islamic streams which have indeed raised the banner of the struggle against Western culture, but which still constitute a militant minority within the Muslim world.

The Muslim world is therefore embroiled in a profound and sharp cultural conflict regarding the character and course to be taken by Muslim society. The consequences of the internal conflict currently dictate the nature of the ties between the Islamic culture and Western and other cultures, and will continue to do so in the future.

To a great extent this phenomenon is also true of the Muslims in the Balkans. Albania, Bosnia-Herzegovina, and Kosovo exist as political or quasi-political entities mainly due to the international forces stationed in the Balkans, and enjoy technological and economic aid provided by the United States and the West. In exchange, they are required to cooperate in the battle against Islamic terror infrastructures that have planted roots in their countries. In this regard there is marked duality in these countries' approaches because they are "torn" between their interest to cooperate with the U.S. and the West on the one hand, and their "moral duty" and solidarity with the Mujahidin that assisted them in the war against the Serbs and currently use their territory for terror purposes on the other.

Islamic fundamentalism makes use of a diversified range of means and tools in order to achieve its goals, starting from education, information, economic aid, and spiritual welfare, to political subversion and culminating in terror and war. An analysis of the conflict focal points indicates that their efforts are primarily focused on changing the political reality inside the Muslim world, and to a lesser extent to bring about change in other cultures as well. The new geopolitical reality in the post-Cold War era is perceived by radical Islamic circles as a reflection of their success, and it places Islam at the forefront of the conflict against its adversaries which are led by the Western culture in general, and the United States—the only remaining superpower—in particular.

In the Balkan arena, Islamic terror organizations rose to the aid of their Muslim brethren, who they believed were in danger of extinction. The mobilization of the entire Muslim world, and particularly the Islamic terror organizations, created an "ad hoc" alliance between adversaries such as Al Qaida and the Saudi regime, and both joined the aid efforts on behalf of the Muslims in Bosnia. Other adversaries—Saudi Arabia and Iran—found themselves cooperating in efforts to aid the Muslims in the Balkans.

The Muslim involvement in the Balkan issue would ostensibly seem to validate Huntington's approach regarding Islam, but the significant change that took place after the end of the fighting in Bosnia makes it difficult to accept his position. After the joint interest had disappeared, the threats and conflicts of interest returned, as demonstrated in Bosnia. After the end of the war, the Muslim regime, headed by Izetbegovic, cooperated with the Mujahidin that fought on its side and granted them Bosnian citizenship. This is what enabled their legal stay in the Balkans. But the terror infrastructures that were established during and after the war years, and which became active in various focal points in Europe, the United States, and Caucasia, evoked a wave of unequivocal demands that Bosnia-Herzegovina and Albania take action against the terror infrastructures. These demands became even more vehement after the September 11 attacks as part of the global war on terror declared by the United States. At this stage, international reality forced the governments of Albania and Bosnia-Herzegovina to choose which side they were on, and they chose the American side. Indeed, the United States and the NATO forces acted in these countries and took steps against organizations and activists suspected of involvement in terror.

It currently appears that the scope of cooperation given by these governments is limited and is largely affected by the contradicting pressures being imposed by Islamic circles and pressure groups on the one hand, and the United States and the West on the other.

## The Conflict between the State-Oriented Concept and the Nomadic Concept

The roots of the confrontation between the nomad and the farmer go back to the Genesis conflict between Cain and Abel. The expulsion from the Garden of Eden transported mankind from a situation of plenty to a reality of meagerness, competition, and force, necessitating him to fight a daily battle for survival. The dramatic confrontation between Cain and Abel is described in the book of Genesis, chapter 4, and culminates in Abel's murder and Cain's sentence; to be a nomad, "thou shalt move and roam in the land," (Genesis, chapter 4, verse 12). This is the first testimony regarding the phenomenon of the nomad and the first mythological explanation for the inherent conflict between the nomad and the permanent inhabitant, between the nomad culture and the territorial, state-oriented culture. Jacque Derrida, Gilles Deleuze, and Felix Guattari regard nomadism as a philosophical concept that, according to their definition, is in perpetual conflict with the state-oriented and tyrannical philosophy.[5] Nomadic society and the nomadic war machine are in constant motion from the conceptual point of view, even if this does not always involve actual physical movement, while the state-oriented philosophy imposes "tyranny" in terms of organization, space, and time. The state-oriented philosophical issue always relates to law, institutions, and contracts that combine to embody the sovereign character of the state that, as previously noted, is regarded by nomadism as tyrannical.[6] To quote Deleuze, even in the Greek city-state (which is perceived as the pinnacle of democracy) there was a philosophical issue regarding tyranny or conceptual force, or at the very least, existence in the shadow of this tyranny.

Nietzsche was one of the first philosophers to raise this complex issue for discussion. He states that philosophical concept and thought must, by nature, be nomadic and free of the restraints of bureaucratic and procedural conception. Therefore, Deleuze argues, Nietzsche turned the thought into a war machine and a battering ram, which reflect a counter philosophy that constantly challenges the state-oriented philosophy.[7]

Deleuze and Guattari point out several essential differences between the state-oriented and nomadic approaches:[8]

- The state-oriented approach, which is founded on the definition of the state's sovereignty, is constructed in the form of a vertical hierarchy. The philosophical and constructive logic are arranged layer upon layer. Thus, by its very nature, the vertical structure creates a dictatorial pattern, since without the enforcement of conceptual and structural order, the vertical structure will collapse. The nomadic approach does not accept the vertical structure and logic. The nomadic system is a horizontal system; on the philosophical and structural level there is no clear hierarchy, and the structural links are amorphous and less structured.
- The concept of territory, permanence, and the connection with location constitute the basic foundations of the state entity, which defines itself through the delineation of boundaries. Boundaries represent a basis not only for the physical definition of the state entity, but also address the conceptual dimensions of this entity. Nomadism signifies conceptual and physical de-territorization, which expresses itself in constant movement while negating the notions of boundaries and state.
- The state does its best to settle its components, and to establish and patrol their movement and organization. The nomadic concept interprets this attempt in terms of compulsion and tyranny on the part of the state entity, and expresses the essence of its existence by opposing any attempt to settle or regulate it.
- The concept of time is perceived differently in the state-oriented entity than in the nomadic culture. While in the state-oriented culture the concept of time is also bound by the entity's conceptual boundaries, constituting part of its definition, the nomadic culture is in constant flow from the aspects of both space and time. In the nomadic perception the concept of time does not serve to set restraints but rather constitutes a reference and direction point in the course of history.

Nevertheless, Deleuze and Guattari point out that there is no "quintessential nomadism," and a paradox exists in the very fact that nomadism defines itself as different than the state entity. Moreover, there is the danger that if the nomadic perception emerges victorious, then it will also turn into a state entity.

In the following sentence Deleuze and Guattari encapsulate the nature of the difference between the state and nomadic entities:[9] "As a non-disciplinary force, the nomadic war machine names an anarchic presence on the far horizon of the state's field of order."

Deleuze and Guattari indicate two types of war: The first is the "real war" and the second is "the pure idea of war."[10] They perceive the pure concept of war as "a war machine that does not regard war as its goal and which maintains a potential or supplementary link with the war."[11] The inherent logic of war contradicts the very existence of the state-oriented entity and constitutes a form of antagonism directed at all forms of sovereignty. The nomadic movement is fed by a fundamental antagonism that opposes any form and regulated stream of normalization and order, much like the calm and regular flow of water in a river as opposed to the turbulent churning of water in whirlpools, which creates a swirling disorder.

*Al Qaida Organization and Bin Laden as a Reflection of the Nomadic Concept.*[12] Osama Bin Laden moved from Saudi Arabia to Pakistan and from there to the Afghan front. In the city of Peshawar in Pakistan, Bin Laden established an organization that dealt with the recruitment, absorption, and training of Muslim fighters from all over the world who volunteered to participate in the Jihad against the Soviet Union in Afghanistan. Already at the beginning of his career, Osama Bin Laden adopted radical Islamic views that state that Islam is involved in an existential struggle against the more powerful forces of the superpowers as well as against secular and corrupt Arab regimes acting according to the interests of their powerful patrons.

According to Bin Laden's tenets, radical Islam is involved in a struggle to banish the corrupt leaders from the Muslim world and found a utopian community of Islamic believers—the "Uma." Bin Laden claims that Islam has no boundaries and that the Muslim national states are the artificial creations of colonialism and imperialism, whose goal was to cause a fake separation within the Muslim world, thus perpetuating the control and involvement of the Western powers. Therefore, radical Islam represents a nomadic concept that negates the state-oriented entity and regards it as an expression of the physical and conceptual tyranny of the Western culture.

Bin Laden adopted the slogan, "not east, not west," which is accepted by those faithful to radical Islam: In 1979, he first focused his struggle upon the Soviet Union, and accepted aid from the U.S., Saudi Arabia, and other "corrupt" Arab regimes to achieve his objective, but even then he never concealed his stand that after victory in this struggle, the West's turn would come.

The war in Afghanistan saliently reflects the conflict between the state-oriented concept and its "war machine" and the nomadic concept of the latter. The Soviet Union and the Communist regime in Kabul reflected the vertical, hierarchial state-oriented concept, both on the philosophical and conceptual level as well as on the practical level. In contrast, the Afghan Mujahidin, who were assisted by the "internacionale" of volunteers from all over the Muslim world, like Bin Laden, saliently reflected the concept of the nomadic "war machine." This machine is structured horizontally and is composed of scores of organizations and groups lacking a regulated or permanent structure as well as defined procedures of cooperation, whose only loose link was the joint goal—defeat of the communist regime and banishment of the Soviet Union's forces from Afghanistan.

The nomadic "war machine" of the Mujahidin is in perpetual movement on various levels:

- Operating a chaotic campaign without a clear delineation of boundaries: Outside of Afghanistan, within Afghanistan in the areas outside of Soviet control, inside Afghanistan behind the Soviet lines, and even inside the government centers in Kabul and other cities. The operation of this type of chaotic campaign is meant to undermine the operative, structured and institutionalized rationale of the state-oriented order.
- A perpetual motion and flow of concepts and ideas all designated to jointly undermine the hierarchial, state-oriented ideology and doctrines prevalent in Kabul, while simultaneously creating new subversive concepts (mostly Islamic) that are free of the state-oriented conceptual tyranny.

The war machine of the Mujahidin undermined the physical and conceptual boundaries of the Afghan state, generated ideas and concepts that were free of the state-oriented, tyrannical rationale, fought a chaotic campaign that neutralized the advantages of the state-oriented superpower, and gave the nomadic machine superiority. And indeed, in 1989 the nomadic "war machine" defeated the Soviet Union, which pulled its forces out of Afghanistan, and three years later the communist regime fell in Kabul leaving control in the hands of the Mujahidin. At the end of the war in Afghanistan, Bin Laden decided to continue the Jihad against the enemies of Islam and named the United States its main target in the campaign.

Deleuze and Guattari foretold the inherent paradox when a nomadic system turns into a state-oriented one. The Afghan case constitutes an interesting example of the opposite phenomenon: Even after their victory over the communist regime and the Soviet Union, the Mujahidin movements continued their nomadic modus operandi. Thus, in the years 1992-1996, Afghanistan remained in a chaotic state, and the attempt to found a vertical, hierarchial system that would result in a state-oriented government failed. In actual fact, Afghanistan was "controlled" by a nomadic "war machine" that perpetuated itself via a complex system of warlords that fought each other, thus preserving the chaotic and non-institutionalized reality that characterizes the nomadic system as an non state-oriented system.

The rise to power of the Taliban regime in Afghanistan during the years 1996-2001 wrought only slight change within the system's structure, because the internal power struggles in the arena persevered. Moreover, during these years two parallel systems existed which were constantly at loggerheads with each other: One system, the quasi state-oriented system of the Taliban regime; and a nomadic system that fought it in the form of the coalition of the "northern alliance." For the purpose of our discussion, the importance of the events in Afghanistan after the victory of the nomadic system is secondary.

At the end of the war an even more salient nomadic "war machine" was shaped and created in the form of the Afghan "alumni," whose most prominent representative is Osama Bin Laden. The Afghan "alumni" are not identified with any particular state or movement, but rather express a radical religious-cultural trend that believes in the relentless struggle of Islam against heretic Muslim regimes and adverse cultures.

One can indicate four main channels of activity adopted by the Afghan "alumni:"

1. Incorporation in the activities and leadership of radical Islamic organizations in their native countries (Egypt, the Magreb countries, Jordan, and others);
2. Establishing new terror organizations such as Al Qaida under Bin Laden's leadership;
3. Establishing "independent" terror cells without a defined organizational link or affiliation while sustaining cooperation with other Islamic terror organizations;
4. Joining areas of conflict involving Muslim populations, e.g., the Balkans, Chechnya, Kashmir, Tajikistan, and more.

As stated earlier, Al Qaida and its leader, Osama Bin Laden, are the most prominent examples of the nomadic concept both from the aspect of its physical dimension and its conceptual aspects. Territory is essential for the promotion of his goals but there is no link with any given territory, and this need is functional and temporary. During the years 1992-2001, Bin Laden "wandered" between Afghanistan, Saudi Arabia, Sudan, and Afghanistan until his "disappearance" following the American offensive in Afghanistan since October 2001.

The same train of thought continued in the establishment of Al Qaida, which was designed as an organization without a clear, graded structure. It is composed of cells and groups spread all over the world and sustains conceptual and organizational links with countries that support terror (such as Sudan, Iran, and more), as well as Islamic organizations that hold similar worldviews. Its goal is to fight an uncompromising battle against the United States, the West, and Zionism which are entities that reflect the state-oriented concept. The organization openly declares war on the rival cultures and mainly on Western culture in all areas:

- On the ideological-religious level it calls for the destruction of the Western rival and the establishment of an Islamic culture in its stead; the organization acts according to the nomadic concept at every place and time and creates a "turbulent" reality that undermines the foundations of the state-oriented rationale.
- On the economic level, it exploits the economic establishment of the Western world for its own purposes and acts through it to demolish this infrastructure, based on the understanding that most of the power of the Western culture is drawn from its economy;
- On the military level the nomadic "war machine" confronts the superior power of the West, and challenges the Western state-oriented "war machine" while rendering it vulnerable and irrelevant. The flexibility, agility and independence of the various components of the nomadic "war machine" constitute an acute problem for the state-oriented "war machine" of the West, which functions within the framework of the restrictions and limits that the graded state-oriented order imposes upon itself.

The terror campaign of September 11 serves as the most prominent reflection of both the conflict between the nomadic war machine and the state-oriented war machine, as well as the confrontation between radical Islam and its enemies. The conflict arena in the Balkans is also a clear example of the modi operandi of the traditional nomadic war.

The collapse of Yugoslavia, and the civil war that erupted in Bosnia, created a campaign arena that enabled the nomadic entity of the global Jihad (including all of the Islamic terror organizations that identify with it) to be incorporated within it and contribute to the creation of a chaotic reality that characterizes the modi operandi of the nomadic war machine. The war in Bosnia enabled radical Islamic factors to pour into the Balkans in covert or semi-covert ways and develop "amorphous horizontal" infrastructures of ostensibly organized fighting frameworks in the shape of the Mujahidin brigades and units. At the end of the war, the latter could be dismantled and converted into covert terror infrastructures whose role was to serve the subversive goals of Islamic terror in the Balkans and Europe. Under the leadership of Al Qaida, and thanks to the support of Muslim states such as Iran and Saudi Arabia, the global Jihad created an "alternative system" to the state-oriented framework which crumbled in Bosnia. This contained civilian and humanitarian components as well as military components that were intertwined within an undefined hierarchy through a loose link. This system included a network of charities which met the population's needs in civilian areas on the one hand, but at the same time served as a channel for financing the military infrastructures, importing Jihad fighters, and cover for the establishment of terror infra structures for after the war.

The Dayton Accords, which brought the war in Bosnia to an end, stipulated the removal of the Mujahidin from Bosnia, but in actual fact some of them remained in the Balkans in the framework of the terror infrastructure that had been erected during the war years. Most of the Islamic charities also continued their activities in the Balkans in the framework of the relief and rehabilitation efforts in Bosnia after the war's conclusion and assisted in the perpetuation of nomadic subversive activity initiated by Al Qaida and other Islamic terror organizations.

In Bosnia, much like in Afghanistan, the war's conclusion did not bring about the creation of an effective state-oriented entity, considering that Bosnia was divided into two states—the first Serb, and the second Muslim-Croatian—and, in actuality, there was no fundamental solution that resolved the root of the controversy. A multinational force positioned in the country enforced the ceasefire upon the adversaries. The situation in Bosnia, and the development of additional combat and tension points in the Balkans, Kosovo, and subsequently in Macedonia, too, have left a chaotic regional reality in which the nomadic entity of Islamic terror continues to take root.

The "Afghan model," in which an "ad hoc" alliance was forged between radical Islam and the West with the aim of defeating a common adversary—the Soviet Union—has recurred in the arena of confrontation between Islam and its Slav enemies in the Balkans. In both conflicts in the Balkans—in Bosnia and with even more intensity in Kosovo—radical Islamic factors and Iran (which is defined as a state that supports terror) chose the same side as the United States and the NATO countries.

Much like in Afghanistan, here, too, the Islamic terror entities did not conceal their intention to continue acting against the West at the end of the joint campaign. Moreover, even at the time when the West and radical Islam were taking the side of the Muslims in the Balkans, in other arenas the same radical Islamic organizations took action against American and Western targets (in Somalia, Yemen, Saudi Arabia, Kenya, Tanzania, and more).

The nomadic subversive concept posed complex dilemmas for the state-oriented rationale which required internal and external sources of legitimizaton in order to aptly contend with the complex challenges of the Balkans and global arena. The United States and the West suffered from "political schizophrenia" vis-a-vis the conflicts in the Balkans, and attained only a "partial and temporary settlement" of the clashes while radical Islam succeeded in laying infrastructures in this region that serve its global requirements and enable it to sow the seeds of chaos that continue to threaten stability and prevent the establishment of stable state-oriented entities in this region.

The case of the Balkans proves that radical Islam has apparently succeeded in developing an effective model in which it harnesses the West to realize the objectives of Islam, as reflected in the "Afghan model" and subsequently in the "Balkan model." With regards to the Afghan case, the West did not comprehend the implications of the success of radical Islam and failed to draw the necessary conclusions, forcing it to pay a heavy toll for its errors (the September 11 offensive). These conclusions were not internalized nor were they applied to the Balkans, and now the West faces new and dangerous challenges that constitute a complicated riddle with which it does not know how to contend.

Proof attesting to the challenge that the Free World faces can be seen in the phenomenon of the "Bosnia alumni" or the "Balkans alumni," which supplements the phenomenon of the "Afghan alumni." All of these aspects contribute to the problem of the global Jihad which has been spreading gradually to every part of the world. In the Iraqi Jihad arena one can currently observe both "Afghan alumni" and "Bosnian alumni" who are continuing their battle against Western culture. In the not too distant future, the term "Iraqi alumni" will be coined as well.

## "Failing States" and "Ungovernable Regions" (UGRs) [13]

The terms "failing states" and "ungovernable regions" have become a pressing issue on the agendas of politicians, military personnel, and academia in the West, due the crystallization of the understanding that these states and regions have turned into a significant threat to the security and interests of the West. Two central threats have positioned these phenomena at the center of international interest, international terror, and international crime.

The reality of the twentieth and twenty-first century has taught us that these two non-state-oriented elements have turned the failing states and the UGRs into havens and activity bases from which they can promote their interests in the regional and global spaces.

During the years of the hegemony of the national-countries, states developed political, military, and economic patterns which were relevant and effective for contact between states and state blocs in the international framework. However, the international terror organizations and the criminal organizations posed new challenges to the national-countries and served as a provocation against the main component of the state-oriented entity—the monopoly over the use of force.

International terror and crime act as networks with global dispersion, while the failing states and UGRs constitute the main infrastructural focal points and bases for action. Due to the lack of an effective central government in these places, the organizations' activities are unrestricted, and they also receive support and protection from warlords and local interested parties with whom they form alliances and ties.

International terror and criminal organizations do not view territory as an asset of moral significance, but rather as a basis which may be temporary and can be swapped with other territories according to evolving circumstances. To a large extent it is possible to define these organizations as entities with a "nomadic" character which clearly challenge the state-oriented entity and its values.

The area of the failing state or the UGR serves as a refuge for criminal and terror organizations, however sometimes it also serves as an arena of confrontation and rivalry vis-à-vis "alien" state-oriented entities acting in the same arena or as a base for attacking neighboring countries.

The provision of solutions by Western countries to these challenges necessitates confrontation on two levels—directly confronting the terror or criminal organization, and also confronting the regime or warlords that offer refuge to these entities.

The provision of an adequate response necessitates the handling of both levels simultaneously as well as preparation for confronting the regional and global alignment of these organizations which exceeds the boundaries of the "failing state" or the UGR.

## Failing States

"Failing states" stem from the collapse of the governmental and political structures in a country and the loss of the state's ability to enforce law and order. The process is initiated and accompanied by manifestations of anarchy and forms of violence. The former secretary-general of the UN Boutros Ghali described this phenomenon as follows:[14] "A feature of such conflicts is the collapse of state institutions, especially the police and the judiciary, with resulting paralysis of governance, a breakdown of law and order, and general banditry and chaos. Not only are the functions of the government suspended, but its assets are destroyed or looted and experienced officials are killed or flee the country. This is rarely the case in inter-state wars. It means that international intervention must extend beyond military and humanitarian tasks and must include the reestablishment of effective government."

The state not only lacks an effective government; the situation includes the collapse of the systems that compose the state entity. Therefore, the term "failing states" actually refers to countries that have disintegrated or collapsed. The term "failing state" addresses a relatively wide range of situations and serves as the starting point for various interpretations vis-à-vis the phenomenon (legal, political, sociological, etc.). The main political and judicial aspects characteristic of a "failing state" are:

- The collapse of the government systems, that is, disintegration of the central government and internal conflicts within its territory. The main processes include disintegration of the central government and the other mechanisms that compose the state institutions (the judicial system, law enforcement authorities, the economic system and more). Disintegration processes take place according to segmentation and cross-sectioning that characterize the society and its political system (interest groups, ethnic and religious groups, etc.), that generate internal conflicts within the country's territorial boundaries;
- The collapse of lawful government, meaning not only disintegration processes, but also disobeying laws and lack of ability to enforce them;
- Loss of the ability to represent the state as a uniform entity within the international system for the purpose of presenting its positions and negotiating with external states and entities.

From the sociological aspect, the "failing state" is characterized by what the sociologist Max Weber calls "loss of the monopoly over power."[15] In this type of reality, the legal system, the police, and other entities that serve the role of maintaining law and order stop functioning or cease to exist. These entities may join various armed groups or criminal elements that take over the state infrastructures and resources for their own needs and establish a "government" of their own within various regions and populations in the state.

This process may be described as a kind of "privatization" of the state, or in certain cases—as criminalization. In this new situation the state ceases to exist and society reverts to a status of pre-state chaos described by Hobbes as "Bellum Omnium Contra Omnes."

Another central sociological characteristic of a "failing state" is the brutality and intensity of violence within the society. Robert J. Bunker believes that historical experience indicates that entities currently defined as criminal and non-legitimate elements, according to our normative standards, may triumph in the struggle with the state entity and form political entities which, in time, will constitute a substitute for today's normative systems and ultimately replace them and gain legitimacy.

As the result of the social and political processes described above, the natures of the confrontations also change. The declared wars between the military forces of the nation state steadily decrease, and we witness the development of new forms of war.

Herfried Munkler[16] argues that in the 1950s and 1960s of the twentieth century many new nations joined the international system that did not succeed in obtaining control when managing war and imposing peace, as European states have achieved since the seventeenth century. Thus, internal conflict (civil wars) became endemic to a series of countries that were established on the ruins of colonial powers, not only in the Third World, but also in Europe itself (the Balkans).

Thus, it is possible to infer that war is no longer waged between countries and armies, but rather through conflicts in which sections of the population defined socially, ethnically, or religiously fight against each other. In this situation partisans or gangs, warlords as well as groups of international mercenaries, are the main players.

The result of this development is the loss of the state's monopoly and a process of "privatization of war." This concept indicates that in the future there will be war between competitive groups on a social and cultural basis, and not necessarily on the basis of state interests. This type of reality currently typifies "failing states," but Bunker points out the inherent threat in the development of violent groups in the United States and the West, such as terror groups or gangs that deal in criminal activity.

Based on the assumption that the future threat against the nation state will stem from the generation of alternative organizations that will undermine the state's monopoly on strength, the latter must formulate organizational frames and operation patterns that will enable adequate defense against internal and external rivals.

From a legal point of view, a failing state is a state that has lost the ability to function as a state entity. A central component of this phenomenon is the lack of a functionary capable of signing agreements with external factors or of actually implementing them.

The scope of failing states is currently relatively low but the numbers are on the rise, and some of the countries that were granted independence after the collapse of the Soviet Union and Yugoslavia are gradually joining this category. There is reason to fear that this is not simply a marginal phenomenon but rather a "pathological" trend of a changing environment and international system.

Robert Bunker points out a cyclical process in human history of order and chaos that alternate with each other. A process of institutionalizing nation states and enhancing law and order in Western states began from the time of the Westphalia peace accords (1648). Bunker claims that the current era is characterized by a change in direction from order to chaos, and we are facing an era that challenges the nation state as a regulator of social order.[17]

Historical experience indicates that when the internal violence in a nation state, which can be described as criminal activity or "a private war," grows to a level that threatens the population of the nation state, this entity may collapse if it does not succeed in suppressing the anarchy.[18] The international reality in the current century points to a decline in the status of the nation state as an entity that regulates and organizes social and political systems in Africa, South America, Asia, as well as areas that were part of the Soviet Union and the Balkans.[19] Bunker maintains that the threat against the nation state will rise from non-state actors:[20] "The challenge to the legitimacy of the nation state will come from armed non-state actors intent on legitimizing forms of behavior that current societies consider to be criminally or morally corrupt."

## Ungovernable Regions—UGR's

The term "ungovernable region" is an amorphous term that generally refers to regions where there is no established government enforcing law and order, and the governmental and administrative structure substantially differs from what is customary in the international system (from the "Western" point of view). In contrast to the term "failing state," which relates to a state entity, the UGR may exist within a state where an effective government prevails in most of its territory, with the exception of a region or regions that are uncontrollable.

Up to the twentieth century these areas, called UGRs, aroused only minimal interest, but in recent years these undeveloped and "remote" areas that are subject to a loose and uneffective central government have come to arouse considerable interest in the West and globally. The dangerous combination of UGRs on the one hand, and the development of the media and modern technologies on the other, have turned these regions into major threats against the West and the international system. They have become a haven for international terror and criminal elements and a source that undermines the stability in the vicinity of their own boundaries and beyond.

These regions can be characterized as follows:

- The lack of a central power capable of enforcing law and order throughout the country or at least in a significant part of its area;
- A backward economic and technological infrastructure;
- Lack of an effective administrative system;
- External warlords acting within the state directly or through internal proxies;[21]
- The internal warlords (proxies) are generally involved in ongoing conflicts;
- There are complex reciprocal links between the exogenic and endogenic powerbrokers, which decrease the possibility of forming an integrative and stable government;[22]
- The state or the UGR itself is involved in conflict with some of the neighboring countries;

The UGR constitutes a confrontation arena for exogenic and endogenic actors. The endogenic actors can be classified in several main categories:

- Violent warlords fighting each other for control of the territory, the population, and the resources;
- Terror organizations exploiting the UGR's area for the construction of an infrastructure and terror activity outside of their territory;
- Criminal organizations that make use of the territory and resources mainly for activity in external markets;
- Ethnic, political, religious, tribal, and other groups struggling for the distribution of the political power and resources in the UGR.

These endogenic actors maintain a reciprocal relationship based on the interests of the various sides, while forming coalitions and alliances that struggle against each other. They also create external threats against both their immediate and distant environments, in the areas of international crime, drugs, and terror.

The director of the CSIS, De Borchgrave states that:[23]

> A wide variety of international threats are now mutating and pose a danger not only to the survival of nations like Afghanistan, Indonesia, the Philippines, and Columbia, but also to the security of American lives and interests. ... The Al Qaida experience in Afghanistan showed the world that the nexus between organized crime, drugs and terrorism can completely undermine a nation and spread tentacles of terror and evil worldwide. ... In the aftermath of 9/11, [the question is] what can and should the U.S. do to save a country caught in the most dangerous nexus.

The terms "failing state" and "ungovernable region" both refer to situations in which the governmental structure ceases to function in the entire state or part of it. However, they are not identical: The term "failing state" usually refers to a complete collapse of the state and its institutions, while the term "ungovernable region" refers to a region within the state territory in which the central government has lost control but no new state substitute has been formed and a chaotic state prevails. Thus, it is possible to state that the UGR constitutes part of the disintegration process of the nation state. There are historical examples of UGRs that did not spread and the parallel existence of the nation state functioning in other areas remained feasible, but in most cases the creation of the UGR constitutes an expression of a disintegration process that causes the ultimate deterioration of the country into the chaotic status of a "failing state."

## The Kosovo Region as an Example of a UGR

In the aftermath of the violent confrontation in Kosovo between the Muslim Albanian majority and the Serbs, a conflict that was tainted by mutual massacres, "ethnic cleansing," and mass expulsion of populations, NATO intervened and forced the Serbs to cease the fighting and pull out of Kosovo. Since 1999, the multinational force (KFOR Kosovo Force) has enforced a tense coexistence between the Muslim and Serb populations in the region. Formally, the region remains part of Serbia, but in actuality a Muslim autonomy has been created in Kosovo in which an independent governmental system exists headed by an elected president which Serbia refuses to recognize.

On both sides of the conflict the reality in Kosovo reflects a shattered economy, unemployment reaching 60 to 70 percent, transportation, educational, and health systems that are only functioning partially, a significant rise in organized crime and the presence of Islamic terror organizations, mainly in the Muslim part of Kosovo.[24] The lack of stability and security in the region prevent the rehabilitation of almost 100,000 refugees who were forced to flee their homes.

The ethnic riots that erupted in March 2004, and which were suppressed with great difficulty by the multinational force after taking a heavy toll on both human life and assets, mainly on the Serb side, serve as a painful reminder of what may happen if the multinational force leaves the region or if it loses its ability to control events.[25]

On July 3, 2005 three explosive devices went off in Pristina, the capital of Kosovo, near the headquarters of the UN delegation. Damage was caused to buildings and vehicles but no one was injured. No party claimed responsibility for the attacks.

These attacks took place the day after the arrival of a Norwegian diplomat who had been dispatched to investigate the possibility of launching talks regarding the future independence of the region.[26]

During the month of August 2005, an assassination attempt against the Muslim president of Kosovo Ibrahim Rugova failed. These attacks must awaken concern regarding the future of the region and illustrate the danger of the collapse of the "temporary quiet" that exists in this fragile and loaded area.

## The Balkans as an Area of "UGRs" and "Failing States"

The disintegration of the Yugoslavian Federation resurfaced internal historical conflicts between peoples and religious, ethnic groups within the Balkans, following their successful suppression under communist rule for forty-six years. States with fairly homogeneous populations and an effective governmental history and tradition, which broke away from the Yugoslavian Federation and declared their independence (such as Slovania and Croatia), succeeded in establishing functional regimes despite Yugoslavian (or more accurately Serbian) attempts to prevent their secession through political and military steps.

In contrast, Yugoslavia's disintegration caused the undermining and collapse of the state mechanism in other sections as well as the establishment of quasi-state entities which in part of the reviewed period (1990-2005) were immersed in the chaotic state of civil war. Even after the battles, the adversaries and international community failed to stablilize the area, and create sovereign and effective state entities, or alternatively restore UGRs to the full control of the functioning states, or create alternative functioning entities. In this category three examples can be presented:

- Bosnia-Herzegovina was embroiled in a civil war for almost four years, which ended due to international intervention. The state was divided into two parts: A Serb state and a Muslim-Croatian state, and the relative stability is being maintained under the auspices of the multinational force there. Three separate armies representing ethnic groups at loggerheads are active in Bosnia. Each national group has separate communication entities and the multiple (national, regional, and local governmental) authorities effectively thwart the possibility of establishing an integrative national entity. Each community views the state's history differently: In the SRPSKA Serb Republic, the residents do not conceal their opposition to the central government's attempts to apprehend the Serb war criminals Ratko Meladich and Radovan Karadzich, who are responsible for the deaths of thousands of Muslim residents and are apparently hiding in the Republic's territory.[27]

- In Kosovo, the attempts of the Albanian-Muslim population to secede from Serbia and establish an autonomy came up against a violent Serb response that was stopped by forceful U.S. and NATO intervention. Since 1999, Kosovo has been under the control of international supervision which maintains the ceasefire there. In actual fact, the political status of Kosovo has not changed, it lacks effective government, and the region's status has not been resolved. Since the offensive launched against Serbia by the international forces in 1999, Kosovo has been recognized as an autonomy. This status has aroused the ire of the Albanian residents in Kosovo due to the fact that they are still recognized as a district of Serbia and are gradually uniting in the name of one central demand—independence. Experts believe that this aspiration is what stood behind the violent riots that erupted in Kosovo in March 2004, when the drowning of three Albanian children sparked attacks against Serb residents.[28] In the aftermath of the attacks, a special UN delegate arrived in Kosovo with the aim of studying the state of mind of the region's residents. A recently submitted report indicates that he reached the conclusion that talks regarding Kosovo's final status cannot be postponed for any length of time, and if the talks do not commence soon additional insurgence by the Albanian residents can be anticipated.
- Albania was under a stringent and strict communist regime until the collapse of the Soviet Union and Yugoslavia. As a result, the communist regime in Albania collapsed as well. The chaotic situation that prevailed in the state was exploited by external parties such as organized crime, Islamic organizations, and sectorial entities in Albanian society. Aside from its internal problems, Albania was also affected by the wars and struggles of the Muslims in Bosnia, Kosovo, and Macedonia, and it took the side of the Muslims both directly and indirectly. Albania continues to exist as a recognized and legitimate state entity but the extent of the regime's effectiveness and its ability to impose its sovereignty and independence on subversive, criminal and terrorist groups are limited.
- Since its secession from the Yugoslavian Federation, Macedonia has functioned as an independent state with a relatively effective government, but its stability is also being challenged by the Muslim Albanian minority, which with external aid from Kosovo (the KLA/KPC) and Albania aspires to achieve autonomy and perhaps even be united with

additional Muslim populations in the Balkans (the concept of "greater Albania").

Due to their inability to achieve their objectives through immediate action, the Muslims are taking gradual steps to drive Serb populations out of areas with a Muslim majority, and to establish "UGR's" bordering on or within areas that are under Serb or Macedonian control. These steps are perpetually eroding the strength and sovereignty of Serbia, Montenegro, and Macedonia. The presence of the mulitnational force in the Balkans effectively restricts the Serbs' ability to respond to the Islamic subversion and largely constitutes an "umbrella" under which the Muslim side can improve and boost its status in the Balkans.

The European Union and the United States aspire to prevent renewed outbreaks of the violent clashes in the Balkans and are avoiding any concrete action that might impede the spreading of Islam. In addition, the steps being taken in the Balkans in the framework of the global war on terror are relativelt limited. It appears that this reality will continue as long as no severe damage is inflicted upon Western interests (such as mega terror attacks) through Balkan sources. A grave development of this kind would force the Western states to take concrete action to restore order in the Balkans and uproot Islamic terror infrastructures in this area.

## Summary

The instability and the chaotic situation that prevailed in the Balkans for many years left their stamp and turned this arena into an optimal operational theater for the Islamic terror organizations and Iran. They view the Balkans as a springboard and a convenient front base for the networking of terror infrastructures on European soil with the aim of exploiting them for the promotion of their activities throughout Europe and at other locations worldwide, including the United States.

While the European Union's interest is to achieve peace and stability in the Balkans, radical Islam, terror organizations, and organized crime all aspire to perpetuate the chaotic situation which gives them ample space and freedom in an area that serves as a springboard to the West.

The "Islamization" processes that the Muslim population underwent in the Balkans during the war years (in Bosnia, Kosovo, and Macedonia), the bitterness against the West that failed to rush to their aid, and the gratitude felt for their "Muslim brethren" who took their side when they were in distress all create a supportive political and social environment for radical Islam. Thus, it would appear that most of the Islamic movements in the Balkans currently strive to establish an independent Islamic state identity, which will be built only after a prolonged and intractable struggle against the Serbs and any other entity (including the West) that constitutes an obstacle.

The Muslim vision in the Balkans fits in well with the global vision of Al Qaida and its affiliates, which aspire to achieve the triumph of Islamic culture over Western culture (and other Islamic foes), and to establish the "Umma"—the community of faithful Muslims which will unite all Muslims and position Islam as the main global force. Until that vision becomes a reality, radical Islam acts as a nomadic subversive entity and the Balkans constitute a crucial arena of activity. The hatred between the Serbs and the Muslims in Kosovo and Bosnia still burns strong and may well lead to renewed conflagaration in the Balkans. Serbia and the Serb minority in Kosovo demand that the current status quo continue, and they are not the only ones who are interested in this balance: The Western countries are well aware that any redefintion of the Balkan boundaries could be the beginning of a slippery and steep decline.

One entity in the Balkans that also aspires to change the existing status quo is located in Bosnia in the SRPSKA Republic or the Serb Republic. The 1995 peace accords regulated the establishment of two state entities in Bosnia-Herzegovina: The Serb Republic and the Muslim-Croatian Federation. These two entities currently subsist alongside each other in a fragile coexistence, and the tension between the Serbs and the Muslims—which were busy conducting massacres against each other only a few years ago—has not abated. The Serb Republic in Bosnia may ignite the next flame in the Balkans: If Kosovo is granted independence, the Serbs in the SRPSKA will demand independence or annexation to Serbia. This possibility of Bosnia's repeated dismantling makes Western leaders shudder—mainly because it might inspire Serbs in other areas of the Balkans to renew their demands to be annexed to Serbia.

Senior entities in the European Union are currently considering a new possibility: If they tempt the Serbs with future membership in the Union, they believe they can neutralize the rising nationalism in the region and replace it with a new force—conomic benefits. Behind this equation lies the hope that future membership in the Union will diminish the hostility, boost sanity and ultimately maneuver the Serb problem by leading all of the states in the region to a Europe without boundaries.

As of the beginning of 2005, it appears that the Balkans are continuing to serve as "a ticking bomb" from two aspects:

- The fear of renewed conflagration in the Balkans between the Islamic entities and their neighbors.
- Escalation of Islamic terror activities based on infrastructures established in the Balkans.

The linking of the Balkans to a "Europe without boundaries" may to a certain extent contribute to the diminishing of internal tensions, but at the same time could also open "Europe's gates" to the Islamic terror infrastructures that took root in the Balkans.

It is clear to the Western countries that as long as the tension between the cultures continues in the Balkans, there will be a constant fear of the renewal of clashes as well as the existence of UGRs and "failing states." The Balkans will continue to serve as a base and bridgehead for the activity of Islamic terror organizations and organized crime. The response to these threats must therefore take the form of an overall response that will deal not only with the symptoms but also approach the roots of the problem. At this time, this type of solution seems very remote.

## Notes

1. Samuel Huntington, The Clash of Civilization and Remaking of World Order, Simon and Schuster, New York, 1996, p. 9.
2. Ibid, p. 23.
3. This section is based on Samuel Huntington's book, The Clash of Civilizations and the Remaking of World Order, Simon and Schuster, New York, 1996.
4. This section is based on Samuel Huntington's book, The Clash of Civilizations and the Remaking of World Order, Simon and Schuster, New York, 1996.
5. John Lechte, Fifty Key Contemporary Thinkers, Routledge, 1994.
6. Gilles Deleuze, "Nomad Thought," in David B. Allison, (ed.) The New Nietzsche, MIT Press, Cambridge, 1998.
7. Ibid, p. 149.
8. Ibid, p. 148.
9. Ibid, p. 148.
10. Ibid, p. 148
11. Ibid, p. 148.
12. This section is based on Shaul Shay's book, The Terror Triangle in the Red Sea—Sudan, Somalia, Yemen, Transaction Publishers, Rutgers University, State University of New Jersey, 2005.
13. Ibid.
14. See the concluding statement delivered by the former UN Secretary-General Boutros Ghali at the UN Congress on Public International Law: Towards the Twenty-first Century: International Law as a Language for International Relations: (13-17 March 1995, New York), Documents, p.9.
15. Max Weber, Staatssoziolgie (ed. Johannes Winchelman), Berlin, 1996, p. 27.
16. Herfried Munkler, The Brutal Logic of Terror:The Privatization of War in Modernity, Constellations, Vol. 9, No. 1, pp. 66-73.
17. Robert S. Bunker, Epochal Change: War over Social and Political Organization, Parameters, Summer 1997, p. 15.

18. Ibid, p. 18.
19. Robert Kaplan, "The Coming Anarchy," *Atlantic Monthly*, February 1994, pp. 44-766.
20. Robert S. Bunker, "Epochal Change: War over Social and Political Organization," Parameters, Summer 1997, p.17.
21. William S. Lind, "Defending Western Culture" Foreign Policy, 84, (Fall 1991), pp. 40-50.
22. Literature refers to the actors' categories: exogenic actors—endogenic actors
23. http://www.csis.org/press
24. Matthew Price, "Kosovo Deep Divide," BBC, Belgrade, October 13, 2003.
25. Thirty people were killed in the riots, mainly Serbs, thirty churches were destroyed and hundreds of houses and vehicles were damaged.
26. Ha'aretz, Tel Aviv, July 4, 2005.
27. Roger Cohen, "The United Nations, the boundaries of the Balkans may need to be redrawn," Ha'aretz, Oct. 17, 2004.
28. Ibid.

# Appendices

## Appendix A: Central milestones in the Balkan Confrontations 1991-1992

| | |
|---|---|
| 15.6.1991 | Croatia declared its independence but postponed its implementation to a later date, and technically Croatia remained part of the Yugoslavian Federation. |
| 10.8.1991 | Realization of the decision to secede from the Yugoslavian Federation and establishment of the independent state of Croatia. |
| 21.8.1991 | The beginning of the war between Serbia and Croatia. |
| 16.12.1991 | The European Union calls upon the republics of the former Yugoslavian Federation—Croatia, Slovania, and Bosnia-Herzegovina—to submit requests for recognition of their independence. A committee appointed by the European Union is to study their requests for recognition by the EU as independent states. (The committee is headed by Robert Bedinter from France). |
| 15.1.1992 | The EU demands that Bosnia-Herzegovina conduct a referendum regarding the issue of independence and secession from the Yugoslavian Federation. |
| 3.1.1992 | A ceasefire between Croatia and Serbia—the Serbs control sections of Croatian territory. |
| 15.1.1992 | The EU recognizes the independence of Slovania and Croatia. |
| 29.2.1992-1.3.1992 | A referendum is conducted in Bosnia-Herzegovina. Two-thirds of the voters support secession from the Yugoslavian Federation and the establishment of an independent state. |
| 6.3.1992 | Bosnia-Herzegovina announces its secession from the Yugoslavian Federation and declares independence. |

| | |
|---|---|
| 4.4.1992 | The beginning of the Serb offensive against Bosnia-Herzegovina. |
| 5-6.4.1992 | The EU recognizes Bosnia-Herzegovina's independence. The beginning of the Serb offensive on Sarajevo. |
| 7.4.1992 | The U.S. recognizes Bosnia-Herzegovina's independence. |
| 22.5.1992 | Slovania and Croatia are accepted as UN members. |

## Appendix B: Main resolutions passed by the UN's Security Council in the matter of the war in Bosnia-Herzegovina (1991-1993)

| | |
|---|---|
| 7.10.1991 | The UN imposes an embargo (resolution no. 713) on the sale of weapons to Yugoslavia, including states that seceded from the Yugoslavian Feeration (Public Notice 1427 – 19.7.1991). |
| 15.12.1991 | UN resolution no. 724, which verifies resolution 713 and calls for its implementation. |
| 8.1.1992 | UN resolution no. 727, which verifies resolution 713 and anchors it in the resolution of the UN secretary-general (S/23363). |
| 21.2.1992 | UN resolution no. 743 clarifies that the embargo does not apply to UN forces acting in Yugoslavia (UNPROFOR). |
| 17.5.1992 | UN resolution no. 752 calls for the withdrawal of the Serb and Croatian forces from Bosnia-Herzegovina territory. |
| 30.5.1992 | UN resolution no. 757, imposing sanctions on Serbia and Montenegro, against the background of the Serb aggression in Bosnia-Herzegovina. |
| 13.8.1992 | UN resolution no. 770 calls for respect for the sovereignty, territorial integrity and the political independence of Bosnia-Herzegovina. |
| 16.11.1992 | UN resolution no. 787, which expresses concern due to the threat against Bosnia-Herzegovina's territorial integrity. |
| 16.4.1993 | UN resolution no. 819, demanding that Serbia refrain from transporting combat means to the Serb militia in Bosnia-Herzegovina. |

A declaration that any invasion of territory by the militia and the expulsion of non-Serb populations (ethnic cleansing) are illegal and unacceptable to the international community. Special emphasis was placed on the activities of the Serbs in the Srebrenica region.

17.4.1993 UN resolution no. 820 repeating the messages in resolutions no. 819, 713, demanding that the embargo on Serbia by neighboring nations be tightened.

4.6.1993 UN resolution no. 836, verifying the territorial sovereignty of Bosnia-Herzegovina and condemning the attacks on the territory of Bosnia-Herzegovina.

20.12.1993 The UN General Assembly expresses concern due to the continuing violence against Bosnia-Herzegovina and the non-implementation of some of the UN resolutions.

The Assembly condemns the Serbs for "ethnic cleansing" being carried out against the Muslim population in Bosnia-Herzegovina.

4.3.1993 UN resolution no. 900, the Security Council reiterates the sovereignty, territorial integrity and political independence of Bosnia-Herzegovina.

## Appendix C:
## The "Mujahid Cassette" about the Mujahidin in Bosnia.

The cassette was made in Bosnia and 2,000 copies were produced in Switzerland. The conversations on the cassette are in Arabic, which attests to the intention of its producers to use it all over the Muslim world and not only in Bosnia where Arabic is not widely spoken. The cassette lauds the bravery of the Mujahidin and their contribution to the war in Bosnia. It documents a meeting between senior Mujahidin, including the Mujahidin commander Abu al Ma'ali (whose face is concealed), the Bosnian commander of the Six Corp of the Muslim Bosnian Army, Sheikh Anwar Shaaban, Sheikh Abd al Rahman, and a colonel from the Muslim Bosnian Army.

In another part of the cassette, Izetbegović, (the president of Muslim Bosnia), who carried the rank of "honorary commander" of the Mujahidin units during the war, is seen surveying a military parade of the Mujahidin.

The cassette features a shocking segment which shows the murder of twelve Serb prisoners—they were decapitated by Mujahidin from the Seventh Muslim Brigade.

## Appendix D

At the end of the war in Bosnia, the Bosnian intelligence agency (AID) helped the Mujahidin that fought alongside the Muslims during the war to remain in the country (in violation of Bosnia's commitment in the Dayton Accords to remove them from Bosnia).

Senior members of the Mujahidin were granted Bosnian citizenship as well as places to live in an area called the "Green Triangle."

Here follow several examples of Islamic terrorists who participated in the civil war in Bosnia and were granted Bosnian citizenship:

- Abu al Ma'ali—former commander of the Mujahidin and a member of the GIA (Group Islamique Armee) in Algeria.
- Hisham Diab—born in Egypt and a member of the New Jihad—this refers to the Egyptian Islamic Jihad under the leadership of Ayman al Zawaheiri, Osama Bin Laden's deputy.
- Abu Hamza Kamel Bin Ali—born on November 16, 1966 in Tunisia and a member of the Jama'a al Islamiyah.
- Suleyman Maherezian—an Algerian called "Abu Jameel" during the civil war in Bosnia, a senior member of the Algerian GIA.
- Fuad Talaat Kassem—a member of the Egyptian Jama'a al Islamiyah. He was arrested in Zagreb in August 1995 and was extradited to Egypt.
- Abdul Hadi al Gahtani—born in Riyadh, Saudi Arabia. He participated in the Jihad in Afghanistan. He subsequently arrived in Bosnia and ran the Agency of the High Committee of Saudi Arabia for Aid to Bosnia and Herzegovina. He was involved in the kidnapping of three English employees of the Overseas Development Agency on January 27, 1994. Gahtani was arrested and sentenced to three years of imprisonment.
- Ahmed Zachariya—a Saudi citizen who was arrested by the Croatian police in February 1996. He was a member of the Organization for Islamic Revolution.

## Appendix E:
## Islamic organizations and groups suspected of links with terror organizatons:

- Elbarad Bosnia (Free Bosnia) – the organization was active in Zenica and included a group of former Mujahidin and radical Bosnian Muslims.
- The Wahhabis – a religious organization established in the Balkans in 1995 which is financed by Saudi Arabia.
- The Red Rose – The group is responsible for several assassination attempts including against Fikret Abdic.
- The Setra organization was linked to several attacks against opponents to the SDA Party.
- The Patriotic League was supposedly a political party at the outbreak of the war. The league's main force lay in several units of Bosnian fighters. In 1991, in cooperation with Croatia, the Patriotic League began arming the Muslims in the Mostar area. At the same time, Muslim fighters were secretly dispatched to Croatia in order to undergo training.
- "From Three to Nine" is a Muslim organization whose name attests to its objective, which is to replace the Christian Trinity with the Nine Holy Signs of Islam.
- The Active Islamic Youth – the Bosnian branch of the organization was run in Zenica. The organization has branches in almost every large town in Bosnia.
- The Muslim Youth Union – the youth movement of the radical "Young Muslims" organization which is connected to the Al-Fatih Mujahidin unit based Sarajevo.
- Hamas Turabe – a radical Muslim organization in Gorazde.
- The Pharaohs – a militia established in September 1996 that acted in cells with three to five members.
- Oric's Militia – which acted under the command of Naser Oric in Tuzla.
- The Black Swans Militia, with 600 members, who served as the bodyguards of senior SDA officials.

## Appendix G:
## A list of terror attacks in Kosovo 1996-1998

This appendix is meant to provide at least a partial picture of the nature and scope of attacks perpetrated by the KLA during the years 1996-1998.

### Attacks in 1996:

1. On April 22, a Serb refugee from Croatia was shot and killed by a masked KLA terrorist at a café. The Serb refugee was the KLA's first victim.

2. On April 22, a student of Albanian origin was killed by a sniper.
3. On June 16, a Serb police patrol was attacked near Poduyevo. One policeman was seriously injured.
4. On June 17, a Serb police patrol was attacked in the town of Siplje at around midnight. One man was killed and another was injured.

   On the same night a bomb was thrown at the Serb police station in Luzani. Automatic weapon fire was opened against policeman who were in the station at the time but no one was hurt.
5. On July 11, terrorists attacked a group of police officers in central Poduyevo at one a.m. One policeman was seriously injured.
6. On August 2, three police stations—in Pristina, Poduyevo, and Krpimej—were attacked by armed groups.
7. On August 28, at 3:00 a.m. three bombs were thrown in the town of Celopek—no one was hurt.

   On the same day an Albanian police detective was shot and killed in the town of Donje Ljupce.
8. On the night of August 31, two bombs were thrown at a Yugoslavian army base in the Vucitrn area.

   That same day an armed group attacked the police station in Rudnik.

   On the same day shots were fired at two police officers at the Pristina-Poduyevo-Kursumli intersection. No one was hurt. In addition, fire was opened from an automatic weapon at the police station in Glogovac.
9. On October 25, two police officers were shot and killed near the town of Surkis.
10. On November 16, a group of terrorists attacked the police station in Rznic at 22:30. No one was hurt.
11. On December 26, a citizen of Albanian origins was shot and killed.

The total number of attacks in 1996 came to between 11-15. (This figure includes several different attacks on the same date).

**Attacks in 1997:**

1. On January 9 at 17:30, a member of the local council was shot and killed in the center of Poduyevo.
2. On January 11 at 19:00, shots were fired (over 26 bullets) in the town of Mijalic in the Watcherin area. No one was hurt.
3. On January 13 at 8:00, a citizen of Albanian origins was murdered after being accused of being a "traitor."
4. On January 16 at 8:00, KLA terrorists attempted to assassinate the Dean of the Pristina University with a remote-controlled explosive charge. The Dean and his driver were seriously injured.
5. A civilian was shot and killed and his son was seriously injured in the town of Reketnica on January 17. They were accused of "pro-Yugoslavian leanings."

6. On February 1, KLA terrorists fired from their vehicle at Serb police officers. The policemen returned fire and killed the three terrorists.
7. On May 5, an explosive device exploded opposite Pristina University. Four people were injured. A 4-kg. explosive device was found near the arena of the first attack and was neutralized by police forces.
8. On March 21 at 20:00, a police officer was shot and seriously injured in the center of Poduyevo due to his "anti-Albanian" leanings.
9. On March 25, near Sicevo, a group of armed men killed two Serb civilians and injured an Albanian national.
10. On April 10, an Albanian national was shot and killed in the town of Banjica near Glogovac.
11. On May 6 at 22:30, an Albanian farmer was shot and killed in the town of Lozica.
12. On May 16, two police officers were shot and seriously injured in Serbica near Kosovoska Mitrovica.
13. On June 19, twelve bullets were fired from an automatic weapon at a police patrol on the Pristina-Poduyevo-Nis road near Donje Ljupce. No one was injured.
14. On July 3, an Albanian farmer who was a member of the Serb Socialist Party was shot and killed during the early morning hours on July 3 in the township of Trstenik.
15. On July 21, the deputy chief prosecutor in Pec was shot and killed.
16. On August 3 at 19:00, gunfire was opened at a police vehicle in the village of Bradis near Poduyevo.
17. On August 4, on the road between Rudnik and Serbica, automatic gunfire was opened at a patrol car. Two police officers were seriously injured and one civilian was slightly hurt.
18. On August 23, an Albanian forester was killed in Serbica.
19. On August 24, a civilian of Albanian descent was killed and his brother was wounded in Zub. That same day fire was opened at the police station in Resnich.
20. On September 2 at 22:55, an Albanian "traitor" was killed at his home.
21. On September 12 at 23:00, twelve police stations were attacked in the areas of Pec, Glogovac, Decani and Djakovica.
22. On September 13 at 22:00, a hand grende was lobbed at the police station in Luzano near Poduyevo.
23. On Septmber 14, a hand grenade was lobbed at a police station in Kijevo near Klina.
24. On September 23 at 11:00, shots were fired at a police patrol in Kijevo. The commander of the regional police was in the vehicle at the time, no one was injured.
25. On October 13, the police station in Calopek near Pec was attacked.
26. On October 16 at 01:30, the police station at Klincina was attacked. One person was killed in the shoot out.
27. On October 17 at 01:00, the Serb community in Babaloc (including 120 families) was attacked. The families had fled Albania several years earlier.

28. On October 20, the KLA announced that it was responsible for the attacks on the police stations in Babaloc, Calopek, and Klincina, as well as the police patrols in Gerlica and Balinac.
29. On November 18 at 19:00, a politician of Albanian descent was seriously wounded in the town of Komoran. His driver was injured as well.
30. On November 25, KLA members laid siege on the police station in Serbica for fifteen hours.

    On the same day at 19:00 in the town of Bedceni and again at midnight in the town of Resnich two terror attacks were perpetrated. One police officer was killed and another was seriously wounded. Three civilians died of their injuries.
31. On December 4, the KLA claimed responsibility for an attack at the Pristina airport and stated that organization members had succeeded in knocking down a Cessna 310 and killing its five passengers.
32. On December 15 at 01:00, on the road between Klina and Serbica, three masked and armed men stopped a convoy of three cars with sixteen Serb passengers and threatened to kill them.
33. On December 19 at 18:00, on the road between Serbica and Klina (near the town of Josanica), eight masked gunmen stopped a civilian car, searched it, threatened the passengers and cursed them.
34. On December 25 at 15:00, police officers were attacked on two occasions in the Poduyevo area. In the first incident, gunshots were fired at a police patrol car in the village of Zakut, and in the second, an explosive charge was lobbed at a civilian building that served as barracks for police officers. No one was hurt.

    The total number of attacks in 1997 came to between 34-36 (this figure includes separate attacks that were perpetrated on the same day).

## Attacks in 1998:

1. On January 4, the KLZ claimed responsibility for several attacks in Macedonia: The first was the planting of a bomb near the police station in Prilep. No one was injured in this attack, but five cars were completely demolished: In the second incident, the police station in Kumanovo was attacked; In the third, an attack was launched against the regional courthouse in Gostivar (in December 1997).
2. On January 9, a Serb civilian in the village of Stepanica—near Kijevo (the head of a Serb family that had remained there—only three Serb families were still living there at the time) was shot and killed.
3. On January 12 after midnight, shots were fired at a civilian building used as living quarters for Serb policemen and their families in the village of Stimlje. No one was injured.

    On the same day at 8:00 an Albanian forester was shot and killed in the village of Gredich after he had been kidnapped from his car by three masked terrorists.

4. On January 13, terrorists from the KLA claimed responsibility for attacks in Gostivar, Prilep, and Kumanovo. The organization announced that it was going to expand its activities to Montenegro.
5. In the early morning hours of January 14, the main offices of the Serbian Socialist Party were attacked and all the building's windows were shattered.
6. On January 19, all of the graves in the cemetery of the Serb Orthodox church in Serbica were desecrated.
7. On January 22, after KLA terrorists had harassed Serbica residents the night before, a gunfight developed between the terrorists and a police patrol. The terrorists holed up in the house of one of their supporters. One terrorist was killed and another two were injured in the shooting.

   That same day a cell of three KLA terrorists kidnapped an Albanian civilian along wih his taxi. They told him that he could buy his car back but if he reported the incident to the police he would be killed.
8. On January 23, during the early morning hours a local politician was killed on the road between Serbica and Klina, near the town of Yosnica. At about the same time and on the same road a local resident of the town Lausa was beaten unconscious.

   That night, a KLA terrorist cell harassed and threatened a group of Serb women on their way to the local convent.
9. On January 25, two police officers were seriously injured in the center of the town of Melisbo from terrorist gunfire.

   That same night, KLA terrorists attacked a private home in the town of Grabanica.

   On that same day, a terrorist threw a bomb at the home of a Serb police officer in Urosevac.
10. On January 26, KLA terrorists opened automatic gunfire on a helicopter of the Serb Ministry of Interior near the town of Turicevac.
11. On January 27, a terrorist cell stopped three local residents and beat them near the town of Turicevac. The three paid a ransom and were released.
12. On January 28, police officers on their way to confiscate weapons from a crime family in the town of Decani were trapped in an ambush. The police succeeded in arresting seven of the suspects.

   That same evening KLA terrorists opened fire on a private Serb home in the town of Sibovac.
13. On February 10, a group of terrorists appeared at a fundraising evening for the KLA in New York. They took advantage of the "festive occasion" to announce that they had killed fifty people in the course of 1997, including Serb police officers and "corrupt" Alanian citizens.
14. On February 12, a postal worker of Albanian descent was shot and killed in the town of Gornji Obrinj in front of twenty passersby, after he had been warned repeatedly to leave his position as a civil servant.
15. On February 15, a civilian of Albanian origins employed by the Serb electric company was killed while working in the town of Staro Cikatovo.

16. On February 18, KLA terrorists confiscated weapons from Albanian citizens suspected of disloyalty in the town of Dernica.

    The same day a police barrier near the town of Dobre Vode was attacked by automatic gunfire.
17. On February 19, a security employee was shot and killed in the town of Luzani.

    On the same day, in the town of Poduyevo, terrorists threw bombs at the center for Serb refugees in Croatia.
18. On February 20, one civilian was shot and killed and a second was seriously wounded on the road between Serbica and Klina, near the town of Lausi. On the same day, terrorists shot at a vehicle, injuring the driver and killing an Albanian passenger, on the same road near the town of Yosnica. That night, KLA terrorists erected a barrier on the road between Klina and Djakovica, stopped a police officer and beat him.
19. On February 22, a civilian of Albanian descent who worked in a Serb store in Dobre Vode was shot and killed after refusing to leave his job.
20. On February 26, terrorists attacked a refugee camp of Serbs from Albania in Babaloc with hand grenades and automatic weapons. This was the third attack against the camp.
21. On February 27, KLA terrorists attacked houses where Serb refugees from Croatia were staying in the town of Serbica. The same day, a group of terrorists harassed the mother superior of an abbey in Devic for half an hour and threatened to butcher the nuns. That day the Serb security forces discovered an arms depot in the town of Prizen and several suspects were arrested.
22. On Febraury 28, a private residence in the Serb town of Donji Ratis was bombed. That day a gunfight developed between KLA terrorists and the police in the town of Dernica. Four police officers were killed and two were seriously wounded. It is unclear how many terrorists were hurt in the incident.

## Summary

- These figures relate to the period between April 1996 and February 1998.
- These figures are based on a Serb source.
- A review of the data indicates that there was a sharp increase in the scope of the attacks from eleven to fifteen attacks in 1996 to thirty-four to thirty-six attacks in 1997, and culminating in twenty-two attacks during the first months of 1998 (eleven attacks a month in comparison to a monthly average of approximately one attack each month in 1996 and three attacks a month in 1997).

# Index